ADOLESCENT LITERACY
IN THE ACADEMIC DISCIPLINES

Adolescent Literacy in the Academic Disciplines

General Principles and Practical Strategies

edited by
Tamara L. Jetton
Cynthia Shanahan

THE GUILFORD PRESS
NEW YORK   LONDON

© 2012 The Guilford Press
A Division of Guilford Publications, Inc.
72 Spring Street, New York, NY 10012
www.guilford.com

Printed in the United States of America

This book is printed on acid-free paper.

Last digit is print number: 9   8   7   6   5   4   3   2   1

Library of Congress Cataloging-in-Publication Data

Adolescent literacy in the academic disciplines: general principles and practical strategies /
[edited by] Tamara L. Jetton, Cynthia Shanahan.
   p. cm.
  Includes bibliographical references and index.
  ISBN 978-1-4625-0283-7 (hardback)—ISBN 978-1-4625-0280-6 (paper)
  1. Language arts (Secondary)   2. Language arts—Correlation with content subjects.
I. Jetton, Tamara L.   II. Shanahan, Cynthia.
  LB1631.A344 2012
  428.0071′2-dc23

                                                                          2011035689

About the Editors

Tamara L. Jetton, PhD, is Professor in the Department of Teacher Education and Professional Development at Central Michigan University. A former public school teacher for 10 years, she is interested in three particular areas of literacy: strategic reading to improve comprehension in the academic disciplines, learning through classroom discussions, and writing processes. Her research agenda also mirrors this interest through her publications, which include the book *Adolescent Literacy Research and Practice;* articles in *Reading Research Quarterly, Review of Educational Research,* and *Journal of Educational Psychology;* and book chapters in *Bridging the Literacy Achievement Gap: Grades 4–12, Handbook of Discourse Processes, Handbook of Research on Literacy in Technology at the K–12 Level,* and *Handbook of Reading Research, Volume III.* Dr. Jetton has dedicated her professional career to the goal of helping teachers improve the reading comprehension of adolescents who struggle in the academic disciplines.

Cynthia Shanahan, EdD, is Professor of Literacy, Language and Culture; Executive Director of the Council on Teacher Education; and Associate Dean of Academic Affairs at the University of Illinois at Chicago. In her role as professor, Dr. Shanahan prepares preservice and inservice teachers to teach middle and high school literacy. She previously taught college students to meet the reading and study demands of their college courses at Georgia State University (1984–1986) and the University of Georgia (1986–2000). Her research and teaching interests are in disciplinary literacy. Through a project funded by the Carnegie Corporation, Dr. Shanahan has investigated the differences among the disciplines in the ways they approach reading and writing. Currently, she is working on Project READi, a Reading for Understanding grant funded by the Institute of Education Sciences for studying argumentation in science, history, and literature in grades 6–12.

Contributors

James Batcheller, DMA, School of Music, Central Michigan University, Mount Pleasant, Michigan

Larry Burditt, MFA, Department of Art and Design, Central Michigan University, Mount Pleasant, Michigan

Roni Jo Draper, PhD, Department of Teacher Education, Brigham Young University, Provo, Utah

Zhihui Fang, PhD, School of Teaching and Learning, University of Florida, Gainesville, Florida

Sue Gamble, EdD, School of Music, Central Michigan University, Mount Pleasant, Michigan

Alan J. Gumm, PhD, School of Music, Central Michigan University, Mount Pleasant, Michigan

Troy Hicks, PhD, Department of English Language and Literature, Central Michigan University, Mount Pleasant, Michigan

Tamara L. Jetton, PhD, Department of Teacher Education and Professional Development, Central Michigan University, Mount Pleasant, Michigan

Richard Lee, Department of Teacher Education and Professional Development, Central Michigan University, Mount Pleasant, Michigan

Kathleen Moxley, PhD, Department of Teacher Education and Professional Development, Central Michigan University, Mount Pleasant, Michigan

Johanna Paas, MFA, Department of Art and Design, Central Michigan University, Mount Pleasant, Michigan

Cynthia Shanahan, EdD, College of Education, University of Illinois at Chicago, Chicago, Illinois

Daniel Siebert, PhD, Department of Mathematics Education, Brigham Young University, Provo, Utah

Susan Steffel, PhD, Department of English Language and Literature, Central Michigan University, Mount Pleasant, Michigan

Judy Thurston, MA, Department of Art and Design, Central Michigan University, Mount Pleasant, Michigan

Bruce VanSledright, PhD, Department of Reading and Elementary Education, University of North Carolina at Charlotte, Charlotte, North Carolina

Preface

Research in the past 10 years points to the urgent need for increased attention to adolescent literacy. According to Biancarosa and Snow (2006), some high school graduates are ill prepared for college writing courses or for the literacy skills required by employers, despite evidence that the fastest growing professions have increased literacy demands. Likewise, the Rand Reading Study Group (2002) found that comprehension scores are not improving, despite the increasing level of complexity and technicality of content-area texts. According to the 2005 results of the National Assessment of Educational Progress, 8th- and 12th-grade students' performance has not shown any significant gains since 1992. Eighth-grade students scored higher on average in 2005 than in 1992, but this increase was not statistically significant (National Center for Education Statistics, 2005a). The results for 12th graders are even more alarming. The percentage of students performing at or above the basic level decreased from 80% in 1992 to 73% in 2005, and the percentage of students performing at or above the proficient level decreased from 40% in 1992 to 35% in 2005 (National Center for Education Statistics, 2005b).

Given these troubling statistics, educators must be concerned with the improvement of literacy education for adolescent readers. The Carnegie Corporation has implemented the Advancing Literacy program to "seed a new field" of researchers and practitioners focused on developing competency in reading and writing skills for middle and high school students. Over the last few years, the Advancing Literacy program has invited a select number of teacher preparation programs to develop innovative instructional materials, build up a cadre of adolescent literacy researchers, and enrich existing secondary school literacy programs.

Biancarosa and Snow (2006) suggest key elements to improving middle and high school adolescent literacy programs. They call for direct, explicit instruction of comprehension strategies that are embedded within the content areas. They also call for text-based collaborative learning, reading a diversity of texts, and intensive writing. The International Reading Association (IRA) recommends that adolescents engage in motivating reading material: instruction that encompasses reading comprehension, critical reading, and study strategies across the curriculum. In addition, the IRA advocates for qualified teachers to respond to each adolescent learner's uniqueness and for reading specialists to assist individual adolescents.

At present, several publications describe the kinds of literacy strategies for adolescent learners that cross multiple content areas (e.g., Alvermann, Phelps, & Gillis, 2009; Beers, 2002; Irvin, Beuhl, & Klemp, 2006; Moore, Hinchman, & Vacca, 2005; Readance, Bean, & Baldwin, 2004; Unrau, 2007). These books detail particular strategies—such as activating prior knowledge, questioning, summarizing, and visualizing, to name a few—that enhance students' abilities to glean content from their subject-matter texts. Called *general strategies*, these can be broadly applied to a range of tasks in many domains (Jetton & Alexander, 2004). Whether students are reading a history text or mathematics book, their learning benefits from predicting what is to come, summarizing what was read, and questioning their understanding of the material.

While these strategies are important and effective, they are not enough. Students must also understand the special nature of each academic discipline. Academic disciplines are powerful means of organizing vast bodies of related knowledge and experience. Each academic discipline necessitates certain processing strategies that are quite specific to the discipline and its typical tasks or problems. For example, in English a student needs to understand how the bird's death in "The Scarlet Ibis" is used by the author to foreshadow the death of one of the main characters in the story (Hurst, 2000). This is a domain-specific literacy strategy. That is, analyzing the text for the use of foreshadowing is not a strategy that this student can transfer to her mathematics class. Unfortunately, few books exist that focus on these discipline-specific literacy strategies.

The purpose of this book is to delve deeper into these academic disciplines by examining the trends in learning from text and those discipline-specific strategies that increase adolescents' understanding of these texts. The first few chapters explore the general principles involved as adolescents engage with text. Chapter 1 looks at the trends in adolescent literacy research over the last decade that relate to learning from text in grades 4–12. Chapter 2 focuses more specifically on the nature of texts that adolescents encounter and the linguistic and academic challenges that these texts pose. In order for educators to understand how to teach students to effectively read disciplinary texts, they must first examine how experts read within their own disciplines. Thus, Chapter 3 examines how discipline experts learn from texts in their fields and the processing required to engage with these academic texts. Chapter 4 then describes a model for teacher planning with text that accounts for the many variables involved as adolescents engage with text in these academic disciplines.

The second part of the book details the discipline-specific strategies that guide adolescents in their ability to learn from text in specific academic disciplines. In designing this book, we have divided the chapters according to those disciplines with which our school systems recognize and regularly assess adolescents' abilities. Thus, the chapters focus on learning with text in the disciplines of English language arts, science, mathematics, history, and the arts. Each chapter explores learning within a particular discipline from the perspectives of both a literacy expert, who understands the reading and writing challenges that adolescents encounter, and a discipline expert, who understands the nature of the discipline and how literacy processes operate within it.

REFERENCES

Alvermann, D. E., Phelps, S. F., & Gillis, V. R. (2009). *Content area reading and literacy: Succeeding in today's diverse classroom* (6th ed.). New York: Allyn & Bacon.

Beers, G. K. (2002). *When kids can't read: What teachers can do.* Portsmouth, NH: Heinemann.

Biancarosa, C., & Snow, C. E. (2006). *Reading next—A vision for action and research in middle and high school literacy: A report to Carnegie Corporation of New York* (2nd ed.). Washington, DC: Alliance for Excellent Education.

Hurst, J. (2000). The scarlet ibis. In *Elements of literature: Third course* (pp. 315–323). Austin, TX: Holt, Rinehart & Winston.

Irvin, J. L., Buehl, D. R, Klemp, R. M. (2002). *Reading and the high school student: Strategies to enhance literacy.* New York: Allyn & Bacon.

Jetton, T. L., & Alexander, P. A. (2004). Domains, teaching and literacy. In T. L. Jetton & J. A. Dole (Eds.), *Adolescent literacy research and practice* (pp. 15–39). New York: Guilford Press.

Moore, D. W., Hinchman, K. A., & Vacca, R. T. (2005). *Teaching adolescents who struggle with reading: Practical strategies* (2nd ed.). New York: Allyn & Bacon.

National Center for Education Statistics. (2005a). *Nation's report card: Reading 2005.* Washington, DC: U.S. Government Printing Office. Retrieved from *nces.ed.gov/nationsreportcard/pdf/maIn2005/2006451.pdf.*

National Center for Education Statistics. (2005b). *Reading: Overall performance in reading declines in comparison to 1992.* Retrieved from *nces. ed.gov/nationsreportcard/pdf/maIn2005/2007468_2.pdf.*

Rand Reading Study Group. (2002). *Reading for understanding: Toward an R&D program in reading comprehension.* Santa Monica, CA: Rand.

Readance, J., Bean, T. W., & Baldwin, R. S. (2004). *Content area literacy: An integrated approach* (8th ed.). Dubuque, IA: Kendall Hunt Publishing.

Unrau, N. (2007). *Content area reading and writing: Fostering literacies in middle and high school cultures* (2nd ed.). New York: Prentice Hall.

Contents

1

Learning from Text

Adolescent Literacy from the Past Decade

Tamara L. Jetton *and* Richard Lee

At the beginning of the 21st century, national education organizations have turned their attention toward adolescent literacy for a number of reasons. For example, U.S. Department of Education (2005) published a survey of college graduates and found that high school dropouts were easily the most prone to lack basic literacy. Other studies examined specific data related to how adolescents learn from text. For example, the RAND Reading Study Group (Snow, 2002) found that comprehension scores were not increasing, and this lack of improvement could be due to the increasing level of complexity and technical difficulty of content-area texts. In a recent report on the National Assessment of Educational Progress (NAEP) scores, only 74% of the 12th-grade students tested in 2009 scored at the basic level, compared to 80% in 1992, and only 38% of the 12th-grade students assessed scored at the proficient level, compared to 40% in 1992 (U.S. Department of Education (2010).

The RAND Reading Study Group (Snow, 2002) also found that secondary teachers were woefully ill prepared to teach literacy strategies necessary for comprehension of content-specific texts. When Ness (2007) examined instruction by four secondary teachers, she found that out of the 40 hours of classroom observation, only 82 minutes of instruction, or 3% of instructional time, was devoted to the explicit teaching, modeling, and scaffolding of students' comprehension of text. Of the 3% of instructional time on comprehension that she observed, teachers spent the majority of their time asking literal questions and assigning a written summary of the text, rather than teaching students how to summarize text effectively. In another study of eight science and social studies teachers, Ness (2009) observed 2,400 minutes of classroom instruction, and once again, she found only 3% of instructional time was spent on comprehension. The most common comprehension strategy was question answering, with some time spent teaching text structure and summarization. The social studies teachers incorporated more comprehension instruction than the science teachers.

Given the aforementioned statistics and research, a focus on adolescent literacy and how adolescents learn from text is certainly warranted. In this chapter, we explore the trends and issues that have emerged in the last decade in relation to how adolescents learn from text. We have examined various articles about adolescent literacy published within the last 10 years and garner some key findings concerning how adolescents learn from text. Our search for these findings began with a database search in both ERIC and PsycINFO for articles published during the last decade that focused on adolescent readers and learning with text. Our keyword search included such terms as *comprehension*, *comprehension instruction*, *learning with text*, and *understanding text*. Narrowing our search to adolescent literacy in grades 4–12, we read each article gathered from the databases and examined the references in each one in order to find additional articles that focused on adolescent literacy and learning with text. From the 43 articles that we garnered in our search, we then grouped each article according to the particular focus and goal of the article. While articles focusing specifically on comprehension and comprehension instruction in 4–12 classrooms were sparse, we were able to determine some common themes, which we report here.

THE NATURE OF TEXTS AND LEARNING

As adolescents progress through the grade levels, texts become more specialized by discipline and are, therefore, much more technical in nature. Students find it difficult to transition into these complex texts as they move from the primary grades to the intermediate grades and into middle and high school. Because of this difficulty, researchers are exploring the unique characteristics of these texts, in particular the expository texts used in science, social studies, and mathematics (Coutant &

Perchemlides, 2005; Fang, 2008; Fang, Schleppegrell, & Cox, 2006).
One of their findings is that the words used in disciplinary texts, such as
science and math books, can be difficult to understand for two reasons.
First, words that students might normally know and use in their everyday language have very specialized meanings in disciplinary texts. For
example, the word *domain*, which students might know as "land that
one owns," means something very different in mathematics. They learn
that the domain of a function is "the set of all possible input values (usually x), which allows the function formula to work." Second, disciplinary
texts contain words that are highly specialized to the relevant discipline,
such as *meiosis* and *mitosis* in biology. When adolescents encounter even
small sections of text with a concentration of these specialized words,
their comprehension is often compromised (Fang, 2006).

Disciplinary texts are replete with abstractions that can prove difficult for adolescents. Fang et al. (2006) emphasize that authors often
create abstract nouns to express a value or theory from which discussion can ensue. These abstractions do not allow students to comprehend
concrete and tangible ideas within the text. In addition, these highly
technical and abstract words occur frequently per sentence, which, in
turn, makes the text dense with information. Adding to the density are
the embedded phrases and clauses that writers use to clarify information
in text. Disciplinary texts can also be daunting to adolescents because
of the impersonal and authoritarian tone taken by the authors in order
to lend credibility and an objective stance to their texts. This is accomplished through a third-person, omniscient narrator who uses technical
language, declarative sentences, and passive voice. It is no wonder that
adolescents become disengaged from these kinds of texts.

Fang (2008) offers some suggestions that can mediate the comprehension problems that occur with disciplinary texts. First, readers need
to be exposed to a variety of expository texts as they progress through
elementary school. They can also learn to deconstruct those long nouns
that contain so much information, and they can learn how writers expand
nouns to add information. Adolescents can learn how to transform and
paraphrase the sentences in the text into their own writing, which contains everyday language that they can then interpret more easily.

Coutant and Perchemlides (2005) offer other suggestions for helping adolescents grapple with complex disciplinary texts. They point to
the importance of providing adolescents with the requisite prior knowledge to read these dense texts and increasing their understanding of the
various text structures found in expository materials. Adolescents must
be encouraged to interact with these disciplinary texts by noting important headings or subheadings, and confusing or surprising information.
They can also note important terms and summarize dense sections of

text. In order to make the text less distant and authoritarian, students can be encouraged to determine the accuracy of the author's information and question the author's information and ideas.

The current research on academic texts clearly shows the need for teachers to understand the difficulty that adolescents encounter with these texts and the need to provide adequate scaffolding for effective comprehension. Teachers in the disciplines cannot send students home with the textbook and guarantee that they have read and understood it. For most adolescents these disciplinary texts are much too difficult to read on their own, and they need practical strategies for grappling with the complex density of information they contain. The focus of future research on academic texts should be an exploration of discipline-specific strategies. For example, reading a history text requires readers to move back and forth between a present-day historian who authors the chapter and the primary sources that he or she cites within. These readers not only have to judge the credibility of the historian's ideas, but also frame the ideas set forth in the primary source within the context of the time and space in which they were written. This is a difficult challenge indeed.

READING COMPREHENSION STRATEGIES VERSUS INSTRUCTIONAL STRATEGIES FOR READING

Since the early 1980s, researchers have been studying reading comprehension strategies that effective adolescent readers employ to understand text. Reading strategies, in particular, involve conscious, deliberate plans that readers use flexibly to understand text (Alexander & Judy, 1988). In 1989, Pressley, Johnson, Symons, and McGoldrick provided a framework for understanding these strategies. They included summarization, in which students determine the most important content in text; imaging, in which students create representational images or pictures of the text material; story structure, in which students use their knowledge of story structure to determine important elements in the literature; student questioning in which students question the text to clarify their understanding and glean the content; and activating prior knowledge, in which students use knowledge they already possess to help them learn the new content in the text.

Later, Dole, Duffy, Roehler, and Pearson (1991) provided a review of comprehension strategies and linked those strategies directly to what they called "teaching strategies" (p. 239). In their article, Dole and her colleagues reviewed 20 years of research on effective comprehension strategies such as determining importance, summarizing, making inferences, student-generated questioning, and comprehension monitoring. Making inferences involves students using the text information and their prior knowledge to arrive at new ideas that are not directly stated in the text. Comprehension monitoring refers to students recognizing when they are understanding the text and, when their comprehension breaks down, applying fix-up strategies for increasing their understanding, such as rereading the text to clarify meaning.

With the publication of the *Handbook of Research on Reading Comprehension* (2009), two chapters appeared that focused specifically on comprehension in the middle grades and adolescent comprehension (Wharton-McDonald & Swiger, 2009; Conley, 2009). Wharton-McDonald and Swiger (2009) relate the important variables that lead to effective comprehension with text. They emphasize that automatic word recognition and fluency are requisite to comprehension. They support their assertion with data from Rasinski and colleagues (2005), who reported a strong correlation between fluency and comprehension. In their study, fluency accounted for 28% of the variance in comprehension. The other variables that relate to comprehension include the use of comprehension strategies, metacognition, vocabulary, and prior knowledge.

Researchers such as Biancarosa and Snow (2006) emphasized the importance of teaching these reading strategies explicitly to students. Explicit instruction began as early as 1983 when Pearson and Gallagher proposed a model of explicit strategy instruction. According to their model, the teacher begins the strategy instruction with an explanation of what the strategy is and the process readers use to employ the strategy. The teacher explicitly models how she would process the text, using the particular strategy. While the teacher models, she points out how the students can use this strategy on their own when they are reading independently. Following the modeling, the teacher facilitates guided practice in which the students process text using the strategy with the teacher monitoring their strategy use and providing scaffolding. As students continue the guided practice over time, the teacher fades by providing less and less support until the students can begin to employ the strategy independently. Here is an excerpt of how a teacher might begin explicit teaching of the strategy, activating prior knowledge:

> "Before we begin reading for information, it's a good idea to think about what we already know about the topic. We call this strategy activating prior knowledge. We're about to read a chapter about the earth's atmosphere, and I want you to remember the information about the atmosphere (setting a purpose). One way to better remember the information is to think about what you already know about the layers of the atmosphere and the gases, particles, and other sub-

stances that are found in the atmosphere before you read, so you can connect the information to what you already know."

The teacher then models how to activate one's own prior knowledge:

"When I think of the layers of the atmosphere, I immediately think about what I know about the ozone because that is one of the layers. I also think about how many layers there must be and what their functions are. I know that if objects enter the atmosphere, sometimes they burn up before they reach earth, so one of the functions of the atmosphere is a protective layer against foreign objects. I also know that the atmospheric layers do not necessarily consist of the same gases as the layer of air we breathe. Lastly, I know from studying science that the layer of atmosphere we breathe consists mostly of nitrogen, followed by oxygen. I can apply all of this knowledge that I already have as I read the text, so I can get the most information out of what I read. Let's see what you know about the earth's atmosphere by activating your prior knowledge."

The teacher would then have students generate their own prior knowledge about the topic while he or she provides prompts as scaffolding to elicit their knowledge. The teacher might provide prompts by stating, "John, you just said that you thought the atmosphere might have more substances than just gases. Search your prior knowledge and try to think of what those substances might be." Then, the teacher fades and lets John continue conveying his prior knowledge of the contents of the atmosphere.

As the research about these reading strategies and the model for explicit strategy instruction were published, educators began examining particular instructional strategies that teachers can use in the classroom to teach these reading strategies. For example, in 1981, Langer created the Prereading Plan (PReP) to encourage students to elaborate their prior knowledge before they read. Likewise, Stauffer created the Directed Reading Thinking Activity (DRTA) to aid students in the strategy of predicting as they read the text (Stauffer, 1969). In fact, from the early 1980s until the present day, educators have been designing effective instructional strategies to teach reading comprehension strategies.

We have noticed, though, over the last 20 years, that many of the articles that discuss these reading and instructional strategies have started confusing the two. Here is an example of what we mean. Ogle invented the K-W-L instructional strategy for increasing reading comprehension for informational text (Ogle, 1986). K-W-L is not a reading strategy. It is an instructional strategy to teach the reading strategies of activating prior knowledge (K, W), asking questions (W), and determining importance (L). Yet, in the literature, we often see the K-W-L instructional strategy expressed as a reading strategy. We also see the instructional strategy DRTA represented as a reading strategy, but the reading strategy that it teaches is prediction.

The reason there needs to be a clear understanding of the difference between a reading strategy and an instructional strategy is because teachers need to understand the reading strategies that they need to teach explicitly. Readers do not need to know the instructional strategy explicitly; they need to know the reading strategies that are taught through them. Thus, if a teacher wants to use K-W-L, he should explicitly teach activating prior knowledge, questioning, and determining importance to his students. Because there is so much confusion in the field about the difference between a reading strategy and an instructional strategy for reading, teachers think that teaching K-W-L and having students state what they know, what they want to know, and what they learned is explicit strategy instruction. At the end of this chapter, we provide a chart that lists the reading strategies, followed by the instructional strategies that are used to teach the reading strategies explicitly, and a short example of how the reading strategies would be introduced through explicit instruction (see Appendix 1.1). We encourage teacher educators to point out the difference between the reading comprehension strategies that must be taught explicitly and the instructional strategies teachers can employ to teach students the strategies.

COMPREHENSION MODELS

Over the last three decades, researchers began to propose and test models of comprehension that attempt to explain the variables involved in this complex process (Kintsch, 1988, 1998; Perfetti, 1985). More recently Cromley and Azevedo (2007) hypothesized the Direct and Inferential Mediation Model of reading comprehension (DIME). In designing this model, the researchers provided research to support the inclusion of particular variables that relate to comprehension. These variables were background knowledge, inference, reading comprehension strategies, vocabulary, and word reading. Using the Gates-MacGinitie Comprehension and Vocabulary subtests (Level 7/9, Form S; MacGinitie), the researchers tested the model with 175 9th-grade adolescents to determine the direct and mediated effects of these five predictor variables on comprehension. The DIME model accounted for 66% of the variance in comprehension, with background knowledge and vocabulary making the largest contribution to comprehension. These variables were followed by inference, word reading, and strategies. The researchers found these variables to have direct and mediated effects on comprehension and, thus, illustrate the complex interplay among these variables that explains comprehension. The researchers suggested that instruction which builds background knowledge and vocabulary for adolescents has the best utility for improving literal and inferential comprehension for adolescents like those in their study. Their results also showed that when a text demanded inferential understanding, reading comprehension strategies were needed.

The DIME model and those reported in previous research provide interesting and important information about the variables critical to reading comprehension. What is missing in these studies is the impact of the discipline. We wonder what the interplay of these variables may be when adolescents read specialized disciplinary texts in science, social studies, or mathematics. We encourage future studies that explore comprehension models within the context of disciplinary learning.

INSTRUCTIONAL STRATEGIES FOR TEACHING COMPREHENSION STRATEGIES TO ADOLESCENTS

In our search for articles during the last decade, we did find that educators are continuing to extend and elaborate on these instructional strategies in order to increase comprehension (Raphael & Au, 2005). For example, Szabo (2006) detailed the KWHHL instructional strategy that she used with her 8th-grade students. As she modeled with science and social studies texts, Szabo taught students to brainstorm the information they already knew (K), ask questions about information they want to know (W), note "head words" that confuse them (H), note "heart words" that triggered emotions (H), and note information they learned (L).

In 2008, Hagaman and Reid elaborated on the RAP instructional strategy that encourages students to paraphrase the text to determine important information (Schumaker, Denton, & Deschler, 1984). Through this strategy, readers followed a three-step process of reading a paragraph, identifying the main ideas and two details, and paraphrasing the content in their own words. Hagaman and Reid used the RAP strategy within the framework of the Self-Regulated Strategy Development model (SRSD), a six-step strategy-instruction model (Harris & Graham, 1996). The 6th-grade struggling readers' comprehension of expository texts increased following the training. Most specifically, the students improved in text recall and correct responses on short-answer questions about the texts. They also found the SRSD to be a useful model for delivering the strategy instruction.

Alfassi (2004) examined how multiple-strategy instruction pro-vided through Reciprocal Teaching and direct explanation impacted adolescents' comprehension and their literal and inferential question and answering. In the first study, Alfassi examined how the two instructional models affected students' comprehension in an English language arts classroom. She found that those students in the treatment group significantly outperformed the students in the control group on comprehension over time. In the second study, she investigated how the two instructional models affected adolescents' question and answering with content materials from their school curriculum. She found that the Reciprocal Teaching and direct explanation model led to increased performance on both explicit and implicit question answering.

As the field of adolescent literacy began focusing more on learning within particular disciplines, Jones and Thomas (2006) detailed several instructional strategies to improve adolescents' understanding of social studies texts. They show how students can use word maps (Santa, Havens, & Maycumber, 1996) in social studies by defining vocabulary in their own words, noting synonyms for the word, using them meaningfully in a sentence, and illustrating the words. They also provide examples of how students can use concept definition maps for understanding their social studies words (Schwartz, 1988). Using this instructional strategy, adolescents learn social studies concepts through definitions, comparisons, examples, and self-written definitions. Jones and Thomas (2006) also show how they adapted three writing instructional strategies to increase comprehension of social studies text. For example, they provide several examples of how to use the RAFT (Santa et al., 1996), paragraph frames (Nichols, 1980), and story maps to increase comprehension in social studies. Through RAFT, adolescents assume the role of a bill (Role) writing to other bills (Audience) through a travelogue (Format) about how it became a law (Topic).

INSTRUCTIONAL FRAMEWORKS FOR ENGAGEMENT AND LEARNING WITH TEXT

In the last three decades, several instructional frameworks have appeared that led to increased comprehension scores for adolescents. One of the first frameworks to show promising results was Reciprocal Teaching, in which the strategies of prediction, questioning, clarifying, and summarizing were taught and modeled for students with a gradual release of responsibility from the teacher to the student (Palincsar & Brown, 1984). Almost a decade later Pressley and his colleagues (1992) introduced transactional strategy instruction, in which readers are taught to use multiple strategies flexibly in order to achieve self-regulation. This framework was followed by Klingner and Vaughn's (1999) collaborative strategic reading, in which readers participated in a collaborative learning environment with four strategies, each taught separately prior to employing a multiple-strategy approach to reading. Readers were taught to brainstorm and predict (preview), monitor their understanding (Click and Clunk), determine important information (Get the Gist), and generate questions and review important content (Wrap Up). Since 2000, Guthrie and Wigfield have researched the interplay of motivation and comprehension as young adolescents learn with text. Their engagement model proposes that both motivation and cognitive strategies are crucial to increasing students' understanding of text. For students to be engaged with text in the classroom, they need to have learning goals, interesting text, opportunities for collaboration, and strategy knowledge they use as they read (Guthrie & Wigfield, 2000). These researchers developed an instructional framework that incorporates these variables, known as concept-oriented reading instruction (CORI).

CORI is a powerful instructional framework for increasing students' comprehension and motivation to read. Within this framework, readers utilize specific cognitive strategies that include activating their prior knowledge, generating questions, searching for information, organizing new knowledge, and monitoring their comprehension (Guthrie, 2004). This framework also emphasizes that readers work toward reading goals, and they exert considerable effort with enthusiasm, even when the reading becomes difficult, to achieve those goals. Another important facet of the framework is that readers are working with interesting text in a classroom environment in which they engage in discussion with others about the ideas in the text.

In one study with young adolescent readers in fourth grade, Wigfield at al. (2008) examined the effects of three instructional frameworks on reading comprehension in science. They investigated the differential effects of CORI, strategy instruction, and traditional instruction on students' comprehension of informational text. The strategy instruction model was different from CORI in that teachers did not explicitly include the motivational support for students that was evident in the CORI model. The teachers in the traditional instruction model were the control group in that they received no training, and they used their existing instruction with text. The results illustrate the powerful impact that CORI can have on students' reading comprehension. The CORI student group performed better than the other two groups on all comprehension measures, including a standardized test, and a multiple-text comprehension task. The CORI group also outperformed the other group in strategy use as measured by the strategy composite, a sum of scores for activating prior knowledge and questioning.

In another study of young adolescents, Guthrie at al. (2009) investigated the effects of CORI on both high-achieving and low-achieving fifth graders' reading comprehension, word recognition, and fluency. Results showed that both low- and high-achieving students benefited from CORI. They also found that the CORI group outperformed the traditional instruction group on both word recognition speed and reading comprehension. Thus, there is strong evidence that CORI is an effective instructional framework for increasing reading comprehension for young adolescents.

Souvignier and Mokhlesgerami (2006) also examined an instructional framework for increasing reading comprehension in young adolescents called the text detective program. Their program focused on teaching fifth-grade students self-regulation of strategies within a 20-lesson framework in which students read both narrative and informational text. The framework began with lessons about goal setting and an introduction of two strategies: activating prior knowledge and forming mental images. Following these lessons, the students were taught to clarify unknown words and generate questions in order to check their understanding of the text. By following these strategies, students learned how to determine importance by underlining key ideas, summarizing text information, and checking their recall of the important text information. These lessons were followed by several lessons in which students used all of the comprehension strategies together as they engaged with text so they could learn to make decisions about how to use the strategies flexibly according to their goals and tasks. The adolescents in the text detective program significantly outperformed both the strategy and the control groups.

The three studies above illustrate the utility of providing instructional models that explicitly teach comprehension strategies and provide the motivational support for adolescent readers as they interact with one another and with text. More research needs to explore how these instructional models can be utilitized in high school classrooms when adolescents are engaging disciplinary learning. While much of the research with CORI has focused on reading in science, less emphasis was placed on the interplay between the discipline of science and the instructional strategy. We still know very little about how CORI mediates or is mediated by the discipline of science. There are also unanswered questions as to how an instructional framework for reading like CORI mediates or is mediated by the disciplines of history and English language arts. For example, search strategies that are an important part of CORI might operate differently in science than in history since history involves the use of primary and secondary documents. Thus, we need a better understanding of the academic disciplines themselves and how to construct instructional frameworks that meet the particular goals for learning with text in those disciplines.

DIGITAL LITERACIES AND COMPREHENSION OF ONLINE INFORMATION

With the proliferation of technology, the nature of adolescent literacy has changed a great deal in the past two decades. Adolescents have embraced this technology to interact with friends and strangers across the globe through Facebook, online games, and various other popular technologies. The Internet has become an integral part of adolescents' lives both inside and outside school. Studies have begun to consider the various literacies involved when adolescents engage with technology, and researchers have explored the social practices that occur as readers engage with new literacies (Street, 1999). Others have examined the discourses that emerge when people interact with such technologies as video games (Gee, 2003). Some researchers have explored the new cultural contexts that emerge through these new technologies (Kress, 2004). More recently, researchers have called for more studies that examine how students learn with online information (Coiro & Dobler, 2007; Kymes, 2005).

In their study of sixth-grade adolescents, Coiro and Dobler (2007) focused on the apparent comprehension differences between traditional printed texts and online information. One of the marked differences is that online information is linked in so many more ways than traditional text. For one to link texts within traditional text, writers might use excerpts within the text itself or cite a reference for which the reader must search. In contrast, online textual information is linked to other online information in multiple ways. For the reader to pull all of this interconnected information together into a coherent whole can be a very complex process. Thus, intertextuality becomes a critical variable as readers navigate through several information sources on several levels to construct meaning. Furthermore, the navigational process is much more complex than traditional text. In traditional text, the reader is guided through the material in a linear way, but with online information, readers choose their navigational paths, so the process of meaning making is a highly personal endeavor. The navigational process becomes an integral part of the meaning that an individual constructs. As readers navigate through the seemingly endless amount of information, they, too, must determine the credibility of their sources. The traditional textbook publishers have tried to ensure that the information found in their texts is from credible sources, but the online information that students encounter may or may not be a credible source, and students must learn strategies to determine the credibility of sources as they encounter various websites online. Another difference is in the nature of the inferences readers make with traditional and online texts. With traditional text, readers might have to tie ideas together from within a particular chapter of their book, but with online information, readers must make inferences between links that may not be explicitly provided. Last, the linguistic cueing system is different in that online information includes icons and dynamic image maps that show the relationships among ideas (Kinzer & Leander, 2003).

In their study of 11 skilled readers in a school of white middle to high socioeconomic students, Coiro and Dobler (2007) found that the existing strategies for learning with text were apparent as these adolescents engaged with hypertext and the Internet. For example, prior knowledge was still a critical variable in processing information, but they found that these adolescents needed knowledge of particular website structures and Web-based search strategies to be successful. They also found that readers were still using inferences, such as when students made predictions about which website might provide the information they needed. However, the students often needed to make these inferences and hold them in abeyance as they dealt with several sources of information, so the inferences themselves became as multilayered as the layers of information online. Students might find this multilayered inferencing difficult as they try to maintain their inferences across many layers of information. Coiro and Dobler (2007) also found that the need for self-regulated learning was tantamount to online text processing. Self-regulated strategies such as monitoring and evaluating involved such behaviors as clicking hyperlinks and search buttons and typing key phrases.

Another article that focused on online strategies and adolescents cited several important strategies for learning with online text (Kymes, 2005). Establishing a purpose for reading becomes even more critical in an online environment. Students with a clear purpose find it easier to establish navigational paths to reach their desired outcome, while students with no clear purpose can get lost in the navigation as they become overwhelmed by the volume of information or sidetracked by interesting information. Thus, readers with no purpose make several attempts at beginning the learning process and may become frustrated with the task (Brandt, 2000). Another strategy readers often used online was skimming and scanning because due to the sheer volume of information, readers often have to search rapidly to find the particular information they need. Kymes described this process as a "snatch and grab" approach (p. 494), in which readers snatch a particular website and quickly scan it for information without reading word for word until they determine those Internet sites that give them the information they need. Another strategy critical to online processing of text is using one's prior knowledge as a framework for learning new information. Since much of the information online is not elaborated or placed in a larger structure of information, the reader must possess that knowledge framework in order to understand the quality and credibility of the information he or she encounters. Vocabulary knowledge is also necessary online, not only in the online texts themselves but for the hyperlink words needed to search for information. Last, the text structures of online information are numerous and require a different understanding of how text is organized online. For example, many online texts enable readers to embed their own ideas through writing, and thus they are constructing the text structure at the same time they are using it to learn information.

DISCUSSION AND TEXT COMPREHENSION

In the 1990s and 2000s, researchers investigated the impact of discussion in the classroom with particular attention to peer-led discussions (Almasi, 1995; Almasi, McKeown, & Beck, 1996; Chinn, Anderson, & Waggoner, 2001). These studies found that rich discussions can enhance students' learning in the classroom (Murphy, Wilkinson, Soter, Hennessy, & Alexander, 2009). When we examined the discussion research conducted during the last decade in middle and high school classrooms, we found a preponderance of studies conducted in English language arts classrooms. For example, Applebee, Langer, Nystrand, and Gamoran (2003) examined discussion practices and student literacy performance in 64 English language arts classrooms in 19 middle and high schools. They found that high academic demands and classroom discussion practices led to increased spring semester performance. Likewise, Fall, Webb, and Chudowsky (2000) examined the impact of discussions on 10th-grade students' understanding of literature. Their study showed that when adolescents engaged in 10-minute discussions, their understanding of the literature increased significantly.

In another study of literature discussions, Rice (2005) investigated the influence of sixth-grade adolescents' sociocultural perspectives as they read and interpreted multicultural literature. Her findings illustrate the powerful impact that class, race, and gender have on adolescents' interpretations of multicultural literature. Thus, stories are socially constructed through the sociocultural lens of the adolescent readers. Last, Morocco and Hindin (2002) examined peer-led discussions of literature in middle-grade classrooms. Their analyses investigated the discourse practices of these adolescents as they engaged with literature. These discourse practices included stating and justifying claims, elaborating on others' claims, and providing alternative views to others' claims. The adolescents in this study also used their own funds of knowledge and experiences to interpret the literature they were reading.

Berne and Clark (2006) extended the research on discussions by focusing on how ninth-grade students use comprehension strategies during peer-led discussions of literature in an English language arts classroom. What is particularly valuable about their study is that they focused on the discipline-specific comprehension strategies that students used during their discussion of literature. These strategies included comparing/contrasting, contextualizing, questioning, searching for meaning, noting the author's craft, interpreting, engaging in retrospection, stating confusion, and inserting oneself into the text. They reported that when adolescents were comparing/contrasting they noted how the events of the story were similar to or different from their own existing knowledge. Contextualizing involved discussions of how the story elements fit within the context of the time and space of the novel or the larger milieu. The discussion also involved students searching for meaning by hypothesizing about reasons for the story events or character motivations. When students noted the author's craft, they discussed how the author developed the plot and characters of the story. Students also engaged in retrospection by talking about the thoughts that had occurred to them as they read the text. They also discussed how they would act as one of the characters by inserting themselves into the text.

While Berne and Clark's study (2006) adds to the research on how adolescents use comprehension strategies to talk about text in English language arts, we still need many more studies that examine the nature of these comprehension strategies within disciplinary discussions. What kinds of comprehension strategies are particularly useful to utilize in disciplinary discussions in order to achieve student learning from text? Since science is guided by discussions of inquiry, what kinds of comprehension strategies can students employ during inquiry discussions that will increase their learning? Discussions of history texts would focus on comprehension of both primary and secondary source materials. What kinds of comprehension strategies are evident in adolescents' discussions of these source materials?

PROFESSIONAL DEVELOPMENT AND COMPREHENSION

The findings from the RAND Reading Study Group (Snow, 2002) reported that teachers of adolescents are not effectively prepared to teach literacy strategies for learning with disciplinary texts. As a result, several articles have appeared during the last decade that examine how teachers can be trained to teach comprehension effectively (Fordham, 2006; Grisham, 2008; Hilden & Pressley, 2007). In one article, a university professor illustrated how instructors can teach preservice and inservice teachers to craft questions to increase their adolescents' understandings of disciplinary texts. Through the use of "embedded questions," the instructor encouraged the middle school teachers to frame questions as they were reading the text that would encourage their students to think strategically. The instructor and teachers examined how questions could be asked that encouraged students to activate their prior knowledge, envision the text, and make inferences about the text content. The instructor's goal was to show teachers how they can frame questions that encourage adolescents to grapple strategically with the text rather than use questions that merely assess their understanding. While Fordham's article has merit for increasing the quality of questions asked in content-area classrooms, the article does not focus on the nature of inquiry and how it is unique to each discipline. Future articles should explore how discipline experts craft inquiry questions to learn from their text materials and how adolescents can learn this process.

Hilden and Pressley (2007) studied five fifth-grade teachers as they participated in a 7-month professional development project focused on effective reading comprehension instruction to increase self-regulation. Several comprehension strategies were taught and modeled, including activating and applying prior knowledge, visualizing, summarizing, monitoring and clarifying, asking and answering questions, and previewing the text features. Inservice instruction also included strategies to address comprehension with informational texts. Each of these strategies was modeled through a think-aloud, so teachers could see the kinds of thinking involved in each strategy.

The findings of this study illustrate that despite the positive changes in the teachers' attitudes and uses of comprehension instruction, the researchers discovered that professional development that seeks to change teachers' instructional practices poses many challenges. One challenge was how to provide professional development to a diverse group of teachers with different levels of expertise. Some of the teachers reported feeling highly overwhelmed by the amount of information and the many ways that they needed to coordinate the strategies within their instruction in the classroom. Teacher attitudes were also an impediment to change because they were skeptical of professional development and, in particular, professional development involving comprehension strategies. They also exhibited doubt that some of the instructional approaches would be successful in the classroom. As these teachers began implementing comprehension instruction in their classrooms, they had many concerns about how to effectively incorporate these strategies into the broader curriculum that already existed and about the time it would take to plan the instruction and teach the strategies to the students. Teachers were also grappling with how to structure the classroom so they could achieve small-group strategy instruction without creating off-task student behavior as teachers were working with one small group. The teachers also expressed concern about how to be more explicit in their strategy instruction and how to vary the instructional approaches so that the strategies remained interesting to the students. The students posed some of the challenges to the project because they were not used to participating as active readers who valued the purposes behind the strategies. As the professional development continued, the teachers found it difficult to transition from modeling the strategies with the students to helping students understand how to use the strategies on their own. All of these challenges illustrate why professional development must be an ongoing process over several years, so teachers have the time to work through these many challenges as they plan their instruction.

In another study that explored how to educate teachers to more effectively teach reading comprehension, Grisham (2008) examined the impact of an advanced university reading program on teachers' instructional practices with comprehension instruction. Through 51 surveys and 12 teacher interviews, Grisham found that advanced reading programs can have a positive impact on teachers' knowledge base and implementation of comprehension instruction. One important finding that emerged is that teachers felt confident in their knowledge of the research base behind the strategies. This knowledge base enabled teachers to understand the reasons why they were implementing the comprehension instruction. The teachers in the program also reported that they gained significant knowledge about how to implement the comprehension strategy instruction in their classrooms, and they stated that their instruction was much more intentional as a result of the program. That is, teachers made conscious decisions about the comprehension needs of their students and the selection of strategies to use with particular narrative and informational texts.

Grisham also gathered data from the surveys concerning the frequency and type of reading and instructional strategies that teachers reported using. Inferencing garnered the highest frequency of use, and teachers reported using this reading strategy both before and during the reading event. This strategy was followed by visualizing and predicting. Teachers reported using visualizing throughout the reading process, while predicting was used before and during the reading. Other often-cited strategies were repeated reading to improve fluency and characterization work. Teachers also reported using previewing prior to reading and summarizing during and after the reading. Some of the most frequently used instructional strategies were K-W-L, the cloze procedure, and the DRTA. In contrast, the least-cited strategies included the anticipation guide, ReQuest, structured overviews, graphic organizers, and semantic mapping. Grisham reported that the strategies used most frequently might have been the ones teachers found easiest to implement in the classroom. We believe it would be interesting to interview teachers about their reasons for deciding which strategies to use during comprehension instruction.

Ness (2009) reported that middle school science and social studies teachers cited a lack of understanding and training regarding reading comprehension as their reasons for not incorporating comprehension instruction into the wider science and social studies curriculum. Teachers also believed that content coverage was the most important priority for them, and they didn't have the time to infuse these comprehension strategies into their curriculum. Certainly Ness's study points to the value that professional development could have in promoting the use of these comprehension strategies in disciplinary classrooms. She encourages secondary schools to adopt schoolwide professional development that clearly shows the value these comprehension strategies can have in disciplinary learning with texts. She also emphasizes the need to create a school environment that encourages teachers in the academic disciplines to examine their instructional goals through a literacy lens, conferring with one another about how particular literacy strategies can help students achieve these goals. Last, she stresses the need of active roles for reading coaches and literacy curriculum specialists who can assist teachers in integrating effective literacy strategies in their classrooms.

Current research has begun to examine disciplinary experts' literacy strategies, so we can better tailor comprehension instruction for the academic content in which adolescents are engaged (Shanahan & Shanahan, 2008). We also need to understand disciplinary experts' literacy strategies in order to provide professional development in comprehension that is tailored to their particular disciplines. In this book, we begin to examine literacy from a vantage point emphasizing the goals of each academic discipline and the literacy strategies that can support these goals as adolescents learn with text.

REFERENCES

Alexander, P. A., & Judy, J. E. (1988). The interaction of domain-specific and strategic knowledge in academic performance. *Review of Educational Research, 8*, 375–304.

Alfassi, M. (2004). Reading to learn: Effects of combined strategy instruction on high school students. *Journal of Educational Research, 97*(4), 171–185.

Almasi, J. F. (1995). The nature of fourth graders' sociocognitive conflicts in peer-led and teacher-led discussions of literature. *Reading Research Quarterly, 30,* 314–351.

Almasi, J. F., McKeown, M. G., & Beck, I. L. (1996). The nature of engaged reading in classroom discussions of literature. *Journal of Literacy Research, 28,* 107–146.

Applebee, A. N., Langer, J. A., Nystrand, M., & Gamoran, A. (2003). Discussion-based approaches to developing understanding: Classroom instruction and student performance in middle and high school English. *American Educational Research Journal, 40*(3), 685–730.

Ausubel, D. (1968). *Educational psychology: A cognitive view.* New York: Holt, Rinehart & Winston.

Berne, J. I., & Clark, K. F. (2006). Comprehension strategy use during peer-led discussions of text: Ninth graders tackle "The Lottery." *Journal of Adolescent and Adult Literacy, 49*(8), 674–686.

Biancarosa, C., & Snow, C. E. (2006). *Reading Next—A vision for action and research in middle and high school literacy: A report to Carnegie Corporation of New York* (2nd ed.). Washington, DC: Alliance for Excellent Education.

Blachowicz, S., & Fisher, P. (2000). Vocabulary instruction. In M. Kamil, P. Mosenthal, P.D. Pearson, & R. Barr (Eds.), *Handbook of reading research* (Vol. 3, pp. 503–523). Mahwah, NJ: Erlbaum.

Bleich, D. (1975). *Reading and feelings: Introduction to subjective criticism.* Urbana, IL: National Council of Teachers of English.

Brandt, D.S. (2000). Do the means justify the end-user searching? *Computers in Libraries, 20*(3), 54–56.

Brown, A. L., & Palincsar, A. S. (1984). Reciprocal teaching of comprehension-fostering and comprehension-monitoring activities. *Cognition and Instruction, 1,* 117–175.

Chinn, C. A., Anderson, R. C., & Waggoner, M. A. (2001). Patterns of discourse in two kinds literature discussion. *Reading Research Quarterly, 36,* 378–411.

Coiro, J., & Dobler, E. (2007). Exploring the online reading comprehension strategies used by sixth-grade skilled readers to search for and locate information on the Internet. *Reading Research Quarterly, 42*(2), 214–257.

Conley, M. W. (2008). *Content area literacy: Learners in context* (2nd ed.). Boston, MA: Allyn & Bacon.

Conley, M. W. (2009). Improving adolescent comprehension: Developing comprehension strategies in the content areas. In S.E. Israel & G.G.Duffy (Eds.), *Handbook of research on reading comprehension.* New York: Routledge.

Cromley, J. G., & Azevedo, R. (2007). Testing and refining the direct and inferential mediation model of reading comprehension. *Journal of Educational Psychology, 99*(2), 311–325.

Coutant, C., & Perchemlides, N. (2005). Strategies for teen readers. *Educational Leadership, 63*(2), 42–47.

Dole, J. A., Duffy, G. G., Roehler, L. R., & Pearson, P. D. (1991). Moving from the old to the new: Research on reading comprehension instruction. *Review of Educational Research, 61*(2), 239–264.

Fall, R., Webb, N. M., & Chudowsky, N. (2000). Group discussion and large-scale language arts assessment: Effects on students' comprehension. *American Educational Research Journal, 37*(4), 911–941.

Fang, Z. (2006). The language demands of science reading in middle school. *International Journal of Science Education, 28,* 491–520.

Fang, Z. (2008). Going beyond the fab five: Helping students cope with the unique linguistic challenges of expository reading in intermediate grades. *Journal of Adolescent and Adult Literacy, 51*(6), 476–487.

Fang, Z., Schleppegrell, M., & Cox, B. (2006). Understanding the language demands of schooling: Nouns in academic registers. *Journal of Literacy Research, 38,* 247–273.

Fordham, N. W. (2006). Crafting questions that address comprehension strategies in content reading. *Journal of Adolescent and Adult Literacy, 49*(5), 390–396.

Gambrell, L. B. (1980). Think-time: Implications for reading instruction. *Reading Teacher, 33,* 143–146.

Gee, J. P. (2003). *What video games have to teach us about learning and literacy.* New York: Palgrave McMillan.

Grisham, D. L. (2008). Improving reading comprehension in K-12 education: Investigating the impact of the reading specialist credential on the instructional decisions of veteran teachers. *Issues in Teacher Education, 17*(1), 31–46.

Guthrie, J. T. (2004). Classroom contexts for engaged reading: An overview. In J.T. Guthrie, A. Wigfield, & K.C. Perencevich (Eds.), *Motivating reading comprehension: Concept-Oriented Reading Instruction* (pp. 1–24). Mahwah, NJ: Erlbaum.

Guthrie, J. T., McRae, A., Coddington, C. S., Klauda, S. L., Wigfield, A., & Barbosa, P. (2009). Impacts of comprehensive reading instruction on diverse outcomes of low- and high-achieving readers. *Journal of Learning Disabilities, 42*(3), 195–214.

Guthrie, J. T., & Wigfield, A. (2000). Engagement and motivation in reading. In M. L. Kamil, P. B. Mosenthal, P. D. Pearson, & R. Barr (Eds.), *Handbook of reading research* (Vol. III, pp. 403–422). New York: Erlbaum.

Hagaman, J. L., & Reid, R. (2008). The effects of the paraphrasing strategy on the reading comprehension of middle school students at risk for failure in reading. *Remedial and Special Education, 29*(4), 222–234.

Harris, K. R., & Graham, S. (1996). *Making the writing process work: Strategies for composition and self-regulation.* Cambridge, MA: Brookline.

Heimlich, J., & Pittelman, S. (1986). *Semantic mapping: Classroom applications.* Newark, DE: International Reading Association.

Herber, H. (1978). *Teaching reading in content areas* (2nd ed.). New York: Prentice Hall.

Herber, H., & Nelson-Herber, J. (1993). *Teaching in content areas with reading, writing and reasoning.* Boston: Allyn & Bacon.

Hilden, K.R., & Pressley, M. (2007). Self-regulation through transactional strategies instruction. *Reading and Writing Quarterly, 23*(1), 51–75.

Homer, C. (1979). A direct reading-thinking activity for content areas. In R. T. Vacca & J. A. Meagher (Eds.), *Reading through content* (pp. 41–48). Storrs, CT: University Publications and the University of Connecticut Reading-Language Arts Center.

Jones, R. C., & Thomas, T. G. (2006). Leave no discipline behind. *Reading Teacher, 60*(1), 58–64.

Kintsch, W. (1988). The role of knowledge in discourse comprehension: A construction-integration model. *Psychological Review, 95,* 163–182.

Kintsch, W. (1998). *Comprehension: A paradigm for cognition.* Cambridge, England: Cambridge University Press.

Kinzer, C. K., & Leander, K. M. (2003). Reconsidering the technology/language arts divide: Electronic and print-based environments. In J. Flood, D. Lapp, J. R. Squire, & J. M. Jensen (Eds.), *Handbook of research on teaching the English language arts* (pp. 546–565). Mahwah, NJ: Erlbaum.

Klingner, J. K., & Vaughn, S. (1999). Promoting reading comprehension, content learning, and English acquisition through collaborative strategic reading (CSR). *Reading Teacher, 52,* 738–748.

Kress, G. (2004). *Literacy in the new media age.* London: Routledge.

Kymes, A. (2005). Teaching online comprehension strategies using think-alouds. *Journal of Adolescent and Adult Literacy, 48*(6) 492–500.

Langer, J. A. (1981). From theory to practice: A prereading plan. *Journal of Reading, 25,* 152–156.

Langer, J. (1982). Facilitating text processing. In J. Langer & T. Smith-Burke (Eds.), *Reader meets author/bridging the gap* (pp. 149–162). Newark, DE: International Reading Association.

Luckner, J., Bowen, S., & Carter, K. (2001). Visual teaching strategies for students who are deaf or hard of hearing. *Exceptional Children, 33*(3), 38–44.

Macon, J. M., Bewell, D., & Vogt, M. (1991). *Responses to literature.* Newark, DE: International Reading Association.

Manzo, A. V. (1969). The ReQuest procedure. *Journal of Reading, 11,* 123–126.

Manzo, A. V. (1975). Guided reading procedure. *Journal of Reading, 18,* 287–297.

Manzo, A. V., & Manzo, U. (1990). *Content area reading: A heuristic approach.* Columbus, OH: Merrill.

McGinley, W. J., & Denner, P. R. (1987). Story impressions: A pre-reading/writing activity. *Journal of Reading, 31,* 248–253.

Merkley, D., & Jeffries, D. (2001). Guidelines for implementing a graphic organizer. *Reading Teacher, 54*(4), 350–357.

Morocco, C. C., & Hindin, A. (2002). The role of conversation in a thematic understanding of literature. *Learning Disabilities Research and Practice, 17*(3), 144–159.

Murphy, P. K., Wilkinson, I. A. G., Soter, A. O., Hennessey, M. N., & Alexander, J. F. (2009). Examining the effects of classroom discussion on students' comprehension of text: A meta-analysis. *Journal of Educational Psychology, 101*(3), 740–764.

Ness, M. (2007). Reading comprehension strategies in secondary content-area classrooms. *Phi Delta Kappan, 89*(3), 229–231.

Ness, M. (2009). Reading comprehension strategies in secondary content-area classrooms: Teacher use of and attitudes towards reading comprehension instruction. *Reading Horizons, 49*(2), 143–166.

Nichols, J. (1980). Using paragraph frames to help remedial high school students with written assignments. *English Journal, 24*, 228–231.

Ogle, D. (1986). K-W-L: A teaching model that develops active reading of expository text. *Reading Teacher, 39*, 563–570.

Palincsar, A. S., & Brown, A. (1984). The reciprocal teaching of comprehension-fostering and comprehension-monitoring activities. *Cognition and Instruction, 1*, 117–175.

Perfetti, C. (1985). *Reading ability.* New York: Oxford University Press.

Pressley, M., El-Dinary, P. B., Gaskins, L., Schuder, T., Begman, J., Amasi, L., et al. (1992). Beyond direct explanation: Transactional instruction of reading comprehension strategies. *Elementary School Journal, 92*, 511–554.

Pressley, M., Johnson, C. J., Symons, S., & McGoldrick, J. A. (1989). Strategies that improve children's memory and comprehension of text. *Elementary School Journal, 90*(1), 3–32.

Raphael, T. E., & Au, K. H. (2005). QAR: Enhancing comprehension and test taking across grades and content areas. *Reading Teacher, 59*(3), 206–221.

Rasinski, T. V., Padak, N. D., McKeon, C. A., Wilfong, L. G., Friedauer, J. A., & Heim, P. (2005). Is reading fluency a key for successful high school reading? *Journal of Adolescent and Adult Literacy, 4*(1), 22–27.

Rice, P. S. (2005). It "ain't" always so: Sixth graders' interpretations of Hispanic-American stories with universal themes. *Children's Literature in Education, 36*(4), 343–362.

Rosenshine, B., Meister, C., & Chapman, S. (1996). Teaching students to generate questions: A review of the intervention studies. *Review of Educational Research, 66*, 181–221.

Sadoski, M., Goetz, E., & Kangiser, S. (1988). Imagination in story response: Relationships between imagery, affect, and structural importance. *Reading Research Quarterly, 23*(3), 330–336.

Samples, R. (1977). *The whole school book.* Reading, MA: Addison-Wesley.

Santa, C., Havens, L., & Maycumber, E. (1996). *Project CRISS: Creating independence through student-owned strategies* (2nd ed.). Dubuque, IA: Kendall/Hunt.

Schumaker, J. B., Denton, P. H., & Deshler, D. D. (1984). *The paraphrasing strategy.* Lawrence: University of Kansas.

Schwartz, R. (1988). Learning to learn vocabulary in content area textbooks. *Journal of Reading, 32*(2), 108–118.

Shanahan, T., & Shanahan, C. (2008). Teaching disciplinary literacy to adolescents: Rethinking content-area literacy. *Harvard Educational Review, 78*(1), 40–59.

Short, D. (1997). Reading, 'riting, and social studies: Research in integrated language and content secondary classrooms. In D. Brinton & M. Snow (Eds.), *The content-based classroom: Perspectives on integrating language and content* (pp. 213–232). Reading, MA: Addison-Wesley.

Short, K. G., Harste, J. C., Burke, C. (1995). *Creating classrooms for authors and inquirers* (2nd ed.). Portsmouth, NH: Heinemann.

Snow, C. (2002). *Reading for understanding: Toward an R&D program in reading comprehension.* Santa Monica, CA: RAND.

Souvignier, E., & Mokhlesgerami, J. (2006). Using self-regulation as a framework for implementing strategy instruction to foster reading comprehension. *Learning and Instruction, 16,* 57–71.

Stauffer, R. (1969). *Teaching reading as a thinking process.* New York: Harper & Row.

Street, B. (1999). New literacies in theory and practice. *Linguistics and Education, 10,* 1–24.

Szabo, S. (2006). KWHHL: A student-driven evolution of the KWL. *American Secondary Education, 34(3),* 57–66.

Taba, H. (1967). *Teacher's handbook for elementary social studies.* Reading, MA: Addison-Wesley.

U.S. Department of Education. (2005). Press release. Retrieved January 11, 2011, from *www.ed.gov/news/pressreleases/2005/12/12152005.html.*

U.S. Department of Education. (2010). Retrieved January 11, 2011, from *nces. ed.gov/nationsreportcard/pdf/main2009/2011455.pdf.*

Vacca, R., & Vacca, J. (2004). *Content area reading: Literacy and learning across content areas* (8th ed.). Boston: Allyn & Bacon.

Vacca, R., & Vacca, J. (2008). *Content area reading: Literacy and learning across content areas.* (9th ed.) Boston, MA: Allyn & Bacon.

Valmont, W. (2000). What teachers do in technology rich classrooms. In S. Wepner, W. Valmont, & R. Thurlow (Eds.), *Linking literacy and technology.* Newark, DE: International Reading Association.

Wharton-McDonald, R., & Swiger, S. (2009). Developing higher order comprehension in the middle grades. In S. E. Israel & G. G. Duffy (Eds.), *Handbook of research on reading comprehension* (pp. 510–530). New York: Routledge.

Wigfield, A., Guthrie, J. T., Perencevich, K. C., Taboada, A., Klauda, S. L., McRae, A., et al. (2008). Role of reading engagement in mediating effects of reading comprehension instruction on reading outcomes. *Psychology in the Schools, 45(5),* 432–445.

Wood, K. (1984). Probable passages: A writing strategy. *Reading Teacher, 37,* 496–499.

APPENDIX 1.1 Reading Strategies

		Prereading Strategies	
Setting a purpose, activating prior knowledge, and considering interest	Brainstorming (Taba, 1967; Vacca & Vacca, 2008; Wood, 2001)	Before they read, students make a vertical list of words/phrases that relate to the concept/focus.	*"Skilled readers think about what they already know before they read. We call this strategy activating prior knowledge. We're about to read a text about the Civil War (concept), and I want you to remember the information that you read (setting a purpose). One way to better remember the information is to think about what you already know about the Civil War before you read, so you can connect events in the story to what you already know. For example, I know that my home state, Illinois, was fighting for the North. I also know that Virginia was one of the Confederate states. What do you know about the war? Let's do an activity in which we activate our prior knowledge."*
	List–Group–Label (Taba, 1967; Wood, 2001)	Before they read, students make a vertical list of words/phrases that relate to the concept/focus. Then, they organize the list by grouping/categorizing their list, and labeling each category.	*See above.*
	PReP (Conley, 2008; Langer, 1982)	Before they read, students make a vertical list of words/phrases that relate to the concept/focus. Then, the teacher goes back through the list and asks students to elaborate on each word.	*See above.*

24

Setting a purpose, activating prior knowledge, and considering interest; asking questions; determining importance	K-W-L (Ogle, 1986)	Before they read, students make a vertical list of words/phrases that relate to the concept/focus in the K column. Then they write questions/ statements regarding information they want to know in the W column. As they read, students will write the important information in the L column.	*See above.*
	Semantic Map (Blachowicz & Fisher, 2000; Heimlich & Pittelman, 1986; Luckner, Bowen, & Carter, 2001; Short, 1997)	Before they read, the teacher and students construct an organized map of information they already know about the concept/focus.	*See above.*
	Anticipation Guide (Herber, 1978; Herber & Nelson-Herber, 1993; Vacca & Vacca, 2004)	Before they read, students state what they know and don't know about three to five statements by writing true/false or agree/disagree for each statement.	*See above.*

(*continued*)

APPENDIX 1.1 (continued)

Prereading Strategies

Guided Imagery (Langer, 1981; Sadoski, 1988; Samples, 1977)	Before they read, the students activate their prior knowledge by visualizing a paragraph related to the concept read by the teacher.	See above.
Story Impressions (McGinley & Denner, 1987)	Before they read, students state what they already know about some words from the story chosen by the teacher. The teacher should choose the words according to the setting, character, problem, and solution. Students then write a story using those words. As they read, students compare their written story with the author's story.	See above.
Probable Passage (Wood, 1984)	Before they read a difficult text, students state what they already know about some words from the story chosen by the teacher. Then, students determine whether each word fits in the setting, character, problem, or solution categories. Next, students read a probable passage and determine which words fit in the passage.	See above.
Advanced Organizer (Ausubel, 1968)	Before they read a difficult text, the teacher discusses with students the big picture via concepts related to the reading through a concept map.	See above.

Setting a purpose, activating prior knowledge, and considering interest

During-Reading Strategies

Analyzing text structure	Graphic Map (Ausubel, 1968; Merkley & Jeffries, 2001)	As they read, students construct a graphic map that shows how the author organized the information in the text.	"Let's imagine that you went into a grocery to pick up some peanut butter, jelly, potato chips, and cookies. Then ask students if these items would be in the same place in the store. Would the peanut butter and the potato chips be in the same place? Have students think about the items that would be together with the potato chips. Have students think about whether peanut butter and jelly would be in the same place. Tell students, "The peanut butter and jelly are placed together because the store manager **organized** the grocery store. He put the food items in order, according to the type or kind of food." Then say, "Did you know that book authors organize their books? In this book the author organized the ideas in the book by writing about the types or kinds of storms. We call this classification. Generate kinds of storms with the students. Then tell students, "Now we are going to read the book and look at how the author organized this book about storms."
Predicting	DRTA (Directed Reading Thinking Activity) (Homer, 1979; Stauffer, 1969; Valmont, 2000) DLTA (Directed Listening Thinking Activity)	As they read, students stop at appropriate places in the text and predict what might happen next in the story or what information the author might present next in the informational text. Students then validate/invalidate their predictions at each stopping point.	"One strategy that strategic readers use is **predicting**. As you read, you think about what might happen next in the story or about the information the author might write about next. So let's do an activity in which we practice this strategy."

(continued)

27

APPENDIX 1.1 (continued)

	During-Reading Strategies	
Signal Words (Rosenshine, Meister, & Chapman, 1996)	As they read, students stop at appropriate places and ask questions that begin with who, what, where, when how (reporter's formula).	*"One strategy that strategic readers use is **questioning**. Readers ask many types of questions. For example, you might read and ask: 'Who is the story about?' or 'What did the character say when he had trouble in the story? When does the story take place? Where does the story take place? Is the setting important? How did the character solve the problem in the story?' Good readers pause throughout the text and ask these kinds of questions, so we are going to practice this strategy of asking questions as we read."*
Generic Questions (Rosenshine et al., 1996)	As they read, students stop at appropriate places and ask the following generic questions: "How does this text relate to what I already know? What is the main idea of this text? What are the important ideas that relate to the main idea? How does the author put the ideas in order? What are the key vocabulary words, and do I know what they mean? What special things does the text make me think about?"	*"One strategy that strategic readers use is **questioning**. As students read, they stop at appropriate places and ask the following generic questions: 'How does this text relate to what I already know? What is the main idea of this text? What are the important ideas that relate to the main idea? How does the author put the ideas in order? What are the key vocabulary words, and do I know what they mean? What special things does the text make me think about?' It's really important to keep these questions in mind as you read, so you can pause throughout the text and ask these questions. Let's practice this strategy as we read today."*
Story Grammar Questions (Rosenshine et al., 1996)	As they read, students ask questions related to the story structure such as: 'What is the setting of the story? Is the setting important? Who are the characters? What are the characters like? How do the characters act? What is the problem in the story? How is the problem solved?' And so on …	*"One strategy that strategic readers use is **questioning**. As students read, they stop at appropriate places and ask the following questions about the story: 'What is the setting of the story? Is the setting important? Who are the characters? What are the characters like? How do the characters act? What is the problem in the story?*

Questioning

ReQuest (Manzo, 1969; Manzo & Manzo, 1990; Vacca & Vacca, 2008)	As they read, students stop at appropriate places and ask the teacher "I wonder" or "quiz" questions. The teacher answers each question and models the strategies she used to answer each question (predicting, summarizing, activating prior knowledge, and questioning).	How is the problem solved?' And so on … It's really important to keep these questions in mind as you read, so you can pause throughout the text and ask these questions. Let's practice this strategy as we read."
		"One strategy that strategic readers use is **questioning**. Readers ask many types of questions. For example, you might read and ask 'I wonder' questions. Maybe you're puzzled about the information in the text or about the information that the author hasn't given you, and you might want to know more about it. Another type of question is a quiz or teacher question. Good readers think about questions that the teacher might ask them, or what might be on a quiz."
Somebody Wanted But So (Macon, Bewell, & Vogt, 1991)	As they read, students summarize the story by stopping at appropriate places and stating: Somebody (character) Wanted (character's goal) But (problem) So (what happens)	"As students read, they think about the most important events or ideas in the story. This strategy is known as **summarizing**. When readers summarize a story, first they tell who 'somebody' was in the story. The 'somebody' was a character. This character wanted something, but a problem kept this character from getting what he wanted. **So**, the character usually had three choices. He gave up what he wanted, or he tried harder, or he tried something else. So let's do an activity that practices summarizing."
Most Important Word (Bleich, 1975)	As they read, students stop at appropriate places and determine the most important word according to them or the author. Then, they share the word and why they thought it was important.	"As they read, strategic readers pause during the text and determine the most important information in the text. Let's practice that strategy as we read today."

(continued)

APPENDIX 1.1 (continued)

		During-Reading Strategies	
Monitoring	Save the Last Word for Me (Short, Harste, & Burke, 1995)	As they read, students stop at appropriate places and determine the most important word according to them or the author. When they share their words, one student says his word and the other students have to guess why the student picked that particular word. Then the student gets the last word by stating why he/she picked that word.	*See above.*
	Guided Reading Procedure (GRP) (Manzo, 1975; Manzo & Manzo, 1990; Conley, 2008)	As they read, students stop at appropriate places, turn the book over, and note the ideas/events that they remember reading in the "Ideas I Know" column. Then, they note the ideas/events that they don't remember in the "Fuzzies" column. If students don't have any "Fuzzies," the teacher creates them by probing with the text.	*"As students read, they **monitor** their reading by being aware of ideas or events in the book that they remember very well and those ideas or events that are confusing or that they have forgotten. Let's practice an activity in which we identify ideas or events in the story that we know very well and those ideas that might still be fuzzy to us."*
Activating and building prior knowledge; questioning	New-Knew-Q (Gambrell, 1980)	As students read, they stop at appropriate places and note the information/events/characters/ characters that are new. They also ask "I wonder" and "teacher/quiz" questions.	*"As students read, they **activate their prior knowledge** or think about what they already know about the ideas in the story or text, and they think about the new information they did not know but are learning as they read. Another strategy that strategic readers use is **questioning.** Readers ask many types of questions. For example, you might read and ask 'I wonder' questions. Maybe you're puzzled about the information in the text or about information that an author doesn't give you, and you might want to know more about it.*

Reciprocal Teaching (Brown & Palincsar, 1984; Vacca & Vacca, 2008)

Summarizing, clarifying, questioning and predicting

As students read, they stop at appropriate places and summarize the text, clarify word/paragraphs/parts, ask "I wonder" and "quiz/teacher" questions, and make predictions and validate/invalidate their predictions.

Another type of question is a quiz or teacher question. Strategic readers think about questions that the teacher might ask them, or what might be on a quiz. So let's practice thinking about what you already know as you read and thinking about the new information you are learning. Then we will practice asking questions."

"As students read, they stop and pause several times as they read the story and practice four strategies that good readers use.

"One strategy we call summary. When strategic readers summarize, they try to think about the most important information in one sentence.

"Another strategy that a strategic reader uses is to clarify. Clarify means to make words and sentences more clear, so if there is a word that you don't know or a part of the text that is confusing, you might need to stop and clarify.

"A third strategy that strategic readers use is questioning. Good readers ask many types of questions. For example, you might read and ask 'I wonder' questions. Maybe you're puzzled about the information in the text, or the author doesn't give you the information, and you might want to know more about it. Another type of question is a quiz or teacher question. Good readers think about questions that the teacher might ask them, or what might be on a quiz.

"The last strategy that effective readers use as they read is predicting. As you read, you think about what might happen next in the story or the information the author might write about next. So let's do an activity in which we practice these four strategies."

(continued)

During-Reading Strategies

	During-Reading Strategies	
Say Something (Short, Harste & Burke, 1995)	As students read, they stop at appropriate places and make comments about their interest (what they like/dislike about the story), connect the text to their prior knowledge, ask "I wonder" and "quiz/teacher" questions, and make predictions and validate/invalidate their predictions.	*"As students read they stop every so often and employ four strategies that strategic readers use.* *"The first strategy that strategic readers use as they read is predicting. As you read, you think about what might happen next in the story, or what information the author might write about next.* *"A second strategy that strategic readers use is questioning. Good readers ask many types of questions. For example, you might read and ask 'I wonder' questions. Maybe you're puzzled about the actions of a character, or about information that the author didn't give you, and you might want to know more about it. Another type of question is a quiz or teacher question. Effective readers think about questions that the teacher might ask them, or what might be on a quiz.* *"Another way in which readers are strategic is by commenting on the text. Readers often express their interest in text by commenting on whether they like or dislike the story and identifying a part of the story that was interesting to them.* *"The last strategy strategic readers' use is making a connection or activating their prior knowledge as it relates to the story or text. When readers make a connection, they think about what they already know about the story by thinking about what the story reminds them of, and how the character is like someone they know. So let's do an activity in which we practice these four strategies."*

Considering interest, activating/building prior knowledge, questioning, and predicting

Imaging Chart

As students read, they image/visualize the information in the text.

*"As students read, they picture or **visualize** the information in the text. For example, if you are reading a story about a boy flying a kite, you would picture a boy with brown hair, striped shirt, and blue jeans running fast in a dirt field with a kite shaped liked a plane flying high in the air. Let's practice getting pictures in your minds. Everyone close your eyes and picture yourself riding a bike down a hill. [Wait 2 seconds and then ask students to tell you what they saw.] Now we are going to read a story and picture the events in the story."*

2

The Challenges of Reading Disciplinary Texts

Zhihui Fang

As students move from elementary to middle and high school, the curricular content they are expected to engage with becomes increasingly specialized and complex. This content is typically presented in academic texts that students often find difficult to comprehend and challenging to critique. The 2007 National Assessment of Educational Progress, for example, reports that fewer than one-third (27%) of 8th graders were able to demonstrate an overall understanding when reading texts with grade-level-appropriate content (Lee, Grigg, & Donahue, 2007). Leading literacy organizations (e.g., Alvermann, 2001; Biancarosa & Snow, 2004; Heller & Greenleaf, 2007; Moore, Bean, Birdyshaw, & Rycik, 1999) have recognized the situation, calling for greater attention to adolescent literacy and urging educators to continue reading instruction beyond the elementary grades. What is it about academic texts in secondary content areas that makes them demanding to read for adolescent learners, many of whom have been successful in elementary reading? This chapter identifies some of the linguistic challenges involved in reading academic texts in the key secondary subjects of science, mathematics, and history. An understanding of the linguistic issues involved in reading disciplinary texts can make an important contribution to the improvement of teaching and learning in content areas.

LANGUAGE, KNOWLEDGE, AND DISCIPLINARY LITERACIES

Academic texts in the secondary curriculum are constructed in patterns of language that differ significantly from those that construct the texts students typically read in the elementary school. This difference is a major source of reading difficulty for adolescents. In the elementary grades, students are exposed primarily to everyday knowledge, and the texts they read typically deal with topics that are near and dear to them and with events that occur at specific times and places. The language that constructs such knowledge is, thus, commonsense, close to the language students use in everyday spontaneous conversation with friends, family members, and others with shared experiences and communal understanding. In secondary schools, students are exposed to more advanced, abstract, and complex knowledge, which they are expected to not only assimilate and reproduce but also question and critique. The language used to construct and challenge this specialized knowledge thus becomes more technical, dense, abstract, and hierarchically structured. In this literacy development trajectory, students are expected to develop increasingly sophisticated control over language during the school years, moving from the language of everyday talk to the language for construing and challenging disciplinary knowledge (Christie, 1998; Halliday, 2007; Schleppegrell, 2004).

Not only is the language of secondary schooling distinct from that of elementary schooling, it also varies from one content area to another (Fang & Schleppegrell, 2008, 2010). In science, for example, what we recognize as empirically sound, objective, and authoritative is often expressed in language patterns that are technical and dense and that promote certain ways of thinking and reasoning about the natural world. In history, what is perceived to be uncontroversial fact is often colored by judgment and interpretation. Such judgment and interpretation are often construed in abstract language that effaces the role of the historian as recorder, interpreter, and adjudicator of the past (Coffin, 2006). In mathematics, meanings are constructed in technical and dense language that works in close partnership with visual images and mathematical symbolism. These linguistic differences reflect the fundamental differences in the ways different disciplines produce, communicate, and critique knowledge.

Given the distinct ways different academic disciplines use language to make their own meanings, students need to develop differentiated literacy skills and strategies for interacting with the texts of each discipline. As Unsworth (2001) has argued, "It is no longer appropriate to talk about 'literacy across the curriculum.' Instead there is a need to delineate 'curriculum literacies,' specifying the interface between a specific curriculum and its literacies rather than imagining there is a singular literacy that could be spread homogeneously across the curriculum" (p. 11). This view of disciplinary literacies has gained currency in recent scholarship on adolescent literacy (e.g., Fang & Schleppegrell, 2008, 2010; Moje, 2008; Shanahan & Shanahan, 2008).

The notion of "commonsense" versus "uncommonsense," "everyday" versus "specialized," or "generalized" versus "discipline specific" is at the core of the functional linguistics theory (Halliday & Matthiessen, 2004), a theory about language that informs the discussion of disciplinary literacies in this chapter. From a functional linguistics point of view, language is a principal resource for making meaning; it "construes, is construed by, and (over time) reconstrues the social context" (Martin, 1997, p. 4). Language constructs and reflects different kinds of knowledge in ways that are functional for each discipline, so the grammatical features of texts change as the knowledge they encode varies across disciplines (Halliday, 1993; Schleppegrell, 2004). The commonplace language that serves adolescents well in their daily lives does not suffice for comprehending, challenging, and composing the kinds of texts that present information in science, mathematics, and history at the secondary level. This linguistic variation across disciplines does not just occur at the word level; it also takes place at the level of grammar. Some of these lexical and grammatical differences, along with the challenges they present for reading comprehension, are the focus of discussion in this chapter. Recognizing disciplinary ways of using language is important because one cannot fully comprehend the texts of a specific discipline—where disciplinary knowledge is produced, stored, transmitted, and evaluated—without having a sense of how the discipline organizes knowledge through language.

READING SCIENCE

Science is a form of culture with its own social practices (Gee, 2004). It involves the use of not only scientific methods for observing, identifying, describing, and experimentally investigating natural phenomena, but also a specialized form of language for constructing and communicating scientific theories, principles, processes, and reasoning (Martin & Veel, 1998; Yore et al., 2004). The social practices of scientists are catalogued in a range of text types that students are expected to be able to read and write as part of their schooling experiences. The major text types of school science include procedure, procedural recount, description, report, explanation, and exposition (Martin, 1989; Schleppegrell, 2004; Veel, 1997). The structures and grammar of these texts are necessarily different from those of stories that students are used to reading in elementary school, as they provide the semiotic means with which scientists perform, explain, theorize, organize, and challenge science.

A procedural text consists of step-by-step instructions on how to conduct an experiment or observation. A procedural recount, on the other hand, records the aim, steps, results, and conclusion of a specific scientific activity already conducted. A report text organizes information about things by describing the taxonomy of classes and subclasses or the attributes, properties, and behaviors of a single class. A description text can be considered an instance of report but differs from report in that it is the specific individual, place, or thing that is characterized or described. An explanation text offers an account of how something works or reasons for some phenomenon. It deals with the interaction of factors and processes rather than a sequence of events, and thus has a process, rather than thing, focus. It usually starts with a general statement about the phenomenon in question, followed by a logically organized sequence of explanatory statements. An exposition text is intended to convince the reader of a point of view, judgment, or theory through the analysis, interpretation, and evaluation of data. In such a text, the writer advances a thesis, introduces background information about the issue in question, presents evidence to support or refute the thesis, and sums up the position in light of the argument presented.

As students advance through the school years, there is a gradual shift of emphasis in their textual diet. In the early elementary grades, procedures, procedural recounts, and descriptions are popular, as the structure and organization of these text types reflect the world of physical activity occurring at specific times and places. In the late elementary through secondary grades, students are increasingly expected to handle reports, explanations, and exposition, as these text types are the major resources for constructing the more abstract and complex knowledge that characterizes the curriculum of the later years of schooling. These three more advanced text types are the focus of discussion here.

Table 2.1 presents three texts representing each of the three major text types that are valued in the secondary science curriculum—report, explanation, and exposition. Text 1 is a science report about tornadoes. It is excerpted from *Science Voyages* (Horton et al., 2000), a sixth-grade science textbook. Texts 2 and 3 both come from *Living in the Environment* (Miller, 2004), an environmental science textbook for grades 9–12. Text 2 is an explanation text discussing why we are losing ground in our war against infectious bacteria. Text 3, an exposition text, argues why we should care about coral reefs. These texts use language patterns, or grammar, that students often find unfamiliar and alienating.

In order to highlight the new challenges involved in reading these

TABLE 2.1. Sample Secondary Science Texts

Text 1 (Report)	Tornadoes
	Some of the most severe thunderstorms produce tornadoes. A tornado is a violent, whirling wind that moves in a narrow path over land. It usually moves from southwest to northeast. Most tornadoes form along a front. In severe thunderstorms, the wind at different heights blows in different directions and at different speeds. This difference in wind directions and speed is called wind shear. A strong updraft will tilt the wind shear and produce rotation inside the thunderstorm. A funnel cloud appears. (from *Science Voyages*, 2000, p. 308)
Text 2 (Explanation)	Are We Losing Ground in Our War Against Infectious Bacteria?
	The incredible genetic adaptability of bacteria is one reason the world faces a potentially serious rise in the incidence of some infectious bacteria diseases once controlled by antibiotics. Other factors also play a role, including (1) spread of bacteria (some beneficial and some harmful) around the globe by human travel and the trade of goods, (2) overuse of antibiotics by doctors, often at the insistence of their patients (with a 2000 study by Richard Wenzel and Michael Edward suggesting that at least half of all antibiotics used to treat humans are prescribed unnecessarily), (3) failure of many patients to take all of their prescribed antibiotics, which promotes bacterial resistance, (4) availability of antibiotics in many countries without prescriptions, (5) overuse of pesticides, which increases populations of pesticide-resistant insects and other carriers of bacterial diseases, and (6) widespread use of antibiotics in the livestock and dairy industries to control disease in livestock animals and to promote animal growth.
	The result of these factors acting together is that every major disease-causing bacterium now has strains that resist at least one of the roughly 160 antibiotics we use to treat bacteria infections. In 1998, health officials were alarmed to learn of the existence of a strain of bubonic plague in Madagascar that is resistant to multiple antibiotics. (from *Living in the Environment*, 2004, p. 239)
Text 3 (Exposition)	Why Should We Care About Coral Reefs?
	More than one-fourth of the world's coral reefs have been lost to coastal development, pollution, overfishing, warmer ocean temperatures, and other stresses that are increasing. One problem is coral bleaching, which occurs when a coral becomes stressed and expels most of its colorful algae. This occurs because of stresses such as increased water temperature and runoff of silt that covers the coral and prevents photosynthesis.
	This loss of algae exposes the colorless coral animals and the underlying ghostly white skeleton of calcium carbonate. Unable to grow or repair themselves, the corals eventually die unless the stress is removed and algae recolonize them.
	Coral reefs are sometimes called the aquatic equivalent of tropical rain forests because they harbor such a high species biodiversity with myriad ecological interrelationships. The decline and degradation of these colorful oceanic sentinels should serve as a warning about the health of their habitats. (from *Living in the Environment*, 2004, p. 144)

texts, a narrative text (story) typical of the materials that students read in elementary school is presented below. This text (Text 4) is the opening paragraph in Valerie Hobbs's *Defiance*, a book about an 11-year-old boy, Toby Steiner, who is determined to do normal things on his vacation rather than return to the hospital for cancer treatment. Winner of Kirkus 2005 Best Book for Young Adults and a *School Library Journal* Best Book, the novel was also included in the 2009–2010 Sunshine State Young Reader's Award Program for grades 3–5, which is cosponsored by the Florida Department of Education and the Florida Association for Media in Education.

> Text 4: Toby knew he was in trouble, but the cow didn't. She just kept gazing at him with her huge brown eyes, like she was in love or something. So he went on petting her, even though he wasn't supposed to be there. His mother would have a fit if she knew. She was always having a fit about something, even out here in the country, where they were supposed to be having a vacation. (Hobbs, 2005, p. 9)

Technical Vocabulary

One obvious challenge in reading the three sample science texts (Texts 1–3) in comparison to the story text (Text 4) is the presence of technical vocabulary. Two types of technical vocabulary are relevant here. The first consists of words that are unique to the realm of science. These are terms that have been specifically coined for science and, as such, are essential to the creation and organization of specialized knowledge in science. Without them, science would be incomplete, inaccurate, and imprecise. Words such as *tornado, wind shear, updraft, funnel cloud, antibiotics, pesticides, bacteria, algae, silt,* and *photosynthesis* belong to this category. Because these words are rarely used in students' everyday language, they present problems for both decoding (recognition) and understanding (meaning).

The second type of technical vocabulary involves words that occur with regularity in students' everyday language but assume specialized or metaphorical meanings when used in a scientific context. Words of this type from the three sample science texts include *front, strain(s), stress(es), skeleton, harbor, bleaching, runoff,* and *health*. These words are often taken for granted during reading because they present little challenge for recognition (i.e., decoding). While secondary students may be able to sound out the words, they may not always be aware of the technical meanings associated with these words in the context of science.

Significant comprehension problems can arise when a text contains a high proportion of technical vocabulary, as the following passage from a 10th-grade biology textbook by Postlethwait and Hobson illustrates.

In <u>prokaryotes</u>, <u>transcription</u> and <u>translation</u> occur within the <u>cytoplasm</u>. In <u>eukaryotes</u>, however, <u>transcription</u> occurs in the <u>nucleus</u>, and then <u>mRNA</u> passes through the <u>nuclear envelope</u> and into the <u>cytoplasm</u>, where <u>translation</u> occurs. The physical <u>separation</u> of <u>transcription</u> and <u>translation</u> by the <u>nuclear envelope</u> gives <u>eukaryotes</u> more opportunities to <u>regulate gene expression</u>. (from *Modern Biology*, 2006, p. 424)

This short excerpt contains 21 technical words of both types (underlined) out of a total of 51 words. Such a heavy load of technical vocabulary can make the text taxing to process, disrupting reading fluency and causing comprehension failure.

Long Noun Phrases

Not only are science texts technical, they are also dense. The informational density of science texts is created by the use of long noun phrases. In English, nouns are a major grammatical resource for expanding information (Fang, Schleppegrell, & Cox, 2006), and science exploits this resource to the fullest extent. For example, a noun such as *scientist* can be expanded into a noun phrase like "the first Hispanic woman scientist in the United States who received this honor" by adding premodifiers and postmodifiers. Premodifiers can consist of articles (e.g., *a, an*), determiners (e.g., *the*), and demonstratives (e.g., *these, that*); numeratives (e.g., *first, ten*); adjectives (e.g., *Hispanic*); and nouns (e.g., *woman*). Postmodifiers are typically made up of prepositional phrases (e.g., *in the United States*) and embedded clauses (e.g., *who received this honor*). This way of expanding information is particularly useful in constructing scientific definitions, as it enables scientists to give terse but complete and accurate descriptions of technical concepts (e.g., *A hurricane is <u>a large, swirling, low-pressure system that forms over tropical oceans</u>*). It is also useful for integrating and compacting information that may otherwise be expressed in the more "fragmented" language of everyday speech. For example, the information presented in these sentences—*There is an attack of smallpox. The attack is imagined. It can "infect" hundreds of people. These people work in the health care profession.*—can be transformed into more scientific language as a long noun phrase: *a fake smallpox attack that can "infect" hundreds of people working in the health care profession.*

Texts 1, 2, and 3 are filled with long, complex noun phrases. Text 1 uses one long noun phrase to construct a definition of *tornado* (*a violent, whirling wind that moves in a narrow path over land*) and several others to concentrate information (e.g., *some of the most severe thunderstorms, the wind at different heights, this difference in wind direction and speed*). Texts 2 and 3 also use many long noun phrases to integrate and concentrate information, such as:

- *the incredible genetic adaptability of bacteria*
- *a potentially serious rise in the incidence of some infectious bacteria diseases once controlled by antibiotics*
- *at least half of all antibiotics used to treat humans*
- *the results of these factors acting together*
- *populations of pesticide-resistant insects and other carriers of bacterial diseases*
- *every major disease-causing bacterium*
- *strains that resist at least one of the roughly 160 antibiotics we use to treat bacteria infections*
- *the existence of a strain of bubonic plague in Madagascar that is resistant to multiple antibiotics*
- *more than one-fourth of the world's coral reefs*
- *runoff of silt that covers the coral and prevents photosynthesis*
- *the underlying ghostly white skeleton of calcium carbonate*
- *the aquatic equivalent of tropical rain forests*
- *such a high species biodiversity with myriad ecological interrelationships*
- *the decline and degradation of these colorful oceanic sentinels*
- *a warning about the health of their habitats*

Long noun phrases such as these significantly increase the informational density of the three sample texts. The informational density of a text can be measured by an index called lexical density (Halliday & Martin, 1993). Lexical density can be calculated as the ratio of the number of content words (e.g., nouns, verbs, adjectives, some adverbs) to the number of nonembedded clauses in a text. It is in fact a much more reliable tool for measuring text difficulty than the traditional readability formulas. According to Halliday and Martin (1993), the lexical density of everyday spoken language is between 2 and 3, but that of written texts is around 4 to 6; in science texts, the index can go up to 10 or higher. The lexical density indices for the three science texts are 5.2, 12.5, and 5.8, respectively. These numbers are much higher than that of Text 4 (the story text), which is 1.8. With such high informational density, science texts present considerable processing demands for adolescent readers, who are typically used to the kind of texts that resembles Text 4, where nouns are generally short and simple (e.g., *Toby, he, she, the cow, his mother, a vacation*).

Nominalizations

In reading science, students come into contact with not only technical vocabulary and dense noun phrases, but also abstract entities realized in nominalizations. Nominalizations are nouns that derive from other grammatical structures such as verbs, adjectives, conjunctions, prepositional phrases, or clauses. For example, the nouns *adaptability* and *availability* in Text 2 derive from the verb *adapt* and the adjective *available,* respectively. When a verb (encoding action) or an adjective (encoding quality) is turned into a noun, it becomes a "thing" that also incorporates the action or quality from which it derives. Thus, instead of saying "bacteria adapt very well" and "antibiotics are available," which are more congruent with everyday ways of using language, Text 2 converts them into "adaptability of bacteria" and "availability of antibiotics," which are more abstract modes of expression. One advantage of this grammatical transference is that de-verbal and de-adjective nouns can be qualified by adding pre- and postmodifiers, as in *the incredible genetic adaptability of bacteria* and *availability of antibiotics in many countries without prescriptions*. This creates dense noun phrases with abstractions, which can cause considerable comprehension problems for readers.

Nominalization is a key grammatical resource in scientific writing and reasoning, as it enables scientists to synthesize information, create semitechnical concepts, and develop text flow. Unlike Text 4, which contains no nominalization, the three science texts, particularly the explanation and exposition texts, use many nominalizations. In Text 1, *this difference in wind directions and speed* is a nominalization that summarizes what is said in the sentence prior, *the wind at different heights blows in different directions and at different speeds*, and allows the idea to be discussed further. Other nominalizations such as *heights, directions*, and *rotation* are abstractions that become semitechnical concepts.

Text 2 is perhaps the most linguistically challenging of the three sample science texts. One major reason for this difficulty is that the text is packed with nominalizations, many of which are also embedded in long noun phrases. These noun phrases are listed below, with nominalizations underlined and their verb or adjective counterparts in parentheses at the end of each example:

- *the incredible genetic adaptability of bacteria* (to adapt)
- *a potentially serious rise in the incidence of some infectious bacteria diseases once controlled by antibiotics* (to rise, to occur)
- *spread of bacteria* (to spread)
- *human travel* (to travel)
- *the trade of goods* (to trade)
- *overuse of antibiotics by doctors* (to use too much)
- *the insistence of their patients* (to insist)

- *failure of many patients to take all of their prescribed antibiotics* (to fail)
- *bacteria resistance* (to resist)
- *availability of antibiotics in many countries without prescriptions* (be available, to prescribe)
- *overuse of pesticides* (to use too much)
- *widespread use of antibiotics in the livestock and dairy industries to control disease in livestock animals and to promote animal growth* (to use, to grow)
- *bacteria infections* (to infect)
- *the existence of a strain of bubonic plague in Madagascar that is resistant to multiple antibiotics* (to exist)

The use of nominalizations in this text enables the author to create abstract entities that can then be elaborated through the addition of pre- and postmodifiers. This, in effect, creates a text that is dense and tightly packed with information.

Text 3 also uses many nominalizations, as shown below (again with nominalizations underlined and their verb counterparts in parenthesis at the end of each example).

- *coastal development* (to develop)
- *pollution* (to pollute)
- *overfishing* (to fish too much)
- *coral bleaching* (to bleach)
- *stresses that are increasing* (to stress)
- *this loss of algae* (to lose)
- *myriad of ecological interrelationships* (to interrelate)
- *the decline and degradation of these colorful oceanic sentinels* (to decline, to degrade)
- *a warning about the health of their habitats* (to warn)

Nominalizations such as *development, pollution, overfishing, bleaching, stresses*, and *interrelationships* create semitechnical concepts that are key to the discussion of environmental protection for coral reefs. Other nominalizations allow the author to synthesize the information that has been discussed in the prior text so that they can become the focus of subsequent discussion. This in effect creates information flow and contributes to textual cohesion. For example, *this loss of algae* summarizes the discussion about the impact of human and natural activities (e.g., coastal development, pollution, coral bleaching) on the health of algae in the first paragraph and becomes the subject of the first sentence in the second paragraph. Similarly, the author uses *the decline and deg-*

radation of these colorful oceanic sentinels to summarize the effects of human and natural activities on coral reefs discussed in the preceding paragraphs and to serve as a departure point for saying more about the environmental consequences of human and natural activities. Readers who are unaware of how nominalizations work in scientific meaning making will likely have trouble comprehending the text.

Metaphorical Realizations of Logical Reasoning

An additional challenge in reading science texts is that logical reasoning is often metaphorically realized. In everyday language, logical connections among ideas are typically realized explicitly between clauses through conjunctions of various types (e.g., *however, and, if, because*). This is the case with the story text (Text 4), in which conjunctions such as *but, so, even though,* and *if* explicitly connect ideas in the text. In science texts, however, logical reasoning is not always realized through conjunctions. It is also conveyed through nouns, verbs, prepositional phrases, and nonfinite clauses. This makes logical connections among ideas implicit and difficult to identify for students.

In Text 1, for example, the verb *produce* in "*A strong updraft will tilt the wind shear and produce rotation inside the thunderstorm*" encodes a causal relation, that is, *a strong updraft* causes *rotation inside the thunderstorm*. In Text 2, causal relations are expressed by nouns (e.g., *reason, results*) instead of the conjunction *because*. In the first sentence of the first paragraph, the cause–effect relation between the adaptability of bacteria and the rise in the incidence of infectious bacteria diseases is conveyed through the noun *reason*. Similarly, the noun *results* in the first sentence of the second paragraph also indicates that bacteria resistance is caused by several factors acting together. The logical reasoning behind these two sentences could have been made more explicit had the sentences been rephrased congruently using the conjunction *because*, as in

- *Because bacteria genes adapt incredibly well, we see more cases of infectious bacteria diseases.*
- *Because these factors act together, every major disease-causing bacterium now has strains that resist antibiotics.*

Cause–effect relations can sometimes be indicated via prepositional phrases. For example, the prepositional phrase *at the insistence of their patients* implies a causal relation, meaning that doctors overprescribe antibiotics <u>because</u> their patients insist on using them. Using the conjunction *because* would have made the logical reasoning easier to discern. Prepositional phrases can encode other types of logical reasoning as well. For example, "*with a 2000 study* ... " indicates an additive relationship, giving an example of doctors' overuse of antibiotics. Here, the preposition *with* is equivalent to *for example*.

In Text 3, causal relations are realized through not only the conjunctions *because* and *because of*, but through verbs and other conjunctions. For example, the verb phrase *lost to* in the first sentence of the text suggests that costal development, pollution, and other natural/human activities are the causes of the coral reefs' disappearance. This same idea might be better understood were the sentence reworded as "*Because of coastal development. ..., more than one-fourth of the world's coastal reefs disappear.*" In the second sentence of the text, the conjunction *when*, as in *which occurs when a coral becomes stressed*, also indicates some kind of causality (in addition to conditionality), suggesting that coral bleaching can be caused by corals getting stressed. This conflation of causality and conditionality is not uncommon in academic texts (see also Schleppegrell, 2004). Finally, in the non-finite clause *Unable to grow or repair themselves*, which means "because the corals are unable to grow or repair themselves," the logical meaning of causality is left implicit. Clearly, these ways of using language make logical reasoning more difficult to identify and can hinder readers' understanding of the true causes of—as well as solutions to—environmental problems.

Summary

The grammatical features identified above—technical vocabulary, long noun phrases, nominalizations, and metaphorical realizations of logical reasoning—are potential sources of reading difficulties in science. All of these features tend to co-occur in science texts, resulting in what is recognized as "the language of school science" (Fang, 2006). It is this language that many students find alienating and challenging.

READING MATHEMATICS

Like science, mathematics has its own language that is functional for constructing mathematical meanings. In mathematics, however, language alone is often insufficient for construing mathematical knowledge and reasoning (Lemke, 2003). In fact, mathematical texts are typically multisemiotic, drawing on not only linguistic but also symbolic and visual resources (O'Halloran, 2005). Mathematical symbols—such as Σ, $F(\chi)$, π, η, =, and β—are used to represent concepts, axioms, lemmas, corollaries, theorems, operations, and relationships that are sometimes awkward to express in language. For example, the equation $h = -16t^2 +$

$35t$ gives the altitude (h) a football will reach t seconds after it is kicked with an initial upward velocity of 35 feet per second. The complete pattern of the relationship between altitude (h) and time (t) is described here with both concision and precision, a feat hard to accomplish with language alone. Visual displays such as graphs, charts, and diagrams are also important in mathematical meaning making, as they enable mathematicians to represent the linguistically and symbolically encoded information in ways that are tangible to our perceptual sense. For example, the relationship between time and altitude encoded in $h = -16t^2 + 35t$ can be graphically represented in a parabola such as Figure 2.1. The figure gives the reader instant insights into the nature of this relationship.

The tripartite formation of mathematics texts evolved from everyday language to meet the new needs of mathematical meaning making. O'Halloran (2000) summarized the functions of the three semiotic resources in mathematics this way:

> The mathematical symbolism contains a complete description of the pattern of the relationship between entities, the visual display connects our physiological perceptions to this reality, and the linguistic discourse functions to provide contextual information for the situation described symbolically and visually. (p. 363)

Thus, any discussion of the linguistic challenges involved in reading mathematics texts must take into account the interaction of language with visual and symbolic elements.

Secondary mathematics textbooks are typically made up of chunks of text labeled as a hypothesis, theorem, proof, example, exercise, review, and so on. Table 2.2 includes three such chunks of text excerpted from two popular secondary mathematics textbooks. Text 5 comes from the review section of a chapter on quadratic equations and functions in an algebra textbook for grades 9–10 (Bellman, Bragg, Charles, Handlin,

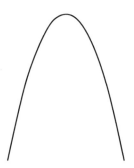

FIGURE 2.1. Parabola.

TABLE 2.2. Sample Secondary Mathematics Texts

Text 5   A function of the form $y = ax^2 + bx + c$, where $a \neq 0$, is a quadratic function. The shape of its graph is a parabola. The axis of symmetry of a parabola divides it into two congruent halves. The vertex of a parabola is the point at which the parabola intersects the axis of symmetry. The axis of symmetry is the line with the equation $x = -b/2a$. The x-coordinate of the vertex of the parabola is $-b/2a$.

     The value of a in a quadratic function $y = ax^2 + bx + c$ determines the width of the parabola and whether it opens upward or downward. The value of c is the y-intercept of the graph. Changing the value of c shifts the parabola up or down.

     When the parabola opens downward, the y-coordinate of the vertex is a maximum point of the function. When the parabola opens upward, the y-coordinate of the vertex is a minimum point of the function. (from *Algebra 1*, 2004, p. 569)

Text 6   Prove that the bases of a trapezoid have unequal lengths.
Given: Trap. PQRS with bases $\overline{PQ}$ and $\overline{SR}$
Prove: PQ ≠ SR

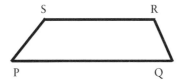

Proof:
Assume temporarily that PQ = SR. We know that $\overline{PQ}$ ‖ $\overline{SR}$ by the definition of a trapezoid. Since quadrilateral PQRS has two sides that are both congruent and parallel, it must be a parallelogram, and $\overline{PS}$ must be parallel to $\overline{QR}$. But this contradicts the fact that, by definition, trapezoid PQRS can have only one pair of parallel sides. The temporary assumption that PQ = SR must be false. It follows that PQ ≠ SR. (from *Geometry*, p. 215)

Text 7   Theorem 9-13: When a secant segment and a tangent segment are drawn to a circle from an external point, the product of the secant segment and its external segment is equal to the square of the tangent segment. (from *Geometry*, 2004, p. 363)

& Kennedy, 2004). Text 6 is a proof listed under the example section of a chapter on geometry inequalities. It comes from a geometry textbook intended for grades 9–10 (Jurgensen, Brown, & Jurgensen, 2004). Text 7 is a theorem from the same geometry textbook.

Technical Vocabulary

One of the challenges in reading mathematics texts is technical vocabulary. Mathematics is a highly technical discipline requiring the use of terms that are uniquely mathematical as well as everyday words that assume technical meanings. Words that are solely mathematical are usually of Latin or Greek origin (e.g., *apothem, cosine, quotient, vector, polynomial, diameter, integer*) and as such, they rarely cause confusion for students, even though they can still be difficult. A variety of such technical words are used in the three mathematics sample texts, including *quadratic, parabola, axis, equation, vertex, symmetry, trapezoid, quadrilateral, parallelogram, secant*, and *tangent*. These words are central to the construction of specialized knowledge in the fields of algebra and geometry.

One of the challenges in learning technical vocabulary words such as these is to understand hierarchies of relationships among the terms. For example, a square, a rectangle, a rhombus, and a trapezoid are all quadrilaterals, with different properties: rectangles and squares are parallelograms, but trapezoids are not; a square is always a rhombus or a rectangle, but a rhombus or rectangle is not a square. The relationships among these terms can be stated as follows: a quadrilateral becomes a trapezoid when there is one pair of parallel sides, but a parallelogram when there are two pairs of parallel sides; a parallelogram becomes a rectangle when its four angles are all right angles, but a rhombus when its four sides are of equal length; a parallelogram becomes a square when all sides are equal and all angles are right angles. Understanding the properties associated with each of these technical terms is important to understanding logical reasoning in mathematics, as students are sometimes required to write the converse, inverse, and contrapositive of *if–then* statements (e.g., "If a quadrilateral is a rhombus, then it is a parallelogram" "If a quadrilateral is a parallelogram, then it is a rhombus") and to judge whether the conditionals are true or false.

The use of everyday, nontechnical items as technical lexis also presents a challenge to the reader. Words such as *face, solid, find, suppose, power, absolute, times, order, acute*, and *volume* belong to this category. These words can cause confusion because students have to distinguish between their meaning in mathematics and their meaning in nonmathematical fields. In the three sample texts, everyday words like *function, value, coordinate, intercept, bases, congruent, segment, product, square*, and *circle* have specifically mathematical meanings.

Semitechnical Terms

In addition to technical vocabulary, mathematics also uses many semitechnical terms, which are created through nominalization. Nominalization is an indispensible tool for mathematical meaning making. It helps create abstract "things," or virtual entities, that can then be elaborated or quantified, reified as mathematical concepts, or put into new relationships with other entities and concepts (Veel, 1999). For example, when mathematical operations such as *add* or *divide* are turned into *addition* and *division*, they become topical areas of mathematics that mean much more than the concrete operations of adding and dividing. Veel (1999) distinguishes between "operational facility" and "conceptual understanding," noting that it is possible for a student to be able to divide but still not fully understand the concept of division. In fact, the development from knowing how to add and divide (as in elementary mathematics) to understanding the concepts of addition and division (as in secondary mathematics) is a giant step that involves induction and abstraction.

Similarly, adjectives such as *long, wide,* and *high* can, when nominalized, become mathematical concepts of *length, width* and *height,* which are key to the discussion of the volume of three-dimensional geometric shapes. These concepts capture more than the properties encoded in the adjectival forms and can be further quantified (e.g., *a width of 50 feet, one-fourth of the height of a square prism*). And when a verb such as *measure* is nominalized, the virtual entity *measure* can then be qualified (e.g., *the measure <u>of each angle of a regular polygon</u>*) or entered into relationships with other concepts or virtual entities (e.g., *The sum of the measures of the interior angles of a polygon <u>equals the product of 180 degrees and two less than the number of sides</u>*).

Nominalization is a salient feature of mathematical discourse, as can be observed in the three sample mathematics texts in Table 2.2. In Text 5, for example, the nominalization *equation* comes from the verb *equate* and is used as a semitechnical term to refer to the symbolic expression $x = -b/2a$. The mathematical concept of *width,* as in *the width of the parabola,* derives from the adjective *wide.* In Text 6, the bases of the trapezoid PQRS are characterized as having *unequal lengths,* a virtual entity that derives from the adjective *long.* Similarly, the word *definition,* as in *the definition of a trapezoid,* evolves from the verb form *define.* The mental process of *assume temporarily* at the beginning of the proof gets turned, at the end of the proof, into an abstract concept, *the temporary assumption,* which is then qualified with the addition of an embedded clause: *that PQ = SR.* In Text 7, *the product of the secant segment and its external segment* and *the square of the tangent segment* can be seen as virtual entities that derive from the mathematical processes of multiplying the secant segment and its external segment and of squaring the tangent segment, respectively.

These ways of using language help create an abstract textual world with semitechnical entities and virtual objects working in conjunction with technical vocabulary to construct specialized meanings in mathematics. Students who are used to the commonsense reality construed through everyday language need experience and guidance when interacting with mathematics texts.

Long Noun Phrases

Technical vocabulary and semitechnical lexis do not occur in isolation in mathematics texts. Rather, they interact with each other and with other grammatical elements to construct meanings (Schleppegrell, 2007). Like other academic texts, mathematics texts are "rhetorical in nature, addressing and attempting to persuade a reader" (Morgan, 1998, p. 9). It is therefore necessary to look beyond the level of vocabulary at the overall grammatical patterns in the text. While the challenges of technical vocabulary and semitechnical lexis may be obvious to students, the challenges associated with the grammatical patternings that these terms bring with them are more difficult to recognize. Mathematics texts in English have a tendency to exploit long noun phrases and linking verbs (e.g., *be, have, equal*). These grammatical resources facilitate the construction of mathematical definitions, theorems, propositions, lemmas, corollaries, proofs, scholiums, problems, and so forth, as they enable mathematicians to include a large number of technical and semitechnical concepts (e.g., *the degree of a polynomial with one variable, the value of the greatest exponent of the variable that appears in any term; a cylinder with a height of 500 feet and a volume of 1×10^6 cubic feet^3, about 89% of the surface area of a square prism with the same height and volume; the absolute value of a real number, the distance between the origin and the point representing the real number*) and then relate them to each other or to other mathematical concepts through the use of linking verbs (e.g., *The degree of a polynomial with one variable is the value of the greatest exponent of the variable that appears in any term. A cylinder with a height of 500 feet and a volume of 1×10^6 cubic feet^3 has about 89% of the surface area of a square prism with the same height and volume. The absolute value of a real number is the distance between the origin and the point representing the real number.*)

Long noun phrases are found throughout the three mathematics texts in Table 2.2. Samples of these noun phrases follow:

- *a function of the form $y = ax^2 + bx + c$*
- *the axis of symmetry of a parabola*
- *the point at which the parabola intersects the axis of symmetry*
- *the line with the equation $x = -b/2a$*
- *the x-coordinate of the vertex of the parabola*
- *the value of a in a quadratic function $y = ax^2 + bx + c$*

- *two sides that are both congruent and parallel*
- *the fact that, by definition, trapezoid PQRS can have only one pair of parallel sides*
- *the temporary assumption that PQ = SR*
- *product of the secant segment and its external segment*

Long noun phrases such as these increase the informational density of the texts. In addition, they often encode mathematical processes and reasoning that must be unpacked in order for them to be fully understood. For example, several mathematical operations are embedded in the long noun phrase *the sum of the angle measures divided by the number of angles in the polygon.* These operations include (1) counting (count the number of angles in the polygon), (2) measuring (measure the degrees of each angle in the polygon), (3) adding (add up the degree measures of the angles), and (4) dividing (divide the result from step 3 by the result from step 1).

Word problems in mathematics often exploit long noun phrases, as can be seen in this example from a mathematics textbook for grades 6–8 (Charles, Branch-Boyd, Illingworth, Mills, & Reeves, 2004, p. 348): Find *the final balance in an account with $1,200 and an interest rate of 5% compounded annually for 7 years.* Here, students are asked to find, or figure out (not physically locate), a virtual object called a "balance," but all the given information related to this virtual object is constructed in a long noun phrase (underlined) that encodes several mathematical processes and assumptions. This long noun phrase can be unpacked into phrases that correspond to the concrete reality of the everyday world: *there is a bank account; the account has $1,200 in it now; the money will earn interest; the interest rate is 5% and it is compounded every year; the money will remain in the account for 7 years; we want to know the amount of money left in the account at the end of the 7th year.* Examples like this show the highly dense and abstract nature of mathematics texts and why it can be challenging for students to read the texts and solve the problems presented in them.

Symbolism and Visual Display

Another challenge in reading mathematics texts is that mathematical symbolism and visual displays are often juxtaposed with language in the construction of mathematical meaning. When mathematical symbolism and visual display are not explicitly included in the linguistic text, it is often necessary to translate the language (e.g., *the volume of a cylinder equals the area of a base times the height of the cylinder*) into mathematical symbols (e.g., $V = \pi r^2 h$, where r is the radius of the cylinder base and h is the cylinder height) and/or visual displays (see Figure 2.2) in order for students to truly understand the information presented and solve the problem posed.

Like mathematical language, mathematical symbolism too can leave many mathematical processes implicit, requiring the reader to unpack the symbols and equations and perform the mathematical operations and reasoning buried in them. Text 5, for example, embeds a quadratic equation, $y = ax^2 + bx + c$ that encodes several arithmetic and algebraic operations, such as addition and multiplication. Students need to know the relevant theorems, corollaries, axioms, and propositions subsumed under these operations in order to make sense of the text. O'Halloran (2000) has likened the structure of equations like this one to the structure of a linguistic clause, showing how mathematical symbols are combined to form operations and equations in the same way that words are combined to form phrases and clauses. From this perspective, the quadratic equation $y = ax^2 + bx + c$ can be conceived of as a linguistic clause, where y, a, x, b, and c (called *atoms*) are combined into x^2, ax^2, and bx (called *expressions*), which are further combined into an *equation*. With each combination in the hierarchical ordering, the reader is taken further away from the everyday construal of meaning. Here, the terms *atom*, *expression*, and *equation* in mathematical symbolism are analogous to *word*, *phrase*, and *clause*, respectively, in language. Deconstructing the "grammar" of mathematical symbolism this way shows that reading mathematics texts often involves "long chains of reasoning that provide little or no indication of the results, definitions, axioms,

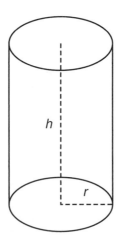

FIGURE 2.2. Cylinder.

operational properties or laws that have been used" (O'Halloran, 2000, p. 377).

Understanding language and symbolism may not be enough to comprehend Text 5. Students also must be able to construct and interpret an appropriate visual display of a parabola, such as Figure 2.1, based on the values of a and c. In short, full comprehension of the text often depends on simultaneous engagement with all three meaning-making resources: language, symbolism, and visual display. The same can be said about Texts 6 and 7, where the ability to comfortably switch among language, symbolism, and visual display is key to understanding the logical reasoning behind the proof or the theorem. In Text 6, mathematical symbols such as — (line segment), = (equality), ≠ (inequality), and ‖ (parallel) must be understood in relation to other symbols within the systems of symbols that are part and parcel of basic geometry. For example, the concept of a line segment is related to, but different from, other concepts such as a line (↔) and a ray (→). Students also need to learn to interpret a visual display, recognizing how order, position, relative size, and orientation may alter its meaning (O'Halloran, 2005). Likewise, an understanding of the theorem in Text 7 would be difficult for students to attain without the aid of a visual display such as Figure 2.3. The visual display renders the technical and abstract language concrete, enabling the construction of a mathematical equation ($QR \times KR = RS^2$) that captures the mathematical processes and reasoning construed in language.

Summary

The foregoing discussion highlights the discursive features of mathematics texts and the potential challenges these features present to reading comprehension. In mathematics texts, language, symbolism, and visual display interact in synergistic ways to construe mathematical knowledge, processes, and reasoning. Students need to develop facility in these three meaning-making resources in order to be successful in reading and learning mathematics.

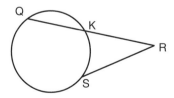

FIGURE 2.3. Visual display of a secant segment.

READING HISTORY

History is a discipline that involves the retelling, analysis, and interpretation of significant past events. It is construed through a distinct kind of discourse that comprises three major text types: recording, explaining, and arguing (Coffin, 2006; Martin, 2002). The recording texts record events of the past as they unfolded naturally through real time; the explaining texts explain the causes, consequences, and significance of historical events; the arguing texts advance a particular interpretation of past events and defend it with a series of arguments and supporting evidence. Each of these text types enables the historian to think and write about the past in a different way (Coffin, 2006). The typical historical texts that students are expected to read in secondary schools (e.g., textbooks, trade books) juxtapose these three text types in different ways, with some texts relying heavily on chronological recounting of past events whereas others focusing on causality or argument (Schleppegrell, 2004).

The three types of historical texts draw on different constellations of lexical and grammatical features that present varied degrees of comprehension challenges to students. The recording texts construct the past as story; they are temporally organized, with a focus on concrete events unfolding in real time and involving specific historical figures. These texts tend be objective, truthful records of the past; however, as Martin (2002) pointed out, the selection and arrangement of events, as well as the attribution of historical significance to these events, may not be entirely objective. Therefore, while students generally find recording texts more accessible because of their prior experience with stories in the elementary grades, they may not always be aware of the bias and interpretations embedded in these texts. The explaining and arguing texts, on the other hand, present explanations and debates about the past. They are organized rhetorically around a set of abstract theses and use language that is metaphorical and evaluative (Schleppegrell, 2004). Thus, the explaining and arguing texts are more challenging for students to read.

In elementary school, history is typically constructed as story-like representations of the past, whereas in secondary schools, it is often constructed as abstract interpretations of the past (Coffin, 2006; Martin, 2002). Even when past events are retold as stories in secondary school history, the stories do not simply record the events as they happened in real time, but usually also include explanations of causal relations among the events and statements regarding their historical significance. This shift from organizing events along a chronological sequence to embedding them as part of a larger sequence of explanation or argument is accomplished largely through linguistic choices that are different from the storytelling language with which students are familiar. Specifically, secondary school history features a greater degree of generalization and interpretation, which calls for the use of more abstract and evaluative language (Coffin, 2006; Martin, 2002; Schleppegrell, 2004; Unsworth, 1999). Some grammatical features of this language are illustrated through three sample texts presented in Table 2.3. Text 8 is a recording text from a high school AP history textbook (Faragher, Buhle, Czitrom, & Armitage, 2007) giving an account of the Panic of 1857. Text 9 discusses why the trial in the Emmett Till murder case received so much national attention. It is an explanation text from *Getting Away with Murder* (Crowe, 2003), an award-winning social studies trade book for middle school chronicling the historically significant trial of two white men who abducted and killed an African American boy named Emmett Till. Text 10 is an arguing text about why Nazi Germany was a genocidal state. It was taken from *The World Must Know* (Berenbaum, 2006), a book about the history of the Holocaust as told in the United States Holocaust Memorial Museum in Washington, DC.

Generic Nouns

As historical discourse moves from simple recounting of past events to analysis and interpretation of these events, there is a shift in focus from specific human actors to groups of people, things, and places (Coffin, 2006; Schleppegrell, 2004). This shift necessitates the use of generic, instead of specific, nouns and enables historians to highlight the impact of historical events on collective groups, rather than on single individuals. Text 8, although a recording text, is unlike many of its textual cousins in the elementary school history. The text is not a simple recounting of what happened during the Panic of 1857; it also introduces explanations of the causes and consequences of the sequence of events that took place in 1857 and 1858. Generic nouns are used to refer to places (*the North, the South*), groups of people (*southerners, some*), and groups of things (*technology, economic system, other financial markets, agricultural exports, cotton exports, northern exports*). When a specific individual (*James Henry Hammond*) is mentioned in the text, it is done to exemplify the collective activity of those who liked to gloat about the superiority of the southern economic system, and this individual is defined in terms of his institutional role as senator from South Carolina.

Similarly, Text 9, an explaining text, uses generic nouns to refer to groups of people (*Blacks in the South, people, entrenched Southern segregationists, all citizens, many African Americans*) who were impacted by the Emmett Till murder case. When specific individuals (*Emmett,*

TABLE 2.3. Sample Secondary History Texts

Recording (Text 8)	Explaining (Text 9)	Arguing (Text 10)
The Panic of 1857	The Boy Who Triggered the Civil Rights Movement	The Wannsee Conference, 1942—The Decision to Kill All Jews

Adding to the growing political tension was the short, but sharp, depression of 1857 and 1858. Technology played a part. In August 1857, the failure of an Ohio investment house—the kind of event that had formerly taken weeks to be widely known—was the subject of a news story flashed immediately over telegraph wires to Wall Street and other financial markets. A wave of panic selling ensued, leading to business failures and slowdowns that threw thousands out of work. The major cause of the panic was a sharp, but temporary, downturn in agricultural exports to Britain, and recovery was well under way by early 1859. Because it affected cotton exports less than northern exports, the Panic of 1857 was less harmful to the South than to the North. Southerners took this as proof of the superiority of their economic system to the free-labor system of the North, and some could not resist the chance to gloat. Senator James Henry Hammond of South Carolina drove home the point in his celebrated "King Cotton" speech of March 1858. (from *Out of Many*, 2007, p. 513)

The trial captured the outside world's interest for several reasons. The *Jet* magazine photo of Emmett publicized the gruesome details of the murder, making it more than just another Southern lynching. The nature of the crime itself, a 14-year-old boy brutally murdered by two men, made it news, but the reason for the kidnapping and killing—Emmett had allegedly whistled at and made "ugly remarks" to a white woman—turned it into big news. The racial context of the case also contributed to its notoriety; at the same time, Medgar Evers and the NAACP were fighting hard to gain equal rights for Blacks in the South, and Emmett's senseless murder seemed to symbolize the plight of Blacks in the region. Finally, the murder indictment against Milam and Bryant was a landmark event in Mississippi, a state where more than 500 lynchings had occurred since 1880, because, as far as people knew, it was the first time white men had been indicted for killing a Black person. The trial gave many African Americans hope that, finally, equal rights for all citizens, regardless of race, might be on the way. For entrenched Southern segregationists, the trial confirmed the fears that had begun with the Supreme Court's *Brown v. Board of Education* ruling: The white-dominated Southern way of life was in jeopardy. (from *Getting Away with Murder*, 2003, p. 22)

Nazi Germany became a genocidal state. The goal of annihilation called for participation by every arm of the government. The policy of extermination involved every level of German society and marshaled the entire apparatus of the German bureaucracy. Parish churches and the Interior Ministry supplied the birth records that defined and isolated Jews. The Post Office delivered the notifications of definitions, expropriation, denaturalization, and deportation. The Finance Ministry confiscated Jewish wealth and property; German industrial and commercial firms fired Jewish workers, officers, and board members, even disenfranchising Jewish stockholders. The universities refused to admit Jewish students, denied degrees to those already enrolled, and dismissed Jewish faculty. Government transportation bureaus handled the billing arrangements with the railroads for the trains that carried Jews to their death. (from *The World Must Know*, 2006, p. 103)

Milam, Bryant, Medgar Evers) are mentioned, they are historically significant figures defined by their institutional roles of, respectively, murder victim, defendants, and NAACP official.

In Text 10, institutional participants, rather than specific individuals, are given priority in support of the argument that genocide was an institutional policy of Nazi Germany, not random acts of specific individuals. This is evidenced in the use of generic nouns that refer to social institutions (*Parish churches, German industrial and commercial firms*) and government agencies (*the entire apparatus of German bureaucracy, the Interior Ministry, the Post Office, the Finance Ministry, the universities, government transportation bureaus*). The text also uses generic nouns to refer to groups of people (*Jewish workers, officers, board members, Jewish stockholders, Jewish students, Jewish faculty, Jews*), suggesting that it is the entire Jewish population, not just single individuals, that was being targeted for extermination by the Nazi government. Taken together, these generic nouns contribute to the argument that Nazi Germany was indeed a genocidal state.

Nominalizations

Another linguistic accommodation that historians make in moving from concrete recounts to abstract interpretations of the past is nominalization. One consequence of nominalization is that information is sometimes lost when verbs or adjectives are converted into nouns. In using verbs or adjectives, we usually have to name the actor who performs the act and the party who is acted upon (e.g., Milam and Bryant killed Emmett Till) or the carrier that possesses the attribute (e.g., the economic system of the South is <u>superior</u> to the free-labor system of the North). However, when the verb *killed* is turned into a noun, as in *the killing,* the information about the party who killed or the party who was killed is buried, and the noun can now be qualified by adding, for example, an adjective, as in "the <u>senseless</u> killing," to encode the author's interpretation of the event. In the same way, when the adjective *superior* is turned into *this superiority,* the carrier of the quality is left unidentified. Historians often exploit the grammatical resource of nominalization to efface historical actors or the writer, inject judgment, and obscure interpretation (Unsworth, 1999). Readers have to understand what nominalization entails in order to read historical texts critically.

Nominalizations are functional in historical meaning making. They enable historians to package a series of events over a long period of time into a "thing" that has ideological connotations (e.g., *the Great Depression, the Great Proletarian Cultural Revolution, the Green Movement*). They also allow historians to construe a specific action (e.g., *criticize*) or quality (e.g., *dead*) as a "thing" (e.g., *criticism, death*), which can then be "colored" with desired ideological perspectives by adding pre- or postmodifiers (e.g., _relentless_ *criticism of the* _gruesome_ *killing*). As such, nominalizations participate in historical processes and reasoning in ways that embed the historian's attitude and naturalize his or her interpretation.

Text 8 is packed with nominalizations. For example, the author bundles together a sequence of events following the failure of an Ohio investment house in August of 1857 and refers to them as "the Panic of 1857," an abstract "thing" that reflects the author's judgment of the historical period. This "thing" is then given a prominent place in the text as a subheading; it also becomes a historical actor with the capacity to inflict harms to the North and the South. This is clearly the author's interpretation of the events of 1857 and 1858, but the interpretation becomes naturalized as facts because the role of the author as interpreter is obscured through nominalization. As Unsworth (1999) points out, nominalization in effect effaces the author as interpreter of events, disguises interpretation as facts, and positions the reader to accept the interpretation as unproblematic.

Other nominalizations in the text also create abstract grammatical participants that foreground the author's interpretation and background the real historical actors (e.g., *the growing political tension, a wave of panic selling, recovery*). Some nominalizations are expanded into long noun phrases that enable the author to add information while also embedding his or her own judgment of the historical events (underlined):

- *the _short_, but _sharp, depression_ of 1857 and 1858*
- *the _failure_ of an Ohio investment house*
- *a _sharp_, but _temporary, downturn_ in agricultural exports to Britain*
- *business _failures_ and _slowdowns_ that _threw_ thousands out of work*
- *the _major_ cause of the _panic_*
- *_proof_ of the _superiority_ of their economic system to the free-labor system of the North*
- *his _celebrated_ "King Cotton" speech of March 1958*

These nominalizations, coupled with other long noun phrases (e.g., *the kind of event that had formerly taken weeks to be widely known, the subject of a news story flashed immediately over telegraph wires to Wall Street and other financial markets*), make the text not only abstract but also dense.

In Text 9, the social and political practices of the South are summarized at the end of the text as *the white-dominated Southern way of life*, an abstract noun that encodes the author's attitude toward the segregated South and that becomes an historical participant to be further qualified (*was in jeopardy*). Some nominalizations in the text create abstract nouns (e.g., *the trial, the kidnapping and killing, the murder indictment*) that are placed in textually prominent positions as the departure point for discussion in the clause. This helps the author develop explanations. Other nominalizations enable the author to inject his judgment into the text (e.g., *its notoriety, Emmett's senseless murder, the plight* of Blacks in the region*) and to construct relationships among them (e.g., *Emmett's senseless murder seems to symbolize the plight of Blacks in the region*). In these cases, the role of the author as interpreter or adjudicator is obscured and the interpretation becomes naturalized as indisputable facts. Sometimes, a nominalization is embedded within another nominalization (e.g., *the fears that had begun with the Supreme Court's Brown v. Board of Education ruling*), creating long noun phrases with layers of abstraction that can hinder comprehension.

In addition to the linguistic indications of judgment, the author also uses intensifiers such as *just* (*more than just another Southern lynching*) to indicate emphasis, and hedges such as *seemed* (*seemed to symbolize*) and *might* (*might be on the way*) to indicate the indeterminacy of history. Wineburg (1991) pointed out that historical writing frequently uses linguistic indications of judgment, emphasis, and uncertainty. Naive readers who are not yet socialized into disciplinary ways of knowing can miss out on these subtle, but important, historical meanings.

In Text 10, the heavy use of nominalizations (e.g., *annihilation, participation, extermination, notifications, definitions, expropriation, denaturalization, deportation, wealth, billing arrangements, death*) makes the text exceedingly abstract to process. These nominalizations become "things" that can be delivered to, taken away, or handled by the various branches of the Nazi government. In this way, they help build up the argument that the Nazi atrocities are not random acts of individuals, but a state policy. Unlike Text 9, Text 10 presents no linguistic evidence of uncertainty, suggesting that the author presents his argument about the Holocaust as an indisputable historical fact.

Causality

Secondary school history texts rarely just record past events. They often juxtapose explanations within the chronology, where logical connections are realized not only explicitly through conjunctions (e.g., *because, therefore*), but also implicitly through nouns (e.g., *reason, effects*), verbs (e.g., *make, lead to*), and prepositional phrases (e.g., *for, through, from*) (Martin, 2002). This metaphorical realization of causality can make it more difficult for students to understand the real causes and effects of historical events. In Text 8, the verb *"adding to"* in the first sentence expresses a causal relation between two abstract "things": *the depression of 1957 and 1858* contributes to *the growing political tension*. The second sentence uses *played a part* to indicate that technology is partially responsible for the depression. Later in the text, *a wave of panic selling* is presented as both the consequence of *the failure of an Ohio investment house* and the cause of *business failures and slowdowns*, which are in turn responsible for making thousands of people lose their jobs. The logical connection between *the downturn in agricultural exports to Britain* and *the panic* is indicated through a noun (*cause*), which is then qualified (*the major cause*). Packaging a causal conjunction (e.g., *because, so*) as a noun (*the cause*) enables the author to give the causal dimension of the event a more prominent position as the subject of the sentence.

It is worth noting that causal relations in Text 8 are realized primarily within clauses through verbs (*adding to, played a part, ensued, leading to*), nouns (e.g., *cause*), and embedded clauses (e.g., *business failures and slowdowns that threw thousands out of work*), but rarely between clauses through conjunctions (*because*). This way of using language necessitates the causes and effects of historical events to be constructed as abstract "things." It can also conflate causality and temporality (Schleppegrell, 2004). For example, the verbs *ensued* and *lead to* construe not only causality but also a temporal sequence of the events happening in real time. Thus, within-clause realizations of causal relations could pose comprehension challenges to students who are used to having causality realized between clauses through conjunctions.

In Text 9, the nonfinite clause *making it more than just another Southern lynching* encodes a consequential relation, suggesting that it is the publication of the gruesome details of the Emmett Till murder that causes the public to view the murder case differently. The cause–effect relation in the text is also constructed in other ways, as shown below:

- ... *the reason for the kidnapping and killing ... turned it into big news* (meaning that the murder becomes big news because of the reason for the murder)
- *The racial context of the case also contributed to its notoriety* (meaning that the murder case gains notoriety because of the racial context)
- ... *because ... it was the first time White men had been indicted* ...

Like Text 8, the causes and effects in Text 9 are also constructed as abstract "things," often realized in nominalizations that are then linked together with verbs (*contributed to*, *turned into*) so as to facilitate further analysis and elaboration of the explanation. The same can be said about Text 10, where *the goal of annihilation called for* (meaning caused) *participation by every arm of the government* and where *the policy of extermination involved every level of German society* (meaning the policy caused every level of Germany society to participate).

Texture

Unlike the typical recording texts of elementary school history that structure the past chronologically (e.g., *By 1820 ... In 1854 ... In 1859 ... The following year ... In December of 1860*), the texts of secondary school history are often organized in what Martin (2002, p. 107) called "waves of abstraction"—that is, the beginning paragraph of a text (topic paragraph) and the beginning sentence of a paragraph (topic sentence) are highly nominalized and abstract, the more narrative recounting of events that follows the introduction becomes less abstract, and the ending paragraph (conclusion) or the end of a paragraph is again highly nominalized and abstract. This "sandwich texture" (Martin, 2002, p. 107) draws on the grammatical resource of nominalization to facilitate prediction (for making an introduction) and summation (for drawing a conclusion).

Text 8, for example, starts with a sentence that is constructed in highly nominalized, abstract language (*Adding to the growing political tension was the short, but sharp, depression of 1857 and 1858*). Following this thesis statement, the text describes a sequence of events in 1857 and 1858 that is later summarized as "the Panic of 1857." The account embeds explanations that are constructed in nominalized and abstract language (e.g., *a wave of panic selling ensued, leading to business failures and slowdowns that threw thousands out of work*; *the major cause of the panic was a sharp, but temporary, downturn in agricultural exports to Britain*). The text ends with a thesis—again constructed in abstract, highly nominalized language—that echoes the one stated in the introduction, *Southerners took this as proof of the superiority of their economic system to the free-labor system of the North*, meaning that the political tension between the North and the South escalated as a result of "the Panic of 1857."

In Text 9, the topic sentence, *The trial captured the outside world's interest for several reasons*, makes predictions about what is to come in the text. As the text unfolds, the author lists four factors that explain why the Emmett Till murder case attracted so much public interest: the gruesome details of the murder publicized through the *Jet* magazine photo, the reason why Milam and Bryant kidnapped and kill Emmett Till (i.e., the Black boy whistled at a white woman), the racial context of the case, and the murder indictment against the two white men. These four factors are not listed in any numerical order (e.g., *first, second, third*), but subtly organized rhetorically as follows:

- The nature of the crime ... *made it news*
- *But* the reason for the kidnapping and killing ... *turned it into big news*
- The racial context of the case *also contributed to its notoriety*
- *Finally*, the murder indictment ... was *a landmark event in Mississippi*

The text concludes with a summary comment, constructed in abstract and generic language, about the impact of the Emmett Till murder case (*The trial gave many African Americans hope* that, finally, *equal rights* for *all citizens*, regardless of *race*, might be on the way. For *entrenched Southern segregationists, the trial* confirmed *the fears* that had begun with *the Supreme Court's Brown v. Board of Education ruling*: *The white-dominated Southern way of life* was in *jeopardy*).

In Text 10, the first sentence makes a thesis statement that establishes a relationship between two abstract entities, *Nazi Germany* and *a genocidal state*. The rest of the paragraph enumerates how every branch of the government (from the Interior Ministry and the Post Office to the universities and transportation bureaus) and every sector of society (from churches to industrial and commercial firms) in Nazi Germany were actively involved in carrying out the goal of annihilation and the policy of extermination. The text is constructed in highly abstract language, with generic nouns and nominalizations used as historical evidence to help the author make the argument.

Summary

Historical discourse in secondary schools is often constructed in abstract language that infuses the historian's ideological perspectives. The abstraction is realized through the use of (1) generic nouns, which refer to groups of people, classes of things, or institutions; (2) nominalizations, which turn a series of events, an action, or time sequences into "things"; (3) evaluative vocabulary to indicate affect, judgment, and valuation; (4) a sandwich texture with layers of abstraction; and (5) within-clause realizations of causal relations that sometimes conflate causality and temporality. Students need to be aware of the ways historians exploit these grammatical resources in order to become critical readers of history.

RETHINKING SECONDARY READING PEDAGOGY

This chapter describes some of the linguistic features of disciplinary texts, their functions in disciplinary meaning making, and the challenges they present to reading comprehension. It shows that secondary content-area texts are constructed in "complex nominal syntax with technical and abstract vocabulary and clause structure that often reasons clause-internally" (Schleppegrell, 2004, p. 136). This language, with its focus on things and relations, is distinct from the more commonsense language of the elementary school texts that typically foregrounds agents and action. This difference is a major source of reading and learning difficulties for many adolescents, including those who have been declared "good readers" in elementary school. Secondary reading pedagogy needs to recognize and respond to this difference. The traditional emphasis on vocabulary and fluency in secondary reading instruction is, while important, woefully inadequate in addressing the new challenges of secondary content-area texts. As this chapter has demonstrated, the difficulties of disciplinary texts lie not just in vocabulary, but more broadly in the discourse grammar, or language patterns. As the content of these texts gets richer and conceptually more complex in secondary schools, their discourse grammar also becomes more complex and challenging. Thus, students need to periodically stop and analyze the language patterns and sort out potential linguistic issues as they read and reason with the text. This suggests that an emphasis on oral reading fluency, while making sense in texts with language that approximates everyday speech, may not be a sound pedagogical practice with secondary content-area texts.

Not only is the language of secondary content-area texts different from the language of elementary school texts, it also varies from one content area to another, as demonstrated in this chapter. For example, while nominalization is a prevalent feature of academic texts in all secondary content areas, it serves quite different functions across the subjects. In science, nominalization helps accumulate meanings so that a technical term can be defined or an explanation sequence synthesized for further discussion. In history, nominalization is often used to portray events as things so that historians can develop a chain of reasoning that simultaneously embeds judgment and interpretation. In mathematics, nominalization helps create semitechnical terms that are then quantified, reified as mathematical concepts, or put into new relationship with other concepts. This variation requires that secondary reading pedagogy pay due respect to discourse grammar as linguistic technology, helping students understand and appreciate how language is used as a creative resource to present information, convey perspective, and structure text in discipline-specific ways. The long-standing emphasis on teaching generalizable strategies such as K-W-L, SQ3R, anticipation guides, and note taking in content-area reading courses in some sense equates, for example, reading texts about DNA with reading about the American Civil War. It fails to take account of the significant linguistic differences between disciplinary texts that emerge from the distinct social practices engaged in by content experts in different disciplines. It is not surprising, then, that although there has been much talk of late about disciplinary literacies, there is still much to be learned about the nature of the pedagogy that can promote the development of discipline-specific literacies.

Recent research has investigated how content experts such as scientists, mathematicians, and historians read and write disciplinary texts (e.g., Shanahan & Shanahan, 2008; Wineburg, 1991; Yore, Hand, & Florence, 2004; Yore, Hand, & Prain, 2002) and described the discursive features of these texts (Coffin, 2006; Halliday & Martin, 1993; O'Halloran, 2005; Schleppegrell, 2004). These studies of disciplinary language and literacy practices have yielded valuable insights into the nature of disciplinary reading and writing that have the potential to guide the teaching of disciplinary literacies. Informed by this body of work, Fang and Schleppegrell (2010) have recently proposed a new approach to secondary reading. The approach, called functional language analysis (FLA), recognizes that disciplinary texts are constructed in patterns of language that adolescents often find unfamiliar and challenging. Grounded in functional linguistics (Halliday & Matthiessen, 2004), FLA offers teachers a set of practical strategies for engaging students in systematically analyzing the language patterns and discussing the meanings of these patterns in disciplinary texts. The analysis and discussion focus on three key comprehension issues that are important to all reading: (1) content (e.g., What is the text about? What does the text tell us?), (2) structure (e.g., How is the text organized? By what logic is the text produced?), and (3) style/voice/tone (e.g., What is the author's perspective? How does the author interact with the reader?). These FLA strategies enable students to learn about the characteristic language patterns that construct the texts of each discipline at the same time they are learning disciplinary content through language. Using FLA, teachers can help students learn to recognize the patterns of language that construe knowledge and value in different ways across different school subjects, enabling adolescents to more effectively engage in the advanced literacy tasks of generalization, abstraction, exposition, reflection, critique, and renovation.

The disciplinary texts of the secondary school curriculum are challenging to read. To engage with these texts, adolescents need to expand the repertoire of reading skills and strategies they have accumulated over the elementary school years, learning to recognize how language is used in different disciplines to present knowledge, provide value, and create specialized texts. This new reading ability is best developed with the help of teachers who are conversant in both disciplinary content and disciplinary language. Unfortunately, most secondary teacher education programs in the United States are at present not in a position to prepare such teacher candidates. This means that the literacy development work must be done, at least for now, through collaboration between content teachers (who are knowledgeable about disciplinary practices and values) and reading/language-arts teachers (who can provide insights into the language that constructs disciplinary texts). The actualization of such collaboration requires a radical revamping of both curriculum and pedagogy in secondary schooling.

REFERENCES

Alvermann, D. E. (2001). Effective literacy instruction for adolescents. *Journal of Literacy Research, 34*(2), 189–208.

Bellman, A., Bragg, S., Charles, R., Handlin, W., & Kennedy, D. (2004). *Algebra 1*. Upper Saddle River, NJ: Prentice Hall.

Berenbaum, M. (2006). *The world must know: The history of the holocaust as told in the United States Holocaust Memorial Museum* (2nd ed.). Washington, DC: United States Holocaust Memorial Museum.

Biancarosa, G., & Snow, C. (2004). *Reading Next—A vision for action and research in middle and high school literacy: A report from Carnegie Corporation of New York*. Washington, DC: Alliance for Excellent Education.

Charles, R., Branch-Boyd, J., Illingworth, M., Mills, D., & Reeves, A. (2004). *Mathematics: Course 3*. Upper Saddle River, NJ: Prentice Hall.

Christie, F. (1998). Learning the literacies of primary and secondary schooling. In F. Christie & R. Mission (Eds.), *Literacy and schooling* (pp. 47–73). London: Routledge.

Coffin, C. (2006). *Historical discourse: The language of time, cause and evaluation*. London: Continuum.

Crowe, C. (2003). *Getting away with murder: The true story of the Emmett Till case*. New York: Phyllis Fogelman Books.

Fang, Z. (2006). The language demands of science reading in middle school. *International Journal of Science Education, 28*(5), 491–520.

Fang, Z., & Schleppegrell, M. J. (2008). *Reading in secondary content areas: A language-based pedagogy*. Ann Arbor, MI: University of Michigan Press.

Fang, Z., & Schleppegrell, M. J. (2010). Disciplinary literacies across content areas: Supporting secondary reading through functional language analysis. *Journal of Adolescent and Adult Literacy, 53*(7), 587–597.

Fang, Z., Schleppegrell, M. J., & Cox, B. E. (2006). Understanding the language demands of schooling: Nouns in academic registers. *Journal of Literacy Research, 38*(3), 247–273.

Faragher, J. M., Buhle, M. J., Czitrom, D., & Armitage, S. H. (2007). *Out of many: A history of the American people* (15th ed.). Upper Saddle River, NJ: Prentice Hall.

Gee, J. P. (2004). Language in the science classroom: Academic social languages as the heart of school-based literacy. In E. W. Saul (Ed.), *Crossing borders in literacy and science instruction: Perspectives on theory and practice* (pp. 13–32). Arlington, VA: National Science Teachers Association.

Halliday, M. A. K. (1993). Towards a language-based theory of learning. *Linguistics and Education, 5*(2), 93–116.

Halliday, M. A. K. (2007). Some thoughts on language in the middle school years. In J. Webster (Ed.), *Language and education* (Vol. 9, pp. 49–62). London: Continuum.

Halliday, M. A. K., & Martin, J. R. (1993). *Writing science: Literacy and discursive power.* Pittsburgh, PA: University of Pittsburgh Press.

Halliday, M. A. K., & Matthiessen, C. (2004). *An introduction to functional grammar* (3rd ed.). London: Arnold.

Heller, R., & Greenleaf, C. (2007). *Literacy instruction in the content areas: Getting to the core of middle and high school improvement.* Washington, DC: Alliance for Excellent Education.

Hobbs, V. (2005). *Defiance.* New York: Square Fish.

Horton, P., Werwa, E., Ezrailson, C., McCarthy, T., Feather, R., Jr., Burns, J. E., et al. (2000). *Science voyages: Exploring the life, earth, and physical sciences* (Level Red, Grade, 6). Columbus, OH: Glencoe.

Jurgensen, R., Brown, R., & Jurgensen, J. (2004). *Geometry.* Evanston, IL: McDougal Littell.

Lee, J., Grigg, W., & Donahue, P. (2007). *The nation's report card: Reading 2007: National Assessment of Educational Progress at Grades 4 and 8* (NCES 2007-496). Washington, DC: National Center for Education Statistics, Institute of Education Sciences, U.S. Department of Education.

Lemke, J. (2003). Mathematics in the middle: Measure, picture, gesture, sign, and word. In M. Anderson, A. Saenz-Ludlow, S. Zellweger, & V. V. Cifarellis (Eds.), *Educational perspectives on mathematics as semiosis: From thinking to interpreting to knowing* (pp. 215–234). Ottawa: Legas.

Martin, J. R. (1989). *Factual writing.* Oxford, England: Oxford University Press.

Martin, J. R. (1996). Waves of abstraction: Organizing exposition. In T. Miller (Ed.), *Functional approaches to written text: Classroom applications* (pp. 87–104). Washington, DC: U.S. Information Agency.

Martin, J. R. (1997). Analysing genre: Functional parameters. In F. Christie & J. Martin (Eds.), *Genre and institutions: Social processes in the workplace and school* (pp. 3–39). London: Continuum.

Martin, J. R. (2002). Writing history: Construing time and value in discourse of the past. In M. J. Schleppegrell & M. C. Colombi (Eds.), *Developing advanced literacy in first and second languages: Meaning with power* (pp. 87–118). Mahwah, NJ: Erlbaum.

Martin, J. R., & Veel, R. (Eds.). (1998). *Reading science: Critical and functional perspectives on discourses of science.* London: Routledge.

Miller, G. T., Jr. (2004). *Living in the environment: Principles, connections, and solutions* (13th ed.). Pacific Grove, CA: Brooks/Cole.

Moje, E. B. (2008). Foregrounding the disciplines in secondary literacy teaching and learning: A call for change. *Journal of Adolescent and Adult Literacy, 52*(2), 96–107.

Moore, D., Bean, T., Birdyshaw, D., & Rycik, A. (1999). Adolescent literacy: A position statement. *Journal of Adolescent and Adult Literacy, 43*(1), 97–112.

Morgan, C. (1998). *Writing mathematically: The discourse of investigation.* London: Palmer Press.

O'Halloran, K. (2000). Classroom discourse in mathematics: A multisemiotic analysis. *Linguistics and Education, 10*(3), 359–388.

O'Halloran, K. (2005). *Mathematical discourse: Language, symbolism and visual images.* London: Continuum.

Postlethwait, J., & Hopson, J. (2006). *Modern biology.* New York: Holt, Rinehart & Winston.

Schleppegrell, M. J. (2004). *The language of schooling: A functional linguistics perspective.* Mahwah, NJ: Erlbaum.

Schleppegrell, M. J. (2007). The linguistic challenges of mathematics teaching and learning: A research review. *Reading and Writing Quarterly, 23,* 139–159.

Shanahan, T., & Shanahan, C. (2008). Teaching disciplinary literacy to adolescents: Rethinking content area literacy. *Harvard Educational Review, 78*(1), 40–61.

Unsworth, L. (1999). Developing critical understanding of the specialized language of school science and history texts: A functional grammatical perspective. *Journal of Adolescent and Adult Literacy, 42*(7), 508–521.

Unsworth, L. (2001). *Teaching multiliteracies across the curriculum: Changing contexts of text and image in classroom practice.* Philadelphia: Open University Press.

Veel, R. (1997). Learning how to mean—scientifically speaking: Apprenticeship into scientific discourse in the secondary school. In F. Christie & J. R. Martin (Eds.), *Genre and institutions: Social processes in the workplace and school* (pp. 161–195). London: Continuum.

Veel, R. (1999). Language, knowledge and authority in school mathematics. In F. Christie (Ed.), *Pedagogy and the shaping of consciousness: Linguistic and social processes* (pp. 185–216). London: Continuum.

Wineburg, S. (1991). On the reading of historical texts: Notes on the breach between school and academy. *American Educational Research Journal, 28*(3), 495–519.

Yore, L., Hand, B., & Florence, M. (2004). Scientists' views of science, models of writing, and science writing practice. *Journal of Research in Science Teaching, 41*(4), 338–369.

Yore, L., Hand, B., Goldman, S. R., Hildebrand, G. M., Osborne, J. F., Treagust, D. F., et al. (2004). New directions in language and science education research. *Reading Research Quarterly, 39*(3), 347–352.

Literature Cited

Yore, L., Hand, B., & Prain, V. (2002). Scientists as writers. *Science Education, 86,* 672–692.

3

How Disciplinary Experts Read

Cynthia Shanahan

Experts in different fields of study such as history, mathematics, or chemistry read texts in their fields in different ways. I asked experts to read texts and then answer a question asking whether or not they paid attention to the identity of the author. Note their answers.

From a historian reading an essay about whether or not Lincoln was a great president:

> "I saw, oh … I don't know him very well, but he [the author] is part of a right-wing group of southern conservatives who is a secessionist. I'm not sure that the best model for thinking about Lincoln as a president is one that comes from a racist. So I have my critical eyes up a little bit, so it's a bit of a stretch to be friendly to, so I wanted to make sure to read it fairly."

From a chemist reading a journal article discussing a scientific experiment:

> "I pay attention in two ways: who wrote it and what is their affiliation, to see, is this somebody I recognize in the field, and also, I suppose, where the affiliation is, which, right or wrong, gives more or less credibility. If it's from a third world country, it may have a little

less—I'd read it with a little more suspicion than if it came from a highly ranked university. I look to see who is the individual and see whether or not I've encountered their research in the past."

From a mathematician reading an algebraic proof:

"Yes, it's interesting [who the author is], but it doesn't really matter. The title and what I know of the review of these papers tells me that these methods are interesting to me. I don't care whether this person has name recognition or not."

The historian's recognition of the author's political stance was a guide to how he should proceed with the reading of the text. He recognized the potential for a particular kind of bias and chose to take this into account while attempting to maintain an objective appraisal of the credibility of the argument the author was making. The chemist wanted to know about how advanced the laboratory was in which the experiment took place. He presumed that a highly regarded chemist from a well-funded laboratory at a competitive research university would engage in high-quality experiments. A chemist without top-notch measurement tools isn't likely to produce the most credible results. The mathematician didn't care by whom the paper was written or where the author did his work, except to satisfy his curiosity. The credibility of a mathematician's proof is evident within the proof itself.

Why does it matter that there is a difference in the way an author is viewed? Researchers have found that an author's expertise is often used to determine whether or not that author's message should be believed (Horai, Naccari, & Fatoullah, 1974; Austin & Dong, 1994). Researchers also know that approaching a text with a particular point of view (based on belief or background knowledge or confidence in the message) affects how individuals read and what they learn from texts. Therefore, the difference matters because it helps to determine the way in which a text is approached, the confidence one has in the information gleaned from reading, and how readers use that information.

This chapter addresses why reading and writing in various disciplines differ, what some of those differences are, and what this approach to reading texts means for teaching and learning.

WHY DO DISCIPLINARY EXPERTS HAVE DIFFERENT WAYS OF READING AND WRITING TEXTS?

Linguists note several possible reasons that differences in language developed among the disciplines (Geisler, 1994). Some argue that these differences came about as a means of insuring that charlatans did not invade a particular field of study. That is, if that field had a unique vocabulary and ways of communicating knowledge in written and spoken discourse, there would be such a long learning curve to engage in that discourse that only experts could participate. Quackery could easily be exposed. The world would be safe from journalists posing as historians, peddlers posing as physicians, mechanics posing as scientists.

Others offer a more negative view of the development of language differences. They suggest that the creation of unique discourses was a way to protect the power and authority of universities from competition. That is, the fields of study weren't protecting the quality of the message, only their rights to be the sole purveyors of it.

But others provide a more benign explanation for how those differences occurred—that they were natural outcomes of the real differences in the kinds of knowledge that was being created in different fields. As knowledge became more specialized, the language describing it had to become more specialized as well. Physicians, for example, needed a level of precision in their vocabulary so that they could make nuanced distinctions among similar phenomena and engage with others who also could make those nuanced distinctions in order to solve problems. *Tachycardia* and *bradycardia* are two kinds of *arrhythmia* of the heart that needed to be distinguished from each other to get at the cause of the disorder. Different traditions for conducting research based on the particular kind of information being studied arose as well. Scientists rely largely on experimentation and systematic observation of phenomena as they occur to examine how the world works. But historians take a different approach. Because they want to describe and interpret the past, they have to rely on documents that have already been created. And theoretical mathematicians don't have to rely on data at all. They use principles of reason and logic to create knowledge. These different ways of performing in a particular discipline lead naturally to different ways that experts discuss what they have learned.

Whatever the cause, disciplines have different ways of writing and speaking about the world. And because of this, discipline experts approach text with sets of expectations, reading strategies, and understandings that are firmly grounded in disciplinary knowledge.

WHAT IS DISCIPLINARY KNOWLEDGE?

Disciplinary knowledge is knowledge of the breadth and depth of a field of study, including knowledge of the way information is created, shared, and evaluated. It is not topical knowledge, although part of discipline knowledge is an understanding of the *range* of topics that comprise it.

The term can be understood better if disciplines are compared and contrasted in terms of their different elements.

Depth and Breadth

Bazerman (1998) found that physicists, when they read, looked at the table of contents and tried to determine what kind of physical science they were reading. Historians, chemists, and mathematicians do this as well (Shanahan & Shanahan, 2008). It matters to a historian, for example, if what she is reading is "grassroots," military, or political history. The chemists I talk to compare their branch with other branches of chemistry. Mathematicians make a distinction between theoretical and applied mathematics and contrast the math they do with the math that physicists do. Experts know whether or not a particular piece of information belongs in their field or not and where it belongs, even if it's not what they study. I know this as an "expert" in secondary literacy. I understand how the topics I am interested in differ from those that an early-childhood literacy expert would be interested in. I know that some individuals are interested in the cognitive aspects of literacy and some in the social aspects (and some in the shades in between), and that different elements of literacy, such as comprehension, word knowledge, fluency, and writing, are sometimes studied together and sometimes separately. I don't have to know all of the information regarding these different topics to know that they exist and how they contribute to the overall knowledge of the discipline. Knowing the breadth of my discipline helps me to search for appropriate information when I open up a journal or click on a website or read a professional book based on my purpose for reading about secondary literacy—to expand my understanding of the field or to add to the *depth* of knowledge about a particular topic in which I am interested. Gaining this depth of knowledge in my particular area of expertise from reading depends on this ability to know what to look for.

The Way Knowledge Is Created

One's level of confidence in information is in large part a function of *what* was created, *how* it was created, and *for what purpose* it was created. We often hear in the field of literacy that "the gold standard" for research into what kinds of instruction works is the *true experiment*. The reasoning behind this makes sense. If we want to know whether using a particular reading strategy raises reading comprehension, for example, it is important to compare the use of that strategy to the use of something else—a control condition, on measurements of comprehension. Researchers studying strategy use try to ensure that when they find gains in reading comprehension, they can attribute them to a particular strategy use, and not some other factor such as differences in the comparison groups on reading ability or topic knowledge. So, when we read the findings of research *about what works* that implements an experimental design, we have more confidence that those findings are generalizable to other like situations more than research that does not meet that standard. However, we know that the findings are not absolute truth. That is, there is likelihood, or probability, that similar findings would occur if the experiment were tried again, but not certainty. In the case just mentioned, the *purpose* of the research is *to determine the effect of strategy use on comprehension*; the *how* of the research is *through experimentation*; and the knowledge that was created (the *what*) is the finding.

If I had another kind of purpose, for example, to find out what students who are engaged in strategy use think about, that would require a different *how* (e.g., *think-aloud protocols*). Think-aloud analysis is usually qualitative, and there is no estimation for probability of generalization. As informative as this analysis is, I might not have the same confidence in the results, and it would not be appropriate for me to make generalizations about what works based on them. Rather, it might make me understand *why* it worked, and it might lead to further hypothesis generation.

The creation of knowledge in the disciplines differs depending on which field or branch of a field one is in. Many *scientists* engage in experimentation, and, as in my example of experimentation in literacy, findings are credible to the extent that an outcome can be predicted within a certain level of confidence. Not all scientists engage in experimentation, however. A botanist, for example, might collect specimens, observe properties, and classify a newly discovered plant based on those properties to understand what is in the world and how it is connected. Sometimes scientific research (such as medical research) must rely on correlation, so that it is not possible to determine if one phenomenon causes another but only whether or not two phenomena are related. Scientists know, however, that no matter how confident they are in the results of research, they are not finding indisputable truth. As measurement instruments become more precise, as knowledge increases, as procedures for observation become more sophisticated, what we once knew is replaced by new knowledge. It is only over time, through the corroborated work of many scientists, that the world comes to be understood, and full understanding is never completely possible. At one time, for example, scientists thought that the Newton's laws of motion were entirely accurate, until quantum theory changed how scientists thought about motion in space. We once thought that smoking cigarettes was harmless but now know that is not the case.

Historians, on the other hand, are not at all confident about historical interpretation; they are much less confident than scientists. Why? They know that the data they rely on and the methods they use are subjective. Although they may be confident that World War II ended in 1945 (because there are so many newspaper articles, newsreels, and personal accounts attesting to it), the factors that determined its end and the effects of the end of the war are open to argument—interpretations that are based on post hoc evidence. Historians must choose what evidence they will pay attention to and what evidence they will ignore, what perspective(s) they want to take when examining the evidence, and how far back in time they want to start their search for evidence. Each of these decision points can be influenced by bias—political, religious, social, and professional. Each of the documents they draw on as evidence is potentially biased as well. A soldier's letter home recounting the bombing of Dresden might be contradicted by the official report. With every document, a historian must decide how credible the information is, what weight he or she wants to give it, and how to interpret it. The credibility of a historical account is measured in terms of plausability rather than probability because of the subjectivity of historical evidence and interpretation.

Mathematicians are unlike either the historians or the scientists. Many believe that they are creating truth, within limits. The answer can be determined, the theorem proved. Truth is determined by reason and accuracy. As long as the rules of logic are followed and there are no mistakes, the answer can be attained. Of course, the burdens of reason and accuracy weigh heavily. Before a mathematician will accept something as truth, he or she has to ensure that no error has occurred, and, as one mathematician said to me, "There is always error." Sometimes it takes years to find. Credibility is a function of how accurate and thorough the solution to a problem is.

How Knowledge Is Shared

Scientific knowledge, like knowledge in other fields, is shared with different audiences in different ways. If a scientist is writing a proposal to a private foundation or making a case to the public for the viability of a research finding, the public discourse will be less technical than if a scientist is writing an article for a scientific journal. However, even given these differences, scientists temporize to a greater extent than experts do in other fields. That is, they qualify what they say, cautioning against overinterpretation of findings. Note the following excerpt from *Popular*

Science, a magazine written for a nonscientific audience: "new research from scientists at Temple University and other institutions *suggests* the technique *is not without* its long-term risks" (Dyer, 2010, p. 1). The term *suggests* is less certain than *finds*, and *is not without* is a lot less certain than *has*. The sentence that follows appears in the premier research journal *Science*: "Given the abundance of silicate minerals, these observations *suggest* that formose-like reactions *may provide* a feasible pathway for the abiotic formation of biologically important sugars, such as ribose" (Lambert, Gurusamy-Thangavelu, & Ma, 2010, p. 984). Note the use of *suggest* rather than *show* or *prove* and the use of *may provide* instead of *provide*. In a high school textbook we find "They came to the conclusion that the stratosphere could be destroyed by CFCs and that they had enough support for their hypothesis to publish their discovery." Note here that instead of *proving* that CFCs destroy the stratosphere, scientists *hypothesized* and proposed evidence. The textbook explains earlier that data supporting a hypothesis only gives a "tentative 'thumbs up' to the idea that the hypothesis may be true."

Temporization is common when scientists describe experiments and observations. Scientists exude caution about the information they get by reading scientific "discoveries." However, scientists have a greater belief in information that has been corroborated and understood over time— the information they think is most credible because of the weight of evidence. They are fairly confident in the information that they place in science textbooks. They are not so confident about the information they get by reading about a scientific experiment in a journal or the discovery of a new species.

Interestingly enough, historical accounts, especially those in textbooks, are usually written in narrative form and are often perceived by naive readers as truth. Cause and effect statements are often made without temporizing. Note the following example: "Roosevelt decided he would join the Allies in the war effort after the bombing of Pearl Harbor." Even though the veracity of this statement is often disputed, there is no indication in the sentence that this is a historian's interpretation, and the reader is not even privy to the evidence on which the interpretation is based. It is written as if it were indisputable. In academic books, this is not quite so true. Historians provide the sources of the information they get and engage in more explicit argumentation about interpretation and meaning, sometimes introducing other interpretations so that they may refute them based on the evidence. However, claims are still more often strongly asserted rather than temporized. In *Gender and the Politics of History* (Scott, 1988), for example, an explicit argument for a "feminist history" is being made. The language is still written as truth: "The seamstresses who articulated and implemented the demands for their trade insisted that women be entirely in charge of their own work affairs" (p. 105). Later in the paragraph, two citations are listed, and the "evidence" can be found in the back of the book. Historians are very interested in having students engage in this kind of historical argumentation, even though the textbooks history students read are not good models for it.

Mathematicians do little temporization, as well. Math textbooks present problems, explain steps for solving the problems, and invite students to practice solving problems using the steps just explained. In a mathematical proof, mathematicians lay out the variables and engage in a logical discussion leading to a solution. As mentioned, answers are considered completely accurate to the extent that the logic was accurate. All one needs to do is engage in problem solution without error. Mathematicians want students to learn how to be logical and accurate and how to find the answer. Credibility is only a function of these things. Therefore, they expect students to read math textbooks carefully, even repeatedly, until the information is understood, and to be satisfied that they have solved the problems posed in textbooks only after they have reviewed their logic and checked for error.

Thus, there are variations in the way information is shared that are dependent on the discipline from which that information comes and the level of confidence one has in that information. The more subject to interpretation the information is, the more need for a critical read.

HOW DO HISTORIANS READ?

My colleague and I engaged in a study of three discipline groups: historians, chemists, and mathematicians (Shanahan & Shanahan, 2008). We formed three focus groups representing those disciplines, each consisting of two experts (researchers and writers), two teacher educators, and two teachers. We then spent a year determining how the experts approached reading within their field of study. We had the focus groups read texts and discuss their processes. We also approached each expert individually and had each one read and think aloud about the processes used in reading several different texts. Finally we shared the transcripts of those experts within the focus group to arrive at shared understandings of the way the experts read.

We drew questions we had about the reading processes of these experts from a study by Wineburg (1991), who had experts and high school students read multiple documents about a single historical event and think aloud about how they read. He found that the students were reading the documents as single entities, choosing facts to remember from each of them but not making any comparisons of the facts across the documents and not mentioning when the different documents disagreed on an interpretation. The historians, on the other hand, besides also paying attention to the facts, engaged in some rather sophisticated processing. For each document they read, they looked at the *source* of information (the author, the publisher, etc.), the *context* in which it was written (the time period and what was happening then, the audience it was written to, and the purpose for writing), and its *corroboration* (level of agreement or disagreement) with the other texts they were reading. Other studies have confirmed that students engage in reading history mainly as a fact-gathering task unless they are explicitly taught to do otherwise (e.g., Stahl, Hynd, Britton, McNish, & Bosquet, 1996; Rouet, Britt, & Mason, 1996), and that historians read in much richer ways, paying attention not only to these elements but to the "subtext" shown by the language used and evidence of other elements of potential bias. Our question for this study was: Do these historians, chemists, and mathematicians engage in sourcing, contextualization, and corroboration?

Our findings were that the three groups differed qualitatively in the way they read, with historians engaging in these processes to a high degree, chemists engaging in them to a lesser degree, and mathematicians not engaging in them in a substantive way at all. We also found other interesting patterns of reading, which I will analyze by discipline.

History Reading

The historians' reading of text could be characterized as nuanced, conscious, critical, and reflective. Of the three groups, these individuals were the most able to explicitly discuss what they were doing as they read and had much more to say about their reading processes. They seemed highly attuned to their responsibility to read in specifically critical ways. What did they pay attention to as they read? I list these elements below.

The Approach to History

The historians wanted to know what kind of historian was doing the writing, and they juxtaposed their own area of history to that which they were reading. For example, a social historian noted that the political history we had him read was not in his area of study. The U.S. political historian reading the same piece (an excerpt that discussed whether or not Abraham Lincoln was the greatest president) noted that he was looking for evidence of the author's approach to history. "I'm weary of the great man in history approach." One historian said that he read for evidence of *pastism* (a view that the past is better than the present and that the world's condition is worsening) or *presentism* (a view that the present is better than the past and that the world's condition is getting better and better). He also said he paid attention to where a story began and where it ended. For example, if a biographer began the story of a person's life as a baby, she might come up with a different interpretation of that life (different cause/effect chains, for example) than a biographer who began the story with adulthood. The historians carefully analyzed the words the historian used to determine bias. Were there positive or negative adjectives, pejorative terms, and so on? Further, the historians engaged in a good deal of discussion about *what was left out.* For instance, when they read excerpts from history textbooks, they first looked at the table of contents to see the range of topics and try to see which perspectives were represented and which were not. All of these elements of reading are an attempt to discover the author's interpretive lens. Once they developed a theory of what that lens was, they felt better able to judge the credibility of what the author said.

They and other historians have explained to me that historians do their work within a framework. History is commonly studied along the dimensions of the rather permanent categories of systems that exist in society, such as social, political, economic, technological, artistic, and religious ones, and historians often choose one of these systems as a research lens. Key understandings about history come from the connections individuals make within these structures. These understandings are conveyed through historical explanation focusing on claims about context (the context of the new world made it easier for democracy to take hold), change over time (democracy in 1800 was confined to propertied males but today it is not), causality (the hardships Germany faced after World War I led to an acceptance of Hitler's message), complexity (numerous interacting factors were involved in the collapse of the Roman Empire), and contingency/coincidence (if Lincoln had not been assassinated, then...; or by a twist of fate). By comparing and contrasting information across time (e.g., ancient to modern) and space (e.g., eastern and western), individuals can reason about phenomena such as the nature of power, the function of the military, or the characteristics of disorder, depending on the lens they have chosen. So, a large part of what they are trying to determine is where the author is located within this framework and what kind of claims he or she is making. Another large part is to determine with what biases the historian enters the framework.

Reading Outside the Text

Historians begin to determine an author's interpretive lens by thinking about what they find that is outside of the text: who the author is, in what time period the author worked, the publisher and intended audience of the text, the topic and its scope, and so on. These are all elements that can be examined before the reading of a text. So, when historians begin to read, they have already done a good deal of thinking about how they will view the text. Note again the historian's point of view about an author seen on the first page of this chapter:

> "I saw, oh ... I don't know him very well, but he [the author] is part of a right-wing group of southern conservatives who is a secessionist. I'm not sure that the best model for thinking about Lincoln as a president is one that comes from a racist. So I have my critical eyes up a little bit, so it's a bit of a stretch to be friendly to, so I wanted to make sure to read it fairly."

The author's stance causes the historian to engage in a more critical reading of the text. At the same time, he is also paying attention to his own reaction to that stance. In other words, while reading the *outside* of the text, he is engaging in theory building about the context of the reading on the basis of who the author is and what his affiliations are; yet, he has still to verify the theory with evidence from *inside* the reading. Therefore, he has to remain open to evidence that both supports and contradicts his theory. Wineburg (1991) refers to this activity as *sourcing*.

Historians can also engage in contextualization by looking *outside* the text. Note the following:

> "I'd want to take up this book. It's a 1984 book, and in Lincoln scholarship, that's ages. There have been many books written since, and I would want to know how the arguments changed since 1984."

Again, the historian is doing some theory building—this time about change over time. But he will refine that theory as he moves into the text.

Reading Inside the Text

Historians also pay attention to what is inside the text—the structure, the wording, and issues of contingency, cause/effect, and so on. Here are a historian's thoughts about the structure of the text.

"The argument was not straightforward, but roundabout, so clearly a part of an attempt to make analytical history a kind of a narrative, to raise big issues indirectly (reader friendly) so I had to be more active in distinguishing the arguments. Her most important statements were at the end, rather than at the beginning, of paragraphs."

In this reading, the historian is using the structure to determine what he has to pay attention to and where that important information is. Since it is narrative and not a straightforward argument, it is harder for him to distinguish what the author wants him to believe. He has to look at the ends of the paragraphs to get the point of the story. But he *is* reading for the argument, not just the story. The historians I worked with read all texts that way, no matter what the structure.

The historians also looked for observations that were new to them: new interpretations or new evidence that they might use to amplify their own understandings of a period in history or an interpretation of events. When these occurred, they read more carefully.

Finally, they looked in the text to verify an author's stance and to critique the way the evidence for that stance was being presented.

"I'm looking kind of carefully at how the author is embedding this argument. In other words, are they [*sic*] trying to undermine the great man in history argument, are they [*sic*] addressing the problem and dealing with the problem or are they [*sic*] letting the problem just kind of fester without addressing it. So I'm looking carefully at how they're [*sic*] kind of wording and locating the individual in history."

Chemistry Reading

The chemists we studied had an approach to reading that could be characterized as flexible, pragmatic, and recursive. That is, the chemists, more than the mathematicians and the historians, changed their approach to reading based on *what* they were reading. And during the reading itself, they would explicitly change their approach depending on whether they needed to learn something they didn't know. When reading, they pragmatically asked of the text, "What can I use in my own work?" or "What is the important chemistry principle I need to learn?" They were also concerned with the quality of methodology and technical sophistication, and, when trying to understand information, they read recursively, moving from text to graph or diagram, or table of numbers, then back to text, and so forth.

The Approach to Chemistry

The chemists we studied sought out reading that would help them in their own work. Said one chemist:

> "I've been researching this subject, so it was something that I sought out. ... I address this problem in my own research, and I wanted to see if he addresses the same problem that I have. Does the first pulse affect the behavior of the second pulse?"

Another explained his choice this way:

> "One of the reasons it caught my attention is that I've been interested in environmental issues. I've taught environmental chemistry. I'm also interested in it because using fluorescence in this way relates to some research that I'm doing, not for sensors, [but for] using fluorescence as a measure of something else."

As noted above, the experts in all three fields did this to a certain extent. However, the chemists explained their reading choices this way more than others.

These chemists approached text with different strategies if they already had a good deal of prior knowledge than if they were trying to learn something about which they knew very little. Unlike the historians, they often expressed the notion that sometimes you just had to sit down and learn what was in the text. As one chemist said,

> "Because I think there is a kind of context ... that says: 'Here are the atomic symbols ... here are the meanings.' Now you could explain that the name *calcium* comes from here and *potassium* comes from here. Some texts do that, but for the majority of texts and for the majority of students it is sufficient to just say: 'Table 2—know it ... there they are.' And we give you a lot of opportunities to use your knowledge and reinforce it ... but we are not going to stop and ask, 'When was the last time you thought about why potassium is here?'"

They were also concerned about focusing only on the important information—"separating the chemistry from the crap." In other words, they believed that one should read chemistry text with the expectation of understanding the chemical principles and were concerned about some of the extraneous information (motivational text, for instance) that could get in the way. I am reminded of a movement to teach physics through narrative text—within the context of a story. These chemists would not have liked that idea at all. To them, it was "hard enough to learn the chemistry." In that vein, they were dismissive of a chemistry text that organized information around real-world phenomena (such as climate change) versus the more hierarchical approach to chemistry that built one chemical concept on another, saying that students had a difficult time learning the chemistry that way.

The author of the text is a determinant of credibility. One of the chemists said about the authors of a research study he was reading,

> "I've known one most of my life—when he speaks everybody listens."

Reading Outside the Text

As mentioned, the chemists did pay attention to sourcing and contextualization, as the historians did. For example, when they read their own materials, usually research and research synthesis journals, they did pay attention to when the research took place. It was important to them whether they knew of (or knew) the authors and the quality of their previous work, their lab, and so on.

> "Every field has its own journals. If you're in the field you know who the good people are. In the first one [the first article he read], the journal is obscure, and I don't think it's a first-ranked journal, and I don't know the authors."

It also made a difference whether or not an article was current.

> "For my kind of science, information loses its relevance, because the principles are changing. In other fields, it may not be that way. The second paper is very driven by theory, as is the field. A paper 20 years old would be totally irrelevant."

As also mentioned, the context has to do with the kind of reading it is—who the audience is, for what purpose it is written, and so on. The chemists approached textbook reading in a different way than they approached journal reading. In textbook reading, they adopted a "reading to learn" approach. One chemist said, that when he was reading to learn, he would "take anything thrown at me" and use that to help him understand the concepts or principles. But when they read journals and even more popular chemistry texts (such as in popular science journals), they read with a much more critical eye.

Finally, before reading an article, the chemists liked to determine what exactly what it was that they were going to read about.

> "And then, I ask, are they doing something in time or frequency? Are they studying a sequence of things? There are two different ways of solving a problem: there are time-domain experiments and frequency-domain experiments. A pulse of sound—short chirp—a bleep will contain all frequencies. A long note (a pure C) will contain only one frequency. If you study time—short pulses—the frequency is not well defined. A frequency experiment does not pay attention to time. The difference is also referred to as steady-state studies versus time-resolved studies."

This is a good example of someone who has a "framework" for chemistry that he uses to help guide his reading.

Reading Inside the Text

The chemists we studied use their frameworks for chemistry as they read the text itself. For example, one chemist listed some of the things he always looks for:

- *Structure:* In an experimental article structure would be indicated by the headings: abstract, problem, hypothesis, answer, and interpretation.

- *Orders of magnitude:* Do the orders of magnitude make sense? Is the distance of the sun 1,000 miles, a million miles? Is the time it takes for a process to occur in a cell, for it to respond to a stimulus, a millisecond, seconds, hours? What is the size of the atom?

- *Violation of well-known principles:* There are certain basic laws of science that can't be violated. Does it make physical sense? Does your answer violate the principle of conservation of energy, for example ... Certain things are canon. Certain things are speculative. Textbooks present canons. And if they get an answer that violates the idea that there is no perpetual motion, they need to rethink.

- *For experimental articles:* Is it done correctly? Are there proper controls described? What are the experimental results? In this case, is the fluorescence directly related to the concentration of mercury? What are the error limits, things like that. And I would suppose that how carefully I read an article depends on how well it relates to my research. If it doesn't relate closely, I'll read it more casually, but if it relates to my research, I want to know what this person has done. I might consider citing this paper in a future manuscript of my own.

The chemists paid attention not just to words, and not just graphs or mathematics. They read recursively, moving from text to graph or formula and back to text. One chemistry educator I worked with discussed this phenomenon as "translation." That is, a key ability in science is to understand information on several different dimensions or forms of representation. A scientist must translate a theory into an experiment with concrete elements and describe phenomena not only in words but numerically and physically. In fact, it is the essence of science to be able to observe everyday objects and see something more.

Mathematics Reading

Reading in mathematics could be described as focused on convergence, repetition, accuracy, reason, and elegance. The mathematicians we studied were keen on not wanting anything to get in the way of the math and, like the chemists, were concerned with textbooks that got too far away from the solution to a problem. They were willing to work hard to understand these solutions—taking years, if needed, to reread and reflect. Unlike the chemists, they were less focused on translation. They did see the necessity for putting formulas into English; but because mathematics is as much a language as a discipline, they seemed to be happy enough dealing mostly in the realm of mathematical language.

The Approach to Mathematics

The reading mathematicians did was dominated by a focus on logic and accuracy. The idea was to engage in complex, abstract problem solving, and the solution, if executed without error, would be regarded as truth. Rather than read divergently, like the historians did, looking for corroboration from other sources and thinking about whose perspective was left out, the mathematicians read convergently, with all attention focused on narrowing to a solution.

> "I look at very small relations. If I write a formula, it must be very simple. If something is complicated, it means it is a bad formula. It must be clear."

Like the chemists, they read because of their interest in and prior knowledge of a particular kind of problem. As one mathematician said,

"I compare what the article is doing with what I know about these issues. Do I know some special cases? Do I deal with similar problems to what is discussed here? Is it interesting to me or not? Is it consistent with what I know? I just want to see if I should continue."

The mathematicians I worked with read with an eye for detail but focused on the concepts rather than simply the formulas. As one said,

"It's about how things are related. I don't think that much in terms of formulas, but concepts. In my work, it's more like how the concepts are related. Like, what is the source of these formulas? Why are they here?"

Reading Outside the Text

The mathematicians I studied paid little attention to sourcing and contextualization. Regarding the author, as already noted, one mathematician said,

"Yes, it's interesting, but it doesn't really matter. The title and what I know of the review of these papers tells me that these methods are interesting to me. I don't care whether this person has name recognition or not."

And it didn't matter to the mathematicians when something was written.

"Sometimes, it takes about 10 to 15 years to find a response to a problem. So, an article written in 1985 is just as important today as it was in 1985, and is not dated, like it is in other fields."

Reading Inside the Text

Reading the actual text was what mattered to the mathematicians I studied. They relied on typical structures to guide them through the reading. One mathematician laid out the process this way:

"The introduction is trying to find out where it all fits together, then there are definitions, and then there are proofs."

Another mathematician said that he tried to memorize the names of the variables defined in the introductory material so that he wouldn't have to go back and reread that section later each time a different variable was introduced. Once the proofs began, they focused on whether the solution to the problem was correct.

"That's the important criteria, and it's by no means assumed."

If the statement is one that can be proven, then

"the matter is closed, and I move forward. If no—if I don't see why this is true, maybe I need to read further to get more explanation."

The mathematicians did try to corroborate or "reconcile" what they read. For example, if one mathematician was reading a particular argument and said that there were other papers making similar arguments, he'd look them up. Another mathematician tried to reconcile what was on the page with what he already knew had been done.

WHAT DOES IT MEAN FOR TEACHING AND LEARNING?

The fact that expert readers in these three fields read texts for different purposes and used different strategies means that students should be guided toward reading their texts differently as well. Previously, my colleague Timothy Shanahan and I have shared a pyramid that has basic reading at the base, intermediate reading in the middle, and discipline-based reading at the top. As students move from basic reading (learning how to read) to disciplinary reading (learning how to read specialized texts), they increasingly use reading strategies that may be idiosyncratic to a particular discipline. For example, a student might engage in contextualization (looking at the time period when a document was written and considering the document in light of the context of that time period) when reading a historical text but would not do that when reading a mathematics text. The new Common Core Standards in English Language Arts acknowledge this difference by specifying different Literacy standards for social studies/history and science and technical subjects than for English (Common Core State Standards Initiative, 2010).

My preference is that instruction in discipline-based reading should be provided for teachers in those disciplines, especially in high school classrooms, in collaboration with reading specialists. Why? Reading specialists know reading but do not have a background in the various disciplines. So much of how reading progresses depends on knowledge of the discipline in terms of how information in that discipline is created, shared, and evaluated. It would be very difficult for reading specialists to obtain knowledge in every discipline in which students take classes. The subject matter teachers would hopefully have a greater sense of the purpose of reading in a particular discipline. These teachers often don't have the background in literacy, however, to determine how and what discipline-specific reading skills and strategies should be taught. Together, these two specialists—in reading and in the subject matter— have a greater chance of determining how students can be taught to read in increasingly discipline-specific ways.

What Should Students Be Taught?

Disciplinary Knowledge

It is unusual for even subject-matter teachers to help students understand the particular discipline in which they are studying as a frame for reading and learning. Yet, I believe that this is a crucial missing element in instruction. That is, it is precisely the approach to the discipline that will help students get the most of what they read. What matters to historians, chemists, literary critics, and mathematicians should be understood by students because it will help them to read with purpose, identify important information, think strategically and critically about what they read, and engage in explanation and argumentation appropriate for the context.

Strategies

I argue that there are at least three types of strategies: general, adaptable, and specific. Some strategies such as SQ3R (Robinson, 1970) or K-W-L (Ogle, 1986) can be applied across a number of texts in different disciplines. These are certainly helpful to students who have difficulty focusing on learning from text. My thought is that they are too general, however, to offer students ways to make nuanced interpretations of text, and their success may be largely due to the fact that they help students pay attention to what they are reading. Other strategies are appropriate across various disciplines because they are adaptable to different contexts. A comparison–contrast chart, for example, is useful if you want to analyze a number of characters in a novel, the perspectives that different authors have on a particular issue in history, or the properties of different hormones. The issue is not whether to use such a chart, but when to use it and for what purpose. To use it in ways that are appropriate for a particular discipline, a student will probably need instruction in how to modify the strategy, because it won't be used the same way in history class that it will be used in science class. It might be useful to teach comparison–contrast charting as a cross-disciplinary strategy, but not unless subject matter teachers teach students its specific discipline-based uses. Other strategies are specific to only a small subset of disciplines. Contextualization—considering the time period and its possible implications before reading a text—is a major strategy engaged in by historians. Even before reading, historians want to know when the document was written, and they think about the social, economic, political, and ideological context of that time period. Among other things, this process helps them to approach the text with historical empathy. For example, the language may be jarring if judged by modern standards (e.g., authors may use terms that are now considered to be vulgar or pejorative), but historians will take into account that these terms were part of everyday language at the time. Contextualization does not seem to be a major strategy in mathematics reading, however. Two of the most often used strategies in mathematics are rereading and close reading (reading for accuracy/reading to identify error). Although rereading and close reading are used in other disciplines to an extent, it would be unwise to teach students to employ them as major strategies across disciplines. Teaching of discipline-specific strategies is best left up to the subject-matter teacher. As students go through school, these discipline-specific strategies become more and more important, because they facilitate the nuanced, skilled reading of texts in a particular field of study. And it is these strategies that are largely not taught in high schools. In short, teachers should (1) show students appropriate uses of cross-disciplinary strategies and (2) teach them discipline-specific strategies.

Multiple Texts

Each discipline creates knowledge employing various genres of text. History, for example, relies on first-person accounts, newspaper articles and editorials, interviews, video, the accounts of other historians, original documents, and so forth. History cannot be understood in the way that historians understand it unless students experience reading about an event from two or more perspectives in different texts. Sometimes the interpretations conflict, which shows readers that history is not a simple description of what happened, but consists of arguments based on historical evidence. Science texts consist of scientific explanations in popular media, lab reports, journal articles, and research proposals, and they are multimodal in the sense that graphs, charts, diagrams, photographs, formulas/equations, and text are interspersed with each other. Students may not understand the role of science unless they read these genres. Multiple texts are important in mathematics because they provide an opportunity to compare and contrast various solutions to problems. Multiple text reading is also the kind of reading that citizens do every day, as they decide who to vote for, what is healthy and what is not, which car to buy, and so on. Citizens are bombarded by multiple, conflicting messages that are more or less credible.

Reading experts, in the past, have been more concerned with the comprehension of a single text than comprehension of multiple texts. But students need to learn to work across texts in order to form more complete and nuanced ideas about the world.

CONCLUSION

This chapter has explored differences among the disciplines, arguing that these differences provide teachers with guidance in how to teach reading in various subject matters. As students advance through the grades, that instruction should become more discipline specific, with a focus on using discipline frameworks to guide the purpose and activity of reading.

REFERENCES

Austin, E. W., & Dong, Q. (1994). Source v. content effects on judgments of news believability. *Journalism Quarterly, 71*(4), 973.

Common Core State Standards Initiative. (2010). Common core standards for English language arts and literacy in history/social studies, science, and technical subjects. Retrieved from *www.corestandards.org.*

Dyer, N. (2010). For test-tube babies, synthetic environment could cause lasting genetic damage. *Popular Science.* Retrieved from *www.popsci/taxonomy/term/23376/all.*

Geisler, C. (1994). *Academic literacy and the nature of expertise:* Hillsale, NJ: Lawrence Erlbaum Assoc.

Horai, J., Naccari, N., & Fatoullah, E. (1974). The effects of expertise and physical attractiveness upon opinion agreement and liking. *Sociometry, 37*(4), 601–606.

Lambert, J., Gurusamy-Thangavelu, S., & Ma, K. (2010). The silicate-mediated formose reaction: Bottom-up synthesis of sugar silicates. *Science, 327*(5968), 984–986.

Ogle, D.M. (1986). K-W-L: A teaching model that develops active reading of expository text. *Reading Teacher, 39,* 564–570.

Robinson, F. P. (1970). *Effective study* (4th ed.). New York: Harper & Row.

Rouet, J. F., Britt, A., & Mason, R. A. (1996). Using multiple sources of evidence to reason about history. *Journal of Educational Psychology, 88*(3), 478–493.

Scott, J. W. (1988). *Gender and the politics of history* (Rev. ed.). New York: Columbia University Press.

Shanahan, T., & Shanahan, C. (2008). Teaching disciplinary literacy to adolescents: Rethinking content-area literacy. *Harvard Educational Review, 78*(1), 40–59.

Stahl, S., Hynd, C., Britton, B., McNish, M., & Bosquet, D. (1996). What happens when students read multiple source documents in history? *Reading Research Quarterly, 31*, 430–457.

Wineburg, S. S. (1991). On the reading of historical texts: Notes on the breach between school and academy. *American Educational Research Journal, 28*, 495–519.

4

A Model for Teacher Planning with Text in the Academic Disciplines

Tamara L. Jetton *and* Richard Lee

Research over several decades has shown that effective teacher planning is an important part of the educational process (Clark & Peterson, 1986; Schumm et al., 1995; Fuchs, Fuchs, Karns, Hamlett, & Katzaroff, 1999; Hall & Smith, 2006). Teacher planning involves both preplanning, in which teachers prepare lessons before they implement instruction in the classroom, and interactive planning, in which teachers make decisions about instruction on the spot as instruction occurs (Schumm et al., 1995). Although teacher planning has a long history of research that we discuss later in the chapter, few studies examine teacher planning and instructional design for literacy lessons in the academic disciplines. Because so little research exists, we are left with many unanswered questions. How do teachers of the disciplines plan for reading instruction? How do teachers think about discussion when they plan for disciplinary learning? What aspects of literacy do teachers of the various disciplines value as shown by their planning process? To address these questions, we wanted to pull together the research on teacher planning and disciplinary literacy in order to construct a model of planning components teachers should consider as they plan instruction with their disciplinary texts. By text, we mean the print, oral, and digital media by which people communicate within a discipline. Thus, text can be print media, including magazines, journals, primary source documents, and traditional academic textbooks, but it can also mean the many discourses with which students engage within the discipline, such as classroom and peer discussions, speeches, and teacher lectures, to name a few, and digital media, including blogs, news articles, and wikis.

TEACHER PLANNING RESEARCH

A number of general findings have emerged about teacher planning and instructional design. As early as 1986, Clark and Peterson found that teacher planning is not always a major consideration when examining teachers' practices. Teachers do not often think about long-term goals and instructional objectives when they plan (Earle, 1998). Rather, they think more about the content, specific activities, and characteristics of students as they plan their lessons. Often, teachers rely heavily on curriculum materials to make planning decisions (Ben-Peretz & Kremer-Hayon, 1990; Clark & Elmore, 1981; McCutcheon, 1981). That is, they rely on the advice from various textbook publishers to determine the content and methodologies for teaching. When teachers plan, they do so for a variety of different reasons (Byra & Coulon, 1994; Clark & Yinger, 1979; Griffey & Housner, 1991; Hall & Smith, 2006). They plan a lesson to ensure that they know the material, and they can determine the course their instruction will take by organizing their materials. Planning also gives teachers the assurance that their instruction will lead to students learning. Planning is also a way to achieve organization, whether it be organizing students or organizing content, so teachers ensure that they have taught the requisite curriculum requirements.

Teachers must consider many factors as they plan, including their own attitudes, beliefs, and conceptions about planning (Remillard & Bryans, 2004; Schumm et al., 1995). Dewey (1933) noted that teachers must be flexible and open to various options as they consider the consequences of their planning. They must also possess an enthusiastic willingness to integrate new ideas into practice. How teachers view the content and how students learn that content influences their planning decisions. For example, in mathematics, teachers who value mathematical reform plan using questions that do not stifle student thinking and consider different ways students might offer solutions to various mathematical problems (Kilpatrick, 2003; Moyer & Milewicz, 2002; Superfine, 2008). Other factors include the teacher's knowledge, experience, and motivation to plan (Schumm et al., 1995). Research has shown planning differences between experienced and inexperienced teachers. Experienced teachers, who have more knowledge about teaching and learning, make many more planning decisions and utilize more skeletal planning frameworks than inexperienced teachers, who produce more elaborate plans (Borko & Shavelson, 1990; Earle, 1998; Hall & Smith, 2006).

Many environmental factors also affect planning, such as state and national mandates for content and teacher development. On a local level, teacher planning is influenced by the budget of the school district and the individual school because the budget can determine such things as the level of resources in terms of technology and texts teachers can use in the classroom. Budgetary issues can also affect class size, for which teachers must plan carefully. Teaching a class of 25 students is quite different from teaching a group of 35. Student factors affect many of the decisions teachers make during planning. Planning is also influenced by ongoing school activities that can disrupt instruction, such as impromptu assemblies (Schumm & Vaughn, 1991). Despite the lack of research in this area, there is some research that emphasizes the need to consider students' social and cultural views about the content (Moje & Hinchman, 2004). Likewise, teachers must consider how those views are relevant to their knowledge about and interest in the content and determine what instructional strategies they may use (Jetton & Alexander, 2004).

In the past, teachers used linear models, including step-by-step procedures, to plan their lessons (Brown, 1988; Taylor, 1970; Yackal & Cobb, 1996). However, researchers have shown that linear models are not sufficient to delineate the planning process, which is largely nonlinear (Superfine, 2008; Yinger, 1977). Yinger (1977) described the planning process as cyclic since planning is affected by previous teaching, and an instructional event can influence future planning. Research also shows that teacher planning involves many different kinds of plans, some of which are determined by time factors, such as short-term plans for the next day's lesson or long-term plans that determine how an instructor will incorporate state objectives into the curriculum during the entirety of the course, whether the course be a semester or full-year course of study.

Teacher planning can involve decisions about the instructional design of a lesson prior to teaching, but it also involves the spontaneous decisions and improvisations teachers make as they engage in lessons (Borko & Livingston, 1989; Hall & Smith, 2006). While planning prior to the lesson is necessary, immediate planning decisions as the lessons are taking place is critical. Suppose a teacher plans to read and summarize a text with his class, but during the summarization lesson, a student asks a question relevant to the topic. The teacher must make the decision whether to continue the summarization and answer the student's question later at a more opportune time; the teacher could also decide that he or she can use the student's question as part of the summarization exercise. The teacher has to weigh these and several other possibilities as the lesson progresses. Often the teacher's flexibility with strategies during instruction can help facilitate the decisions that are made during instruction (Hall & Smith, 2006).

Recent research in teacher planning has shown that the discipline in which teachers plan is another important factor. Teachers must examine the characteristics, structure, demands, and challenges of a particular discipline (Superfine, 2008). Although there are studies on teacher planning in relation to mathematical reform, special education, and physical education, there is a dearth of research that examines how secondary teachers plan lessons for adolescents that incorporate text.

The purpose of this chapter is to provide a model of teacher planning with text that encompasses the various factors that influence teachers as they plan lessons in the various academic disciplines (see Figure 4.1). While we acknowledge that teachers may consider other planning factors related to specific occurrences within their schools and districts, we include seminal planning factors related to literacy planning that appear in the research with adolescent students and their teachers.

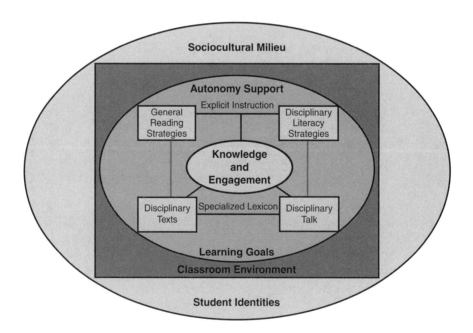

FIGURE 4.1. Model of teacher planning with disciplinary text.

SOCIOCULTURAL FACTORS AND STUDENT IDENTITIES

Contrary to past views of students as receptacles of a subset of skills or strategies, teachers must understand that the sociocultural milieu in which students engage inside and outside of school mediates and is mediated by student identities (Moje & Luke, 2009). Although not all identity theorists view the term *identity* in the same way, such theorists offer vital information to teachers about identity and how considerations of identity are important for teachers as they plan with text in the classroom. One way to think about identity is to think about how students' social and cultural identities mediate and are mediated by text. That is, the social and cultural groups to which one belongs become an integral part of how one develops self and identity. Teachers should be mindful of the social and cultural practices of these various sociocultural groups to which their students belong, particularly if the content of the lessons devalues or disenfranchises students.

Another consideration regarding identity is that it is developed through activity as students and teachers interact socially with one another and the text during classroom practice. Teachers should be mindful that identity is not a static construct; students don't enter the classroom with an identity (Moje & Luke, 2009). Rather, students' identities are fluidly produced and developed through the sociocultural activities in which they participate inside and outside of school. Teachers should also value the fact that identities are narratives or stories that students tell about themselves, and they should find opportunities in the classroom to appreciate and value these narratives rather than marginalizing them. Last, teachers should be mindful that identity also refers to the ways in which students are perceived by others, whether it be recognition of that person as fitting into a particular cultural group or having a certain social position. When students are afforded certain social positions within the classroom the power relationships may become unbalanced, and students might see themselves as having little agency in school. They begin to believe that their ideas, values, and beliefs are undervalued.

One way to value and honor student identities in the classroom is to facilitate instruction with culturally responsive pedagogy that uses "the cultural knowledge, prior experiences, frames of reference, and performance styles of ethnically diverse students to make learning encounters more relevant to and effective for them" (Gay, 2000, p. 29). In one study Jetton, Savage-Davis, and Baker (2009) investigated the use of multicultural literature to mediate student identities about diversity through the writing of tandem stories. Students were encouraged to read quality multicultural literature that explored a variety of adolescent issues. Through this project, students used writing and peer discussion to express their beliefs and views about these issues. Opposing opinions and the expression of novel ideas caused the students to reconsider their own textual interpretations in light of these views and restructure their own beliefs and views about the diversity issues represented in the literature.

Students began the project by constructing their own ideas, views, and experiences regarding the literature through writing. Following this activity, students engaged in peer discussion and tandem story writing in which they brought their unique, individual experiences and understandings of the literature to a small group, incorporating their individual writing ideas into one story ending for the literature. The challenge of the project was to incorporate all of the students' individual ideas into one coherent story ending that valued each student's contribution.

This type of project could easily be adapted to the study of history, in which students are encouraged to gather evidence from primary resources and use these resources to construct their own interpretation of an historical event. Then the students take each of their interpretations to a small group in which they write an interpretive essay on the historical event that honors each of the individual interpretations. Moje and Hinchman (2004) describe another example of culturally responsive pedagogy in their examination of a math class in which a teacher facilitated instruction by drawing her math problems from real-world experiences; students were invited to consider problem sets through inquiry. The teacher's role was to ascertain the students' needs in order to provide the necessary scaffolding for them to reach a level of independence with the problem set.

Teachers who practice culturally responsive pedagogy construct and develop lessons with applications to the various disciplinary content that is relevant to the students. Teachers of science can construct project-based lessons in which students are invited and encouraged to draw on their existing funds of knowledge, values, and beliefs to inquire about a particular topic. One of the examples that Moje and Hinchman (2004) provide is an inquiry project about communicative diseases developed by a science teacher. Rather than begin with a more traditional science text concerning this topic, the teacher began the unit with a text concerning body piercings and tattoos, a topic more relevant to students' experiences. Through this text, the teacher could weave together the students' funds of knowledge and beliefs with the scientific concepts of the unit. By connecting the principles of the scientific discipline with the students' own cultural experiences, the teacher was ultimately helping apprentice students into the scientific discourse communities by drawing from the existing discourse communities in which student engage in their everyday world.

CLASSROOM ENVIRONMENT

The current research on disciplinary literacy stresses the importance of constructing a classroom in which teachers and the students engage in "norms of practice" that are common to each discipline (Moje, 2008, p. 100). Learning in each discipline is a way of understanding the various processes, practices, and discourses that characterize that discipline. Teachers need to consider ways in which they can apprentice students into these norms of practice. For the English teacher, that might mean showing students how to read a piece of literature and engage in literary analysis through critical discussion of an author's use of dramatic irony as a device to create suspense in a play. In science, that might mean developing an inquiry project in order to better understand force and motion. Through this project, students read about force and motion, write their observations about various experiments, and discuss their theories with each other. Thus, within each discipline, literacy becomes a seamless part of the norms of practice as each discipline uses reading, writing, discussing, and visual representation in unique ways to explore its major themes and concepts.

Learning Goals

Part of teaching students the norms of practice within each discipline is helping them understand the learning goals for grappling with the content of each discipline (Guthrie & Davis, 2003). Teachers and students who construct task goals focused on understanding a particular discipline greatly increases students' motivation and self-efficacy in that discipline. As a result, students are more likely to want to learn how one comes to understand in a particular discipline. In contrast, those classroom contexts where the focus is solely on grades and performance relative to other students causes students to focus less on the norms of practice within that discipline and more on achieving higher scores than other students. Teachers can teach students how experts arrive at task goals within their respective disciplines. That is, in science, teachers help students understand that the nature of scientific inquiry is rooted in investigations and evidence, rather than a perfect score on a science test. The questions students ask, the claims they make through their investigations, the reasoning they provide as support for their claims should be stressed as the task goals for apprenticing in the discipline of science.

Autonomy Support

Another important component within the classroom environment is the level of student autonomy that teachers engender as students engage in disciplinary thinking and learning. Guthrie and Davis (2003) state that autonomy support leads to a greater increase in desire, responsibility, and persistence by students as they learn within an academic discipline. Autonomy support means that students "experience an authentic sense of control and decision making" as they engage in learning tasks within the classroom environment (p. 75). Cooperation between teachers and students on decisions regarding unit planning and task choices leads to increased motivation in secondary schools (Zahorik, 1996). Students can make decisions about the amount of work and time required on projects in class; they can also make choices about the order in which they do their assignments, the form by which they construct a project for class, and the rubric for assessing their learning of content.

KNOWLEDGE AND ENGAGEMENT WITH TEXT

All academic disciplines involve a specialized body of knowledge that is organized by core concepts or principles. Knowledge of these disciplines is most often acquired through formal education or training (Alexander, 1998; Jetton & Alexander, 2004). For example, the study of human biology is frequently organized around systems (e.g., circulatory or digestive) and subsystems (e.g., organs tissues, or cells). These core concepts and principles are often determined and sanctioned by experts through sociocultural practices (Phillips, 1987, 1995). Disciplines also have their own lexicon or vocabulary for conveying information relative. For students to be knowledgeable in history, they would need to know such words as *acts, bill*, and *treaties*, which carry specific meanings that may not be obvious or significant to those outside the domain. Likewise, words such as *domain, base ten,* and *order of operation* are central terms for the discipline of mathematics. Students who apprentice within a discipline learn to express their understandings by reading, writing, and discussing concepts with this discipline-specific language. Thus, knowledge is more than just amassing a large quantity of content knowledge about the discipline; it involves students learning the discourse used within the discipline to communicate and engage in discipline-specific activity.

Knowledge within a discipline also means learning the mode of inscription experts use to convey information within a discipline (Goldin, 1992; Kulikowich, O'Connell, Rezendes, & Archambault, 2000). For many disciplines such as history and literature, the mode of inscription is linguistic, as in the language of words, phrases, sentences, and paragraphs. Linguistic knowledge also refers to the understanding of various genres that authors use to convey knowledge within a domain. For example, knowledge of lab reports as a genre is useful to understanding how experts structure inquiry in science. Similarly, knowledge of art criticism as a genre is vital to an art history student. Other domains such as math and science incorporate numeric or graphic modes of inscription along with the linguistic forms. Thus, knowledge of graphs, charts, tables, and equations becomes central to students' understandings of the math and science disciplines.

When teachers think of knowledge within a discipline, they often refer to the subject-matter knowledge that students and teachers construct as they engage in learning a discipline (Alexander, 1998). Subject-matter knowledge refers to the concepts one knows about a particular field of study or discipline, such as knowledge of the Civil War in history and the knowledge of parallelograms in mathematics. Over time, we would expect subject-matter knowledge to increase as students engage within a discipline (Alexander, 2005). However, another type of knowledge is important to consider as students grapple with particular textual material, such as online blogs and primary source documents, within the various disciplines. One can possess a wealth of subject-matter knowledge about the Civil War but encounter a particular topic within that discipline that one might not know. Thus, topic knowledge is also an important factor that teachers should consider in their planning (Jetton & Alexander, 2004). Just because students gained subject-matter knowledge in their biology classroom the previous year does not mean that they will also possess knowledge of more specific topics within that discipline. A student can acquire a great deal of subject-matter knowledge about cells, but encounter a text on which he or she has no topic knowledge, such as an article about occupational exposure to aluminum and its effects on cells.

Just as disciplinary and topic knowledge are important for teachers to consider as they construct lessons for students, they must also plan for engaged learning in the disciplines (Wigfield et al., 2008). As students transition from elementary to middle and high school, their motivation drops (Guthrie & Davis, 2003). This drop may be due to a number of factors, including students' reluctance to read the difficult textbooks they encounter in middle and high school, and their interests outside the school environment. Students also report that as they move up the grade levels, teachers provide fewer opportunities for them to express their opinions on class content and choose topics of interest to them in the various disciplines. Students also report that teachers are less likely to encourage use of strategies that they need to better understand the more difficult texts they may encounter (Guthrie & Davis, 2003). Teachers need to find opportunities to reengage these adolescent learners. We have already noted several ways teachers can accomplish this task: valuing adolescent identities, setting learning goals, and providing autonomy support in the classroom. To increase engagement, teachers should also use interesting texts that tap adolescents' curiosity, and explicitly teach strategies for engaging with these texts. They must also plan instruction that includes social interaction, so students and teachers can employ discourse to grapple with the ideas and theories of the discipline.

DISCIPLINARY TEXTS

One way teachers apprentice students in a particular discipline is through the various discourse practices that characterize that discipline. Each discipline represents unique ways of thinking, talking, reading, and writing, and teachers must explore ways they can show students how the experts in that discipline think, talk, and write. As experts engaged in these disciplines, they offer examples through the various texts they write. Little research to date has explored how texts are used to accomplish specific disciplinary learning goals (Moje, Stockhill, Kim, & Kim, 2010). Recent research has shown that texts are used for different purposes in the various disciplines. As teachers plan, they need to think about how they will apprentice students into the language of their disciplines without sacrificing the everyday language in which students engage in and out of school. Since another chapter in this book is dedicated to the nature of disciplinary texts, we will not provide an in-depth discussion of this topic. However, we do believe that when teachers plan, they need to consider the nature of disciplinary texts and the need to apprentice students into the unique discourses evident in these texts.

One consideration that teachers must contemplate as they plan is the nature of the text itself and the goals they have for using that particular text. Despite the proliferation of reading material in the various academic domains, many teachers still use the standard textbook as the primary reading material for students. While the textbook might be an appropriate vehicle for teaching content, it has its drawbacks. Many academic textbooks in high school are very difficult for students to read because they either contain content that is difficult to understand or the text is difficult to read because of the complexity of its sentences and technical vocabulary (Goldman & Rakestraw, 2000). Some students do not have the requisite prior knowledge to understand the ideas in the text while other students are discouraged by the complex language.

Teachers should consider using texts that are interesting and relevant to the students' experiences and beliefs (Guthrie & Davis, 2003; Jetton & Alexander, 2004). Interest is a critical factor related to academic learning. While some students may have an interest in the academic content that motivates them to learn, many do not. However, students can become situationally interested in text, which in turn can lead to the development of individual interest (Hidi & Renninger, 2006). Situational interest refers to interest evoked by a variety of environmental factors that include the teacher, other students, and the text (Hidi & Renninger, 2006; Linnenbrink-Garcia et al., 2010). Textbooks may not be the best vehicle for engendering situational interest; rather, other texts, including online news articles, blogs, magazine publications, and adolescent fiction, may be more interesting to them. Because some of these sources are not rigorously reviewed, teachers must be careful to determine the credibility of information students will read.

When selecting text materials teachers must also contemplate the learning goals within their academic domain (Guthrie & Davis, 2003). For example, history teachers may be using a text because it is a primary source document for teaching the views and perspectives of people during the time a particular event took place. English language arts teachers may use text to examine cultural and societal themes evident in the literature. When teachers choose to incorporate text in the teaching of academic content, they have to consider the content learning goals, but also the instructional goals for helping students understand the content in the text. These goals operate simultaneously and in coordination with one another. As an example, consider Mike, a high school biology teacher. He wants to use a text that details different types of fungi because the author provides clear, detailed descriptions of the types. At the same time, Mike needs to consider his goals for helping students glean the text content by examining the prior knowledge students bring to bear to the reading task, and how students might use the text structure of the chapter to determine the important information. In another science classroom, Sandra is using a science text to contradict students' long-held misconceptions about the earth's atmosphere. While she realizes that students understand the role of oxygen in the atmosphere, she wants to use the reading to emphasize the role that nitrogen plays in the atmosphere. Her content goal is to learn about the content and layers of the atmosphere, but Sandra also knows that she needs to plan specific reading strategies that students can use to better understand the content they read.

It is also important for teachers to consider the social and cultural views represented in the texts used in the classroom. For example, a group of American history teachers were beginning to plan their unit on western expansion. When they examined the textbook, the focus of the content was the Anglo-American pioneers moving west and the impact this movement had on the Native Americans. The text did not account for people from other cultures who were also part of the great western expansion, such as Asian Americans and Mexican Americans who worked to build the railroads traveling west. Teachers need to be vigilant about incorporating text that represents the views of many cultures and discourse communities. Teachers must also be attuned to the various social and cultural views of their students as they approach a variety of different content topics within their domain. A science text on stem-cell research might evoke a variety of different sociocultural views from students. Various themes within the literature studied in an English language arts class can impact students differentially, depending on their sociocultural background. Teachers need to provide many opportunities for students to feel safe and comfortable sharing their differing ideologies as they pertain to the academic content of the text.

Teachers should explore the many texts within their disciplines and ensure that students are engaging with authentic disciplinary texts that historians, scientists, and experts in other disciplines use. In contrast to classroom textbooks, which often do not engage the student and can become outdated very quickly, authentic disciplinary texts can create the human connection that students seek as they read information, and these texts can provide current information with which disciplinary experts are grappling. In history, for example, teachers can find interesting online and traditional texts in formats such as journals, newsletters, government documents, speeches, historical commentaries, and biographies. Some of these texts might include primary source documents that often are more difficult to read, so teachers should be aware of the scaffolding they must provide so that students can understand and engage with these texts. Art teachers may choose online and traditional texts including art education magazines, art theory articles, art interpretation books, program notes, art gallery postings, and museum reviews. Engaging students in literacy activities revolving around authentic disciplinary texts that experts regularly use in their field will apprentice students into the kinds of thinking discipline experts employ in their work.

GENERAL AND DISCIPLINARY LITERACY STRATEGIES

Although the purpose of this book is to detail discipline-specific literacy strategies that teachers and students engage in within particular academic domains, teachers must also consider the general reading strategies that have been shown to aid students in their understanding of texts. It is our belief that these reading strategies work in tandem with the more discipline-specific literacy strategies to help students achieve their learning goals. Reading strategies, in particular, concern conscious, deliberate plans that readers use flexibly to understand text (Alexander & Judy, 1988). Beginning as early as the 1980s, researchers have examined the nature and effect of reading strategies on students' ability to comprehend texts. In 1989, Pressley, Johnson, Symons, McGoldrick, and Kurita provided a framework for understanding these strategies. They included summarization, in which students determine the most important content in text; imaging, in which students create representational images or pictures of the text material; story structure, in which students use their knowledge of story structure to determine important elements in the literature; student questioning, in which students question the text in order to clarify their understanding and glean the content; and activating prior knowledge, in which students use knowledge they already possess to help them learn the new content in the text. Later, Dole, Duffy, Roehler, and Pearson (1991) provided a review of comprehension strategies, and linked those strategies directly to what they called "teaching strategies" (p. 239). In their article, Dole and her colleagues reviewed 20 years of research on effective comprehension strategies such as determining importance, summarizing, making inferences, student-generated questioning, and comprehension monitoring. Making inferences involves students using the text information and their prior knowledge to arrive at new ideas that are not directly stated in the text. Comprehension monitoring refers to students recognizing when they are understanding or when their comprehension breaks down and applying fix-up strategies for increasing their understanding such as rereading the text to clarify meaning.

When students learn in an academic discipline, these strategies enable them to think about the content in useful ways as they "read, write, talk, and reason as a junior member of a particular discipline" (McConachie & Petrosky, 2010, p. 21). Students are employing these strategies to grapple with the content so they can better inquire about science and history, determine important perspectives in history, discover patterns within the math problems, and explore motivations and themes in literature.

All of these general strategies are used in the academic disciplines to comprehend text, but they might be used differently depending on the particular academic discipline. The next part of this chapter explores how teachers should consider planning for each of these strategies within their particular academic discipline.

Activating Prior Knowledge

Educators know that readers in any academic discipline find it easier to comprehend if they connect the prior knowledge that they possess with the new information in text. In the academic disciplines, activating prior knowledge during reading is used for a variety of different reasons. In a choral music class, students use their prior knowledge of a capella music in order to understand Renaissance music. A cappella music, which is sung without instrumental accompaniment, helps the choral music student imagine Renaissance polyphony, music designed for several different voices. Likewise, students in history are taught to read texts like historians, who use their prior knowledge and a variety of different sources, including primary and secondary sources, to build a credible narrative of historical events. Students in an algebra class use their prior knowledge of order of operations to write and solve complicated equations. Students in a science class use their prior knowledge of observation to help them construct an inquiry project in science.

Determining Importance

Students determine importance in text for a variety of different reasons or purposes. In an English language arts classroom, students choose text to read as part of their independent reading time. As they read, these students are left to their own devices to determine importance in the texts they have chosen. Dole and her colleagues (1991) referred to this as reader-based importance. Students who read with this purpose in mind often find the interesting information the most important to them (Alexander & Jetton, 1996). Students in a history class are reading a primary source document in which a Native American is giving his account of the western expansion, and the treatment of Native Americans by the white settlers. The students are particularly interested in the views of the author in order to build their historical narrative with the views of Native Americans. In this case, the readers determine importance according to the author. The teacher and the task can also drive importance. Students in a science class who are conducting inquiry research task read to determine important information that will support their existing data and observations.

Mental Imagery

Often, students learn from text by constructing representational images of the words and symbols in print (Van Meter, 2001). In English language arts, students are reading "The Most Dangerous Game," a short story about a man who is being hunted for sport. As they read, students are picturing the man running through the jungle, sweating, with a look of fear on his face. In a mathematics class, students read the following word problem:

> Marina has two cakes that she is getting ready to frost. She has two containers of frosting: vanilla and chocolate. The tub of vanilla has more frosting, so she wants to use the vanilla on the cake that has the larger surface area on top. One cake is a 15-inch-by-8-inch rectangular cake. The other cake is circular, with a diameter of 10 inches. Which cake should she frost with vanilla?

As they read the problem, the students are visualizing the two cakes as they consider the principles of circumference that will help them solve the problem. In groups, students work together to draw the images and the appropriate measurements of the cakes as they discuss possible solutions.

Text Structure

Authors organize their ideas in text, and readers use that organization to find the information they need (Meyer & Poon, 2001; Meyer & Wijekumar, 2007). Students involved in a science inquiry project on weather need to find information about the weather cycle; knowing that the author of the article they are reading organizes this information as a step-by-step process helps them remember it better. Researchers have also found that students who know the story structure are better able to glean the important content of fiction (Pressley et al., 1989). Thus, students are encouraged in an English language arts class to consider the setting, the location and time period of the story, and consider how these two elements affect the overall outcome of the story. They are also encouraged to examine characters, their motivations, actions, and the author's descriptions in order to better understand the story. Sequencing the events in the story from the beginning exposition to the climax and through the denouement helps students better remember the important events in the story. In history, the students are studying the aftermath of the Civil War from a variety of different perspectives. As they read one slave's account, they note the effects of the final events of the war from the slave's perspective. Another group of students are reading about the effects of the Civil War on families in Texas and using the authors' cause/effect organization to construct the information they need from a Texan's perspective. Thus, the cause/effect text structure of the passage makes it easier for students to glean the important information they need to understand the effects of the Civil War as seen through the eyes of several participants.

Question Generation

A science teacher is helping students understand that good questions will aid them in their inquiry endeavors, and she shows them how scientists in the field use these questions to guide their own inquiry. Thus, the students are learning that in the discipline of science, they must develop good questioning strategies. Research has found that question generation during reading increases students' understanding of text (Rosenshine, Meister, & Chapman, 1996). Furthermore, student-generating questioning enables students to see the text as a resource for developing and constructing ideas, rather than the authoritative answer (McConachie & Petrosky, 2010). For example, students in a history class are reading about Magellan's voyage to transverse the world in order to find a new passageway to China. To gather information for their historical narrative of this voyage, they have just read the account of Pigafetta, a crew member who kept a journal of the voyage. In his journal, Pigafetta provides information about how the crew greeted the Patagonians in a friendly way. As they begin reading their classroom textbooks, they read that Magellan's crew placed two of the Patagonians in chains and brought them on the ship to bring them back to Europe. As students read both accounts, they begin generating questions about Magellan's crew. One student asked, "Why did Magellan's crew feel it necessary to take the Patagonians back in chains when Pigafetta claimed that they greeted the crew in a friendly and reverent way?" Discussion ensued with students generating other questions that, if answered, would build their narrative, such as "How did Magellan's crew treat other islanders that they encountered?" All of these questions create an atmosphere of inquiry rather than a blind belief in the textbook account of the event, and students develop a more personally driven interpretation of the events through multiple print sources from a variety of perspectives.

Making Inferences

Students in a mathematics class have been examining a graph that shows the composition of the United States Congress, in which they were asked to find the total number of Democrats in Congress in 1985 (Dancis, 2002).

In order to find the answer to this task, students have to infer that the Congress consists of two houses since this information is not directly stated in the table. As they examine the table, students continue drawing several inferences about the data such as how Democrats consistently outnumbered the Republications in both the Senate and House for the 6 years from 1983 to 1989. Research has shown that inference making is a critical strategy for readers as they construct meaning from both informational and narrative text (Peverly & Wood, 2001). Making inferences means that readers are using the text information and their prior knowledge of the content to arrive at ideas that are not directly stated in the text, as shown by the math students who are making judgments about members of Congress in small groups.

Comprehension Monitoring

A student is grappling with a difficult story in her literature class and says, "I can clearly picture the narrator lying in bed, blowing out the candle, and sleeping with a book in his hands. I understand the narrator is looking back at an experience he had. But, I am confused about the book the narrator is reading: it involves a church, a quartet, and a rivalry between Francis I and Charles V. Who are they? Is that Charles V, a king of England?" In this example, the student has realized that her comprehension has broken down, and she employs the strategy of self-questioning to help her make sense of the story she is reading. This is one example of comprehension monitoring. With comprehension monitoring, readers become aware that their comprehension has broken down because they don't have sufficient prior knowledge to understand, as was the case in the example above, or their existing knowledge runs counter to the information in the text. To illustrate, students in science class are reading about gravity and discover that their own knowledge about gravity differs from the resources they are reading. For example, they believe that gravity acts differently on certain matter, that gravity cannot exist without air, and gravity increases with height. When the texts that they are reading contradict their long-held misconceptions, students pause in confusion and realize that they do not understand. They state, "I don't get this. I thought the higher you go, the more gravity there is." Comprehension monitoring is critical to understanding because students need to be able to realize when they don't understand the ideas, and when the teacher and other students may need to aid them in their understanding of the content (Fox, 2009).

Explicit Instruction of General Strategies in Tandem with Disciplinary Strategies

As we have shown in the aforementioned examples, students employ comprehension strategies for different purposes within all of the various academic disciplines. These strategies provide a way for students to think about and use the content they read. Teachers need to apprentice students into the ways of thinking about certain disciplines, so they can learn to think like experts in each field. Thus, students must be able to think like historians, scientists, mathematicians. These strategies are ways that these experts grapple with text content. In constructing a historical record of a period in time, historians think about what they already know about this time period, they determine the important facts and perspectives in several historical documents, and they make inferences about a set of guiding questions they have constructed (Ravi, 2010). Likewise, mathematicians employ these strategies as they think about high-level problem sets. They draw on prior knowledge, create visual representations, and make predictions or conjectures as to the solutions (Bill & Jamar, 2010).

For teachers in these academic disciplines to apprentice students in the types of thinking that these experts do, they need to be intentional about these ways of thinking with their students. Thus, they need to externalize their thinking for students through modeling and discussion, so students grow accustomed to common ways of thinking in the discipline. This is why the explicit instruction of these comprehension strategies is imperative (Biancarosa & Snow, 2006). Rather than just having students participate in an authentic inquiry activity common to the field of science, teachers must be intentional about the kinds of thinking scientists employ as they converse about science (Spiegel, Bintz, Taylor, Landes, & Jordan, 2010). Similarly, English language arts teachers should not just have students read quality literature—they need to engage in discussions using the type of thinking that literary critics engage in, and they must be explicit about the strategies these critics employ to make sense of the texts.

Explicit instruction is not a new concept, but when we go out in the field and observe teachers in their classrooms using text, we see teachers employing these strategies for thinking but not explicitly showing students what they are doing and why they are thinking in those ways. Many years ago Pearson and Gallagher (1983) proposed a model for explicit comprehension instruction that first involved teachers explaining the type of strategy they employed and why the strategy was important to use. Then they modeled the use of the strategy as they read the text. Following the modeling, they provided guided practice for students with the strategy, so students learned how to use the strategy with scaffolded support from the teacher and other students until they could employ the strategy on their own. Almost three decades later, this strategy model is still a powerful model for helping students understand the kind of thinking with text that experts use in all of the academic disciplines.

Let's consider a sample sixth-grade mathematics lesson in which the teacher, Michael Came, is being explicit about the strategies he employs as he models the process of solving a word problem. The word problem reads,

> Patricia is decorating her house for her 12th birthday party with her five best friends. She is particularly interested in decorating the kitchen table for the party because this is where they will eat, play games, and open presents. She wants to paint five stools with circular seats that are each 12 inches in diameter. She wants to paint the tops of all the stools bright red, but needs to know the area she will paint. What is the total area of the tops of all five stools?

Michael models his thinking about the problem to illustrate the strategies that students can use as they participate in mathematical thinking. First, he shows students that he must summarize the goal of the problem before more thinking takes place. He says:

> "One thing I always do is summarize the goal of the problem and determine exactly what is being asked before I do anything else. This helps me establish a starting point for approaching the problem. The goal of this particular problem is to find out the total area of the top surface of five round stools. The word *round* implies that the surface is a circle. In order to accomplish this goal, it helps me to think about what I have already learned about circles and their area. I know that thinking about circles can involve many different concepts such as radius, diameter, and circumference because I have prior knowledge of the unit from last year that I taught. I also know that the formula for the area of a circle is $A = \pi r^2$. So, I now know that I need the radius in order to find the area of one of the stools. Then I will multiply the area by the number of stools to get the total area. Other formulas relating the radius, diameter, and circumference might also be useful in case the radius isn't given. These formulas are $C = \pi d$ and $d = 2r$. Now that I know what I need to extract from the problem, I can get rid of useless information the problem gives me. Determining importance can help me weed out the unnecessary information, including irrelevant numbers, to help me find the most important information that I need to use. I often do this by crossing out the unimportant information. *[The teacher then thinks through the problem, crossing out irrelevant and stressing relevant information.]* Since the important information left is the diameter of the circle, I predict or conjecture that the diameter will be important, and because I apply my prior knowledge to the

problem, I know that I can get the radius from the diameter by applying the formula $d = 2r$. Another important fact is that there are five stools so I know now I have to multiply the area of one circle by 5. Now I have extracted the information best suited to help me solve the problem."

As Michael continues modeling his thinking, he is able to explicitly teach the reading strategies he employs throughout the problem, so students can, in turn, learn to incorporate these strategies and others as they group together to work on another problem in small groups with the teacher floating among groups, listening to their thinking, and scaffolding students' thinking with reading strategies that will further their thinking. While mathematical thinking entails a number of discipline-specific strategies, these general reading strategies are also useful to integrate into students' thinking as they participate in mathematical problem solving.

In conducting professional development with teachers, we have found that when teachers give these strategies a name, students become more consciously aware of the kind of mathematical thinking available to them, and the students understand that these strategies can be employed flexibly with many different kinds of mathematical problems. We also find that when teachers illustrate how they themselves use these strategies by explicitly teaching them through mathematical thinking, students become apprenticed into the kinds of thinking mathematicians use (Bill & Jamar, 2010). Teachers can then follow this instruction with small-group work and teacher scaffolding for the strategies so students can see how to flexibly use these strategies with a variety of different problem sets.

Let's consider a different discipline and how a teacher might scaffold the explicit strategy instruction in a high school biology class in which students are participating in an inquiry project about genetics and Punnett squares. The teacher begins the lesson by explaining to students that they will be investigating authentic cases involving genetic diseases that might occur in their own families. The teacher states:

"When I think genetic diseases or illness, one of the first things that I do is activate my prior knowledge about this issue. I might even think about my own family and whether someone in my family has an illness such as muscular dystrophy or Huntington's disease. I think about when I was pregnant with my child, I had to have genetic testing to determine whether my child might have spina bifida or Down syndrome. Activating prior knowledge helps me pull up requisite knowledge that I can use as I learn new information throughout the unit."

The teacher then asks students to think about what they already know about genetic disorders, illnesses, and disease through a class discussion, so students are using the language of science as they engage in the content. The teacher then tells students that scientists are always participating in inquiry in which they investigate problems by using questions and seeking answers through a variety of methods that include observation, reading, discussion, data gathering, and reflection (Spiegel et al., 2010). The teacher shows how she can take ideas from her prior knowledge and phrase questions for inquiry. She says,

> "As I activate my prior knowledge about my knowledge of genetics, and I think about one of my students whose uncle has Huntington's disease, I begin to realize that there are many gaps in my prior knowledge, and I have many questions that are ripe for investigation."

The teacher then models questions such as "What are the symptoms of Huntington's disease? How is it passed down to family members? Where might I go to find answers to my questions?" The teacher then tells students that a good starting place might be a Web search in which they investigate some of the answers to their questions. The teacher provides students with an inquiry handout about searching the Internet (*www.kumc.edu/gec*; University of Kansas Medical Center, 2010). Students are given questions such as "What is Huntingon's disease?" and "How is the Huntington genome carried down through the family?" The teacher then searches the term *Huntington's disease* on Google and locates a site posted by the Huntington Disease Society of America (*www.hdsa.org/about.html*). The teacher clicks on information about the society and discusses the credibility of the site with her students. She then reads the information on Huntington's and models the strategies she used to answer her inquiries. She states:

> "In order to guide my inquiry, I need to know more about the disease in general, so I am going to read the description of the disease. Did you notice that the information is in the form of answers to questions, so this Internet site is a good example of scientific inquiry in which questions are posed and data is given to respond to the inquiry. This is how I want you to think as you engage in scientific thinking. When I begin reading, right away I am noting things I already know and new information that I didn't know already. For

example, I knew that Huntington's affects the brain, and I already knew that there is no known cure yet. However, I didn't think about how this disease might affect other family members, and I certainly didn't know that it affects more than a quarter million Americans. As I read on, I have more questions such as 'Why is this disease one of the most common genetic disorders?' And 'Why does it not show up until age 30? Is there some sort of genetic time clock that is set off at that age?' As I'm reading the symptoms, I am trying to visualize them so I can remember them better, but I am also realizing that there is so much information to remember that it might be useful to create a data chart to record the most important information on this website before I move on to another site with additional information."

The teacher then proceeds, with student input, to determine the most important information related to the inquiry questions and to note the information on the data chart. After the teacher has modeled her scientific inquiry through this website, she guides students to another website where they will work in small groups to continue their inquiry as the teacher moves among groups, providing scaffolding for how to use these reading strategies flexibly when they read the text to answer their inquiry questions.

As shown by the aforementioned examples, these general reading strategies can and should be used as students explore mathematical problem solving and scientific inquiry and engage in history, English language arts, and the other disciplines. The real issue at hand is making the students fully aware of what these strategies are and the possibilities for using them. Explicit instruction can help accomplish this goal.

DISCIPLINARY TALK

As teachers plan, they should consider pedagogy that responds to the diverse discourse communities in which their students engage both in and out of school, in addition to the discourse communities of particular disciplines with which the teachers want students to become familiar. Teachers can provide the bridge between the everyday-world discourses of an adolescent and the various academic discourses in which students engage in school. Teachers bridge these discourses by apprenticing students in the unique discourses of their academic disciplines. Talking history is very different from talking chemistry or literature, yet students are often unaware of the kinds of discourse that occur within these disciplines because the focus of discussion is a review of the facts for a test. Historians construct narratives of historical events by reading primary and secondary source interpretations of these events. As they build these narratives, historians consider the credibility of each source and how each source fits within the greater discourse of other interpretations about the same event (Shanahan & Shanahan, 2008). Students should have similar opportunities in the classroom to collaborate through discussion by engaging in inquiry about a historical event, weighing the credibility of each source as they accumulate evidence and interpretations of the event to create a narrative that they are constantly changing and revising as they encounter additional voices from historical documents (Ravi, 2010).

To foster discussion in political science classrooms teachers can engage students in thinking beyond their own personal beliefs by using hypothetical simulations (Marks, 2008). For example, in sociology, instructors might use a coin-toss simulation to show unequal distributions despite attempts to achieve more equal outcomes. By participating in this simulation, students begin to understand societal inequality. Another exercise to show inequality, particularly as if affects gender, is to examine and discuss data representing professor salaries by gender. Teachers of history can also use historical case studies for discussions that enable students to talk about power relationships and moral conduct during war (Bald, 1996). Role-playing activities in which students take on the part of political officials during a world event can lead to productive discussions of important historical themes (Asal, 2005; Asal & Blake, 2006).

In science, discussions can focus on observations and reasoning about the topic under study and data or evidence that supports students' scientific predictions or assumptions (Spiegel et al., 2010). Discussion can also focus on new insights students have gained from their investigations and how their ideas and conceptions changed because of their observations and evidence. In its work on informal learning situations that aid our understanding of more formal learning, the Center for Informal Learning and Schools (2007) has emphasized the importance of examining communication within participation structures:

> Language is an essential tool for creating scientific explanations, arguments, narratives, metaphors, and analogies. Through language and discourse people explore and convey scientific and mathematical ideas. When learners engage in constructing and communicating explanations, whether they be scientific claims, mathematical conjectures, theories, interpretations, or representations, they are forced to externalize, clarify, and

restructure their knowledge. It is this process that stimulates individuals' understandings and presents opportunities for learning.

Teachers of science and math should ensure that they construct an environment that facilitates communication as part of the natural experimentation and investigation that are an ongoing part of these disciplines (Marks, 2008). In one study, seventh-grade students were encouraged to engage in several discussions concerning their two-dimensional models of the moon phases in order to develop geometric spatial concepts (Sherrod & Wilhelm, 2009). Through this activity, the students' common misconceptions were addressed by discussion, rather than a focus on correcting errors in the sketches. When students showed their sketches to other class members, discussions ensued that allowed the students to challenge others' ideas about the moon phases, reconsider their understandings of the universe, and elaborate their own explanations (Sherrod & Wilhelm, 2009). For math, discourse can focus on patterns that students find, generalizations that aid them in their problem solving, and explanations that help them explain their reasoning for particular solutions or weigh their reasoning in light of their peers' findings (Bill & Jamar, 2010). Engaging in academic discourse in which the meaning of text is constructed and enacted through the language of group participants will lead to a greater understanding of what it means to learn within a discipline.

FINAL CONSIDERATIONS

While this model of teacher planning may not consider every nuance of instruction that teachers may use as they plan for learning with text in their academic disciplines, we have provided several crucial components that teachers should consider as they prepare their lessons for content learning, and as they enact these lessons with their students. Despite the pressures teachers face to prepare students for high-stakes tests and future learning, we believe teachers should take a step back and consider the larger purposes for learning in the academic disciplines. We believe teachers are engaged in disciplinary teaching to show their students how people in these fields of study think, communicate, and engage with one another and texts. When teachers have this goal in mind as they plan their lessons and they engage students in the habits of thinking and processes of communicating that distinguish a discipline, they enable students to traverse new fields and come to new ways of thinking and learning.

REFERENCES

Alexander, P. A. (2005). The path to competence: A lifespan developmental perspective on reading. *Journal of Literacy Research, 37*(4), 413–436.

Alexander, P. A. (1998). The nature of disciplinary and domain learning: The knowledge, interest and strategic dimensions of learning from subject-matter text. In C. Hynd (Ed.), *Learning from text across contextual domains* (pp. 263–287). Mahwah, NJ: Erlbaum.

Alexander, P. A., & Jetton, T. L. (1996). The role of importance and interest in the processing of text. *Educational Psychology Review, 8*, 89–121.

Alexander, P. A., & Judy, J. E. (1988). The interaction of domain-specific and strategic knowledge in academic performance. *Review of Educational Research, 8*, 375–304.

Asal, V. (2005). Playing games with international relations. *International Studies Perspectives, 6*(3), 359–373.

Asal, V., & Blake, E. L. (2006). Creating simulations for political science education. *Journal of Political Science Education, 2*(1), 1–18.

Bald, S. (1996). The melian dialogue. *Pew Trust Cases in International Affairs.* Washington DC: Georgetown University.

Ben-Peretz, M., & Kremer-Hayon, L. (1990). The content and context of professional dilemmas encountered by novice and senior teachers. *Educational Review, 42*(1), 31–40.

Biancarosa, C., & Snow, C. E. (2006). *Reading next—A vision for action and research in middle and high school literacy: A report to Carnegie Corporation of New York* (2nd ed.). Washington, DC: Alliance for Excellent Education.

Bill, V. L., & Jamar, I. (2010). Disciplinary literacy in the mathematics classroom. In S. M. McConachie & A. R. Petrosky (Eds.), *Content matters* (pp. 63–85). San Francisco: Jossey-Bass.

Borko, H., & Livingston, C. (1989). Cognition and improvisation: Differences in mathematics instruction by expert and novice teachers. *American Educational Research Journal, 26*(4), 473–498.

Borko, H., & Shavelson, R. (1990). Teachers' decision making. In B. Jones & L. Idol (Eds.), *Dimensions of thinking and cognitive instruction* (pp. 311–346). Hillsdale, NJ: Erlbaum.

Brown, A. (1988). Twelve middle-school teachers' planning. *Elementary School Journal, 89*(1), 69–87.

Byra, M., & Coulon, S. C. (1994). The effect of planning on the instructional behaviors of preservice teachers. *Journal of Teaching in Physical Education, 13*, 123–129.

Center for Informal Learning and Schools. (2007). Research framework. Retrieved October 17, 2010, from *cils.exploratorium.edu/cils/page.php?ID=53.*

Clark, C. M., & Elmore, J. L. (1981). *Transforming curriculum in mathematics, science, and writing: A case study of teacher yearly planning* (Research Series No. 99). East Lansing, MI: Michigan State University, Institute for Research on Teaching. (ERIC Document Reproduction Service No. ED205500)

Clark, C. M., & Peterson, P. (1986). Teachers' thought processes. In M. Wittrock (Ed.), *Handbook of research on teaching* (3rd ed., pp. 255–296). New York: Macmillan.

Clark, C. M., & Yinger, B. (1979). Research on teacher planning: A progress report. *Journal of Curriculum Studies, 11*(2), 175–177.

Dancis, J. (2002, September 8). When it comes to math, words count. *Washington Post*, p. B04.

Dewey, J. (1933). *How we think*. Chicago: Henry Regnery.

Dole, J. A., Duffy, G. G., Roehler, L. R., & Pearson, P. D. (1991). Moving from the old to the new: Research on reading comprehension instruction. *Review of Educational Research, 61*(2), 239–264.

Earle, R. S. (1998). Instructional design and teacher planning: Reflections and perspectives. *Educational Media and Technology Yearbook* (Vol. 23, pp. 29–41). New York: Springer.

Fox, E. (2009). The role of reader characteristics in processing and learning from informational text. *Review of Educational Research, 79,* 197–261.

Fuchs, L. S., Fuchs, D., Karns, K., Hamlett, C. L., & Katzaroff, M. (1999). Mathematics performance assessment in the classroom: Effects on teacher planning and student problem solving. *American Educational Research Journal, 36*(3), 609–646.

Gay, G. (2000). *Culturally responsive teaching: Theory, research, and practice.* New York: Teachers College Press.

Goldin, G. A. (1992). Toward an assessment framework for school mathematics. In R. Lesh & S. J. Lamon (Eds.), *Assessments of authentic performance in elementary mathematics* (pp. 63–88). Washington, DC: American Association for the Advancement of Science.

Goldman, S. R., & Rakestraw, J. A., Jr. (2000). Structural aspects of constructing meaning from text. In M. L. Kamil, P. B. Mosenthal, P. D. Pearson, & R. Barr (Eds.), *Handbook of reading research* (Vol. 3, pp. 311–355). Mahwah, NJ: Erlbaum.

Griffey, D. C., & Housner, L. D. (1991). Differences between experienced and inexperienced teachers' planning decisions, interactions, student engagement and instructional climate. *Research Quarterly for Exercise and Sport, 52,* 196–204.

Guthrie, J. T., & Davis, M. H. (2003). Motivating struggling readers in middle school through an engagement model of classroom practice. *Reading and Writing Quarterly, 19,* 59–85.

Hall, T. J., & Smith, M. A. (2006). Teacher planning, instruction and reflection. *Quest, 58*(4), 424–442.

Hidi, S., & Renninger, K. A. (2006). The four-phase model of interest development. *Educational Psychologist, 41,* 111–127.

Jetton, T. L., & Savage-Davis, E. M. (2005). Preservice teachers develop an understanding of diversity issues through multicultural literature. *Multicultural Perspectives, 7*(1), 30–38.

Jetton, T. L., Savage-Davis, E. M., & Baker, M. (2009). Developing culturally responsive teacher practitioners through multicultural literature. In J. C. Scott, D. Y. Straker, & L. Katz (Eds.), *Affirming students' rights to their own language* (pp. 219–231), New York: Routledge.

Kilpatrick, J. (2003). What works? In S. Senk & D. Thompson (Eds.), *Standards-based school mathematics curricula: What are they? What do students learn?* (pp. 471–488). Mahwah, NJ: Erlbaum.

Kulikowich, J. M., O'Connell, A. A., Rezendes, G., & Archambault, F. X. (2000, April). Many theories, many methodologies: Blending quantitative and qualitative procedures in the study of classroom studies involving technology. In K. Squire (Chair), *The merits of multiple theories of learning in the study of technology use in classroom settings.* Symposium presented at the annual meeting of the American Educational Research Association, New Orleans, LA.

Linnenbrink-Garcia, L., Durik, A. M., Conley, A. M., Barron, K. E., Tauer, J. M., Karabenick, S. A., et al. (2010). Measuring situational interest in academic domains. *Educational and Psychological Measurement, 70*(4), 647–671.

Marks, M. P. (2008). Fostering scholarly discussion and critical thinking in the classroom. *Journal of Political Science Education, 4,* 205–224.

McConachie, S. M., & Petrosky, A. R. (2010). Engaging content teachers in literacy development. In S. M. McConachie & A. R. Petrosky (Eds.), *Content matters* (pp. 1–11). San Francisco: Jossey-Bass.

McCutcheon, G. (1981). On the interpretation of classroom observations. *Educational Researcher, 10*(5), 5–10.

Meyer, B. J., & Poon, L. W. (2001). Effects of structure strategy training and signaling on recall of text. *Journal of Educational Psychology, 93*(1), 141–159.

Meyer, B. J., & Wijekumar, K. (2007). A web-based tutoring system for structure strategy: Theoretical background, design, and findings. In D. McNamara, (Ed.), *Reading comprehension strategies: Theories, intervention, and technologies* (pp. 347–374). Mahwah, NJ: Erlbaum.

Moje, E. B. (2008). Foregrounding the disciplines in secondary literacy teaching and learning: A call for change. *Journal of Adolescent and Adult Literacy, 52*(2), 96–107.

Moje, E. B., & Hinchman, K. (2004). Culturally responsive practices for youth literacy learning. In T. L. Jetton & J. A. Dole (Eds.), *Adolescent literacy research and practice* (pp. 321–350). New York: Guilford Press.

Moje, E. B., & Luke, A. (2009). Literacy and identity: Examining the metaphors in history and contemporary research. *Reading Research Quarterly 44*(4), 415–437.

Moje, E. B., Stockdill, D., Kim, K., & Kim, H. (2010). The role of text in disciplinary learning. In M. L. Kamil, P. D. Pearson, E. B. Moje, and P. P. Afflerbach (Eds.), *Handbook of reading research* (Vol. IV, pp. 453–486). New York: Routledge.

Moyer, P. S., & Milewicz, E. (2002). Learning to question: Categories of questioning used by preservice teachers during diagnostic mathematics interviews. *Journal of Mathematics Teacher Education, 5*(4), 293–315.

Pearson, P. D., & Gallagher, M. C. (1983). The instruction of reading comprehension. *Contemporary Educational Psychology, 8*, 317–344.

Peverly, S. T., & Wood, R. (2001). The effects of adjunct questions and feedback on improving the reading comprehension skills of learning-disabled adolescents. *Contemporary Educational Psychology, 26*, 25–43.

Phillips, D. C. (1987). *Philosophy, science, and social inquiry.* Oxford, UK: Pergamon Press.

Phillips, D. C. (1995). The good, the bad, and the ugly: The many faces of constructivism. *Educational Researcher, 24*(7), 5–12.

Pressley, M., Johnson, C. J., Symons, S., McGoldrick, J. A., & Kurita, J. A. (1989). Strategies that improve children's memory and comprehension of text. *Elementary School Journal, 90*(1), 3–32.

Ravi, A. K. (2010). Disciplinary literacy in the history classroom. In S. M. McConachie & A. R. Petrosky (Eds.), *Content matters* (pp. 33–61). San Francisco: Jossey-Bass.

Remillard, J. T., & Bryans, M. B. (2004). Teachers' orientations toward mathematics curriculum materials: Implications for teacher learning. *Journal for Research in Mathematics Education, 35*(5), 352–388.

Rosenshine, B., Meister, C., & Chapman, S. (1996). Teaching students to generate questions: A review of the intervention studies. *Review of Educational Research, 66*(2), 181–221.

Schumm, J. S., & Vaughn, S. (1991). Making adaptations for mainstreamed students: General classroom teachers' perspectives. *Remedial and Special Education, 12*(4), 18–27.

Schumm, J. S., Vaughn, S., Haager, D., McDowell, J., Rothlein, L., & Saumell, L. (1995). General education teacher planning: What can students with learning disabilities expect? *Exceptional Children, 61*(4), 335–352.

Shanahan, T., & Shanahan, C. (2008). Teaching disciplinary literacy to adolescents: Rethinking content-area literacy. *Harvard Educational Review, 78*(1), 40–61.

Sherrod, S. E., & Wilhelm, J. (2009). A study of how classroom dialogue facilitates the development of geometric spatial concepts related to understanding the cause of moon phases. *International Journal of Science Education, 31*(7), 873–894.

Spiegel, S. A. , Bintz, J., Taylor, J. A., Landes, N. M., & Jordan, D. L. (2010). Disciplinary literacy in the science classroom. In S. M. McConachie & A. R. Petrosky (Eds.), *Content matters* (pp. 87–127). San Francisco: Jossey-Bass.

Superfine, A. C. (2008). Planning for mathematics instruction: A model of experienced teachers' planning processes in the context of a reform mathematics curriculum. *Mathematics Educator, 18*(2), 11–22.

Taylor, P. (1970). *How teachers plan their courses.* New York: National Foundation for Educational Research.

University of Kansas Medical Center. (2010). *Human Genome Project exercise II.* Retrieved November 15, 2010, from *www.kumc.edu/gec/onlinx2.html*.

Van Meter, P. (2001). Drawing construction as a strategy for learning from text. *Journal of Educational Psychology, 93*(1), 129–140.

Wigfield, A., Guthrie, J. T., Perencevich, K. C., Taboada, A., Klauda, S. L., McRae, A., & et al. (2008). Role of reading engagement in mediating effects of reading comprehension instruction on reading outcomes. *Psychology in the Schools, 45*, 432–445.

Yackal, E., & Cobb, P. (1996). Sociomathematical norms, argumentation, and autonomy in mathematics. *Journal for Research in Mathematics Education, 27*, 458–477.

Yinger, R. J. (1977). *A study of teacher planning: Description and theory development using ethnographic and information processing methods.* Unpublished doctoral dissertation, Michigan State University, East Lansing.

Zahorik, J. A. (1996). Elementary and secondary teachers' reports of how they make learning interesting. *Elementary School Journal, 96*, 551–565.

5

Learning with Text in English Language Arts

Troy Hicks *and* Susan Steffel

Place: A high school English classroom in the United States

Time: Present day

Situation: As she has done for a number of years, Mrs. Smith begins her new unit by passing out books and preparing for a brief discussion of the major novel to be studied this marking period: Steinbeck's *Of Mice and Men* (1937).

No stranger to professional conferences, journals, and books, Mrs. Smith has attempted to craft a unit that is responsive to student needs, yet still meets curricular demands and incorporates instructional strategies for reading and writing. Given that this is the first day of the unit, and that students have been studying American literature sequentially through the year, she will give an introductory lecture on the Great Depression, including a brief video from a reputable website streaming educational video, and will share major events from Steinbeck's life leading up to the writing of the book. During this class period, she will also read the first chapter aloud, inviting students to preview the rest of the text, and will then assign reading questions for homework that will initiate a class discussion tomorrow.

Over the course of the next 3 weeks, students will be expected to read a few chapters each night, periodically participate in online and face-to-face discussions, take quizzes, and learn about some strategies for comprehending the text as well as study some specific vocabulary. As a culminating project, they will write an essay that compares the text to the 1992 film adaptation, which they will watch in class; this essay will focus on character development, in particular, and Mrs. Smith will integrate instruction about transitional words and phrases to help students organize details and make comparisons. Since her students are working in a college-preparatory curriculum and preparing to take both the ACT and, eventually, the AP literature exam, Mrs. Smith feels this course of study is both appropriate and efficient, as it has been adopted by the school's English department as a model for others teaching American literature.

This unit aligns with the broad goals outlined in her state content standards, as well as the new national standards for reading and writing in English language arts in the Common Core State Standards (Common Core Standards Initiative, 2010). Mrs. Smith understands the content and context of American literature, specifically for the book *Of Mice and Men* as well as the Great Depression. Using multiple forms of media, she invites students to compare the original text with a film adaptation and gives them opportunities to participate in discussions about the book. Within the context of this unit, Mrs. Smith is also teaching general instructional strategies for comprehension of a literary text as well as individual vocabulary words. On the surface, this snapshot provides us with a glimpse of what many would consider to be a well-structured, progressive English classroom.

However, we disagree.

Mrs. Smith's unit is strong, no doubt. Yet—as English teacher educators who are responsible for teaching preservice and inservice teachers both how to engage students in functional literacy practices and to apprentice them in becoming scholars of the English language arts—we argue that Mrs. Smith's curriculum and instruction could, and must, do more for her students as readers and writers, listeners and speakers, viewers and producers of visual texts. Building on a history of research that values "literacy," writ large, as both a developmental and functional aspect of human communication and a socially situated and purposeful series of acts in which people engage, we recognize the limitations in Mrs. Smith's approach, an approach that we feel is present in many secondary English classrooms. In many others, sadly, the level of professionalism and engagement that Mrs. Smith offers her students may not exist even to this degree, as students participate in mundane reading exercises and formulaic writing. Either way, the typical course of study in secondary English classrooms—one that focuses almost exclusively on canonical texts and general writing strategies in response to literature—does not acknowledge the complexities of what it means to be literate, nor does it teach our students to fully engage as novice experts who are learning to be scholars in the English language arts. There are many English educators and researchers whose work supports this contention, and we know that recent summaries of research on adolescent literacy *(Reading Next, Writing Next)*, policy statements from our professional organizations (the National Council of Teachers of English [NCTE]), and the NCTE/ IRA standards aim for a broader vision of what it means to teach and learn English.

In this chapter, we describe the dual, and sometimes competing, nature of what it means for our work as English teachers to help our students become "literate" (in the sense that they can comprehend what they read and view as well as create written, oral, and visual texts) and help them understand both content and critical approaches in English studies (in the sense that they can analyze and critique existing texts, as well as imagine new texts in a variety of genres and media). We describe these two approaches to teaching in the English classroom not necessarily as an either/or dichotomy; instead, understanding the dual nature of what it means to teach both literacy (as a multifaceted set of skills) and a body of knowledge (in the sense of studying canonical and contemporary literature, genres, and approaches to writing, and other types of texts such as film, graphics, and of digital media) brings more to our English classrooms than either approach would alone.

No sooner can we say that we will explore this dual nature of teaching English than we need to provide a disclaimer. Teaching "English," and we use the quotes purposefully here, is difficult and contested work. Any discussion of what it means to teach someone to be literate in the sense that they can understand and create texts is both a practical and ideological pursuit. The past 30 years of literacy studies have shown us that we cannot teach students to understand literature, create a written composition, or design a new media text—as well as to use any of the particular literacy skills involved in any of those tasks—without engaging in a socially constructed activity. We all bring our own experiences to these literacy activities and, at any given moment, make numerous decisions about how to gain meaning from texts that we consume, as well as how to infuse meaning into the texts that we create. In short, people act as agents in their own literacy, an idea we elaborate on below.

While it is beyond the scope of this chapter to delve fully into the history of literacy studies and examine exactly how and why scholars have arrived at this point, we later examine three literacy frameworks as a way to discuss our vision of functional literacy skills and ways to better teach students the content of English. For those of us interested in studying the ways that language works have, in the past 30 years, come to understand the ways in which reading and writing, listening and speaking, viewing and producing visual texts are socially situated acts. For the reader who would like to trace the emergence of the "social turn" in literacy studies, the following scholars offer a solid foundation from which to start, although there are certainly many others: Barton and Hamilton (1998), Brandt (2001), Gee (1996), Graff (1991), Heath (1983), the New London Group (2000), and Street (1984). In particular, we also rely on the work of Rosenblatt (1994, 1995) who was first to describe the belief that meaning resides in the transaction between the reader and the text.

To return to the case at hand, this social perspective on literacy informs our thinking on the vignette above, in which Mrs. Smith has worked to provide context for the study of a novel, Steinbeck's *Of Mice and Men*, and appeal to her students' adolescent interests and sensibilities in her initial approach and overall construction of the unit. We appreciate that her teaching builds sequentially over time, culminating in an essay that invites students to compare the original text to a modern film version, a medium presumably interesting to adolescent learners, who are often portrayed or perceived as disengaged. On the one hand, Mrs. Smith's work is compelling in that it differs from what many of us may have experienced as students when we were simply assigned the reading without any development of background knowledge and told to answer basic comprehension types of questions, culminating in a final exam and/ or essay. To her credit, Mrs. Smith scaffolds her unit and includes the explicit teaching of comprehension strategies, and even brings in different forms of media. She is, in a sense, integrating the types of functional reading and writing that we would expect to see in an English classroom with other, more innovate approaches to adolescent literacy instruction in the English language arts such as media integration.

On the other hand, we make the claim in this chapter that Mrs. Smith (despite her best intentions) is not really teaching the literacy skills that her students need for success as readers and writers, nor is she really teaching the literary content well, if she is teaching it at all. We suggest this criticism at risk of both incriminating ourselves as teachers who have not lived up to our own expectations over the years, as well as potentially alienating our colleagues in secondary schools who face up to 150 students a day, in short blocks of time, and with piles of papers to grade. These are colleagues whom we both trust and admire, and our claim is in no way meant to discredit the work that they do with students or their dedication to the profession. Still, what we will argue in this chapter is that English teachers, even strong teachers like Mrs. Smith, need to rethink instruction in light of significant shifts, some very recent, in the ways we conceive of literacy. What research in the teaching of literacy skills in general and in relation to the content of English language arts has shown us, as teachers, is that we need to reimagine both what literacy is as well as how it should be taught.

In other words, connecting to the social turn mentioned above, there are deep, sometimes tacit, understandings about how literacy, both in terms of function and form, is defined, situated, and enacted, especially in classrooms. We are not interested in setting up a good teacher/ bad teacher dichotomy, as we understand the role of "teacher" and the definition of "literacy" to be both historically constructed and highly politicized; instead, we want to frame our discussion of literacy in the English language arts in light of the broader conversation about what it means to be literate. Uncovering, acknowledging, and investigating our understanding of literacy is central to the work of creating students who are both functionally literate as well as skilled, novice scholars in the content of English language arts such literary analysis and the construction of rhetorically effective texts. We turn our attention to this task now.

LITERACY SKILLS AND THE CONTENT OF ENGLISH

As teachers of the English language arts, we would be remiss to begin a discussion of content-area literacy—as well as to offer a series of practical suggestions for helping adolescents to become more proficient at being literate—without first exploring the ways in which literacy has been defined, especially in relation to the English language arts. In a single chapter, we have little space to fully outline the radical changes of the last 30 to 40 years and politicized nature of what it means to be literate, in terms of functional literacy skills and to describe our changing conceptions of what it means to study English as a field that integrates all of the "language arts," including reading, writing, listening, speaking, viewing, and producing visual texts (Myers, 1996).

So, we will be brief and direct. First, literacy, as a broad concept, can be defined as the ways in which we understand how to participate in communicative acts. There are some skills that transfer across different contexts and certain strategies that we can use in all areas of our literate lives including social, academic, and work environments. Yet, having functional literacy skills is only a beginning.

Second, and equally important, there are a variety of content-specific concepts in the study of English, specifically concepts related to reading and analyzing literature as well as composing and evaluating the written word. These range from thoughtful analysis of plot and characters, to comparing canonical and contemporary works, to writing in a variety of genres for different audiences and purposes. Moreover, in today's increasingly media-saturated world, being literate also means interpreting multiple message streams, managing a great deal of information, and producing compositions that include textual, audio, and visual components.

Over the past few decades, teachers and researchers in the field of English education have implemented programs, researched classrooms, and described the many ways in which effective literacy learning can happen. For instance, Langer (2001) describes six features of literacy instruction that are demonstrated in stronger classrooms, including the use of multiple lesson types, connections that are made across curriculum and life, and engaging in specific instruction so that students are being taught strategies for doing the work. Gere, Fairbanks, Howes, Roop, & Schaafsma (1992), Morris and Tchudi (1996), and others also address what effective literacy learning involves, citing many of the same types of approaches as Langer in that we actively model reading and writing for our students and that we invite them to read, write, and speak about significant themes and issues.

To put a finer point on this, we return with a quick example from the vignette above to show the literacy strategies being used as well as the approaches to understanding literature, thus helping students become scholars of English. Mrs. Smith aims to have her students both comprehend *Of Mice and Men* at a literal level (involving a variety of literacy skills such as decoding words, inferring an author's intent, and comprehending texts) and appreciate the book as a work of literature, created by a particular author and situated in a particular historical time frame, an approach that blends the English language arts of reading, writing, and viewing.

In terms of general literacy skills, Mrs. Smith takes an instructional strategies-based approach. One current example of a strategies-based approach come from Daniels and Zemelman, two longtime collaborators with an interest in content-area literacy and best practices who have recently published both *Subjects Matter: Every Teacher's Guide to Content-Area Reading* (2004) and, with Steinke, *Content-Area Writing: Every Teacher's Guide* (2007). Filled with specific ideas, these books are indicative of a larger collection of professional resources in our field that make the following argument: literacy is a set of skills that can be employed across different contexts, and teachers can help students become more literate by employing a variety of strategic approaches to texts such as asking questions, predicting, understanding the structure of textbooks, using literature circles (Daniels, 2004), creating double-entry notes, using the writing workshop, and using writing-to-learn activities to teach unfamiliar ideas. These are, indeed, useful strategies, built on the ideas of teachers and researchers engaged in the study of adolescent literacy, and Mrs. Smith attempts to use them in a way that will support her students' literacy learning.

Second, in relation to the broader subject of English, by taking an integrative approach to the teaching of the English language arts, Mrs. Smith recognizes and attempts to respond to the many standards for teaching and learning, such as these two from the National Council of Teachers of English (1996): "Students apply a wide range of strategies to comprehend, interpret, evaluate, and appreciate texts" and "Students employ a wide range of strategies as they write and use different writing process elements appropriately to communicate with different audiences for a variety of purposes." Mrs. Smith's approach is nuanced and useful. She considers the various ways in which she wants students to interpret and respond to texts, such as adopting different reading-response theories, making personal connections, comparing and contrasting to other versions of the text such as films. In thinking about the ways that students can represent their understanding more fully in written responses, she is, to some degree, asking them to engage with the text as novice scholars of English.

So, in many ways, Mrs. Smith understands the dual-faceted approach that recognizes the needs of students to learn literacy strategies while, at the same time, engaging in the study of literature, film, and writing. Yet, this is where our concerns begin. Even in Mrs. Smith's approach to teaching both literacy skills and the content of English, she has, tacitly or overtly, taken a stance on how and why texts come into existence, how they function, and how we as readers and writers should respond to those texts. Having neither examined her own assumptions nor acknowledged that there are multiple and sometimes competing aims and visions for what it means to be literate, Mrs. Smith has not fully engaged in the study of English, and her curriculum and instructional approach are both problematic. To better understand why and how, we turn now to examine some of the assumptions we make about literacy instruction.

EXAMINING OUR APPROACHES TO LITERACY INSTRUCTION

To understand these assumptions, we turn to Cadiero-Kaplan (2003), who describes four types of literacy ideologies: functional, cultural, progressive, and critical. Building on the work of a number of researchers and theorists, Cadiero-Kaplan summarizes these ideologies and encourages us as English teachers to understand how these frameworks guide our teaching, our curriculum, the books we choose, and the choices we make in our instruction. In brief, she describes and critiques functional, cultural, and progressive literacy in the following manner:

1. "A *functional literacy* ideology is reflected in a curriculum that teaches students the skills deemed necessary to successfully participate in school and society, specifically, skills to be a productive citizen or member of the workforce and, as such, to support marketplace ideologies" (p. 374). We can see echoes of the functional literacy perspective in modern calls from stakeholders in business and industry for students with career and workplace readiness. In the vignette above, Mrs. Smith is (either tacitly or explicitly) providing her students with opportunities to become functionally literate in terms of comprehending vocabulary and the novel more broadly.

2. "A *cultural literacy* ideology focuses on the teaching of morals and values, with a curriculum that includes the classics or 'Great Books' " (p. 375). Cadiero-Kaplan cites a number of educational researchers, most notably E. D. Hirsch (1988), who advocates for this approach as a means for students to develop "core knowledge" about the people, events, and concepts that form the basis of Western literature and thinking. In Mrs. Smith's unit, she clearly recognized the need for some context on the Great Depression and Steinbeck's life, as well as for students to understand the importance of the text itself.

3. "A *progressive literacy* ideology requires students and teachers to engage in the process of learning to read and write based on themes and topics of interest to students, with vocabulary related to their lives" (p. 376). Built on the progressive ideals of Dewey (2011) and others, this perspective recognizes the needs of students in terms of their ages and capabilities and attempts to engage them in learning styles that are timely and useful. In this vignette, Mrs. Smith connects the classic work of literature with a contemporary film, a move she expects will make students more interested in the unit and willing to write at the end.

Fortunately, Cadiero-Kaplan and many other scholars of literacy have questioned these three perspectives. If we accept functional, cultural, or even progressive literacy to be a set of skills that include the ability to decode, comprehend, interpret, and compare, incorporating both reading and writing, then we risk leaving our students at the level of the text. Approached this way, literacy is stagnant. Readers and writers are not encouraged to go beyond, to apply these literacy skills in other situations, or to critique dominant discourses of power. These literacies are foundational, for sure, yet are not nearly enough to teach *Of Mice and Men*, or any other text, if we wish to make the claim that our students can be literate or be informed, thoughtful, and engaged young scholars of English. To achieve this, we must incorporate even more into the curriculum, activities that encourage our students to use higher-level thinking skills in ways that direct their thinking outward and forward—as Morris and Tchudi (1996) say, "the ability to act from the content and context of a text" (p. 12).

Ultimately, scholars who have created the social turn in literacy studies show us that none of these three ideologies provides the kind of thinking that, ultimately, is useful in thoroughly reimagining a literacy ideology. Yet, as Cadiero-Kaplan explains, there is an additional ideology that we must use to embrace literacy as a socially situated practice, enacted by people for a variety of purposes. Building on the work of Freire and Macedo (1987), as well as others, she describes how a "critical literacy" ideology invites students to "read the world and the word, by using dialogue to engage texts and discourses inside and outside the classroom" (p. 377). Because "literacy curricula decisions are often the result of conscious choices tied to the political and economic structures of a country" (p. 378), teachers must examine the hidden ideological positions embedded in those curricula, as well as the instructional choices they make. Critical literacy provides one such lens through which teachers and students can better understand both how, and more importantly why, texts are constructed (and can be constructed) in particular ways. To return to Mrs. Smith's vignette one more time, and to show why critical literacy matters, there is no time at which she invites students to question why and how they are reading this text, or the types of oral presentation and writing they must perform in response to the text. Moreover, despite the inclusion of the 1992 film, there is no opportunity for students to openly critique *Of Mice and Men* by comparing it to other classic and contemporary texts, let alone to question the issue of injustice raised in the book. And, while they may watch other media, they are not invited to produce it.

We do not necessarily think the ways Mrs. Smith is using strategies and literary approaches to study the book are terribly off the mark, and in many ways they feel consistent with what we would expect to see in the high-performing English classrooms described by Langer. However, we think that the visions of literacy outlined in her approach are limited. There is much more to becoming literate or engaging in the content of English studies than simply employing a single instructional strategy to comprehend or create a text, even if that strategy is creative. Moreover, there are many ways to interpret, critique, and respond to a text. In other words, there is much more to teach when we think about reading and writing texts in English classrooms—both in terms of the specific skills of literacy and the ways in which students engage in literature and rhetoric. A perspective on critical literacy helps us see that Mrs. Smith's approach, while generally useful and engaging, could be different and, most likely, better.

We should note here that the term *critical literacy* has a long history. Many scholars of the subject argue that in order to be considered critically literate, teachers and students must actively examine and critique power structures evident in language use. We admire the scholars, teachers, and students who embrace and embody this approach in their writing, through parody and criticism, by integrating popular culture into the classroom, and by engaging in service learning and, at times, direct political action. For purposes of this chapter, we will take critical to mean an informed and multifaceted stance, even though we know adopting that stance, as Borsheim and Petrone suggest, may cause students to be uncomfortable and potentially resist engaging in critical literacy (2006, p. 82). In relation to literacy, then, we believe that teachers must invite their students to actively critique and challenge existing notions of what it means to both produce and consume texts.

Finally, making this change in the classroom also necessitates that we change the way we assess learning. We recognize that many transitional changes have taken place already, both in formative and summative measures of literacy. When using formative assessment, which takes place during the process or lesson, it is much easier to implement the types of approaches that help students become both functionally and critically literate. Teachers can use response logs, incorporate creative activities, and use small, interactive groups within the lesson. With summative assessment, at the end of the process or lesson, we face a greater challenge. Compared with the unlimited ways that teachers can measure their students' learning, such as papers, portfolios, projects, and performances, the recent importance placed on the use of standardized tests severely limits these practices. Within the scope of this chapter, we are focusing more on strategies for engaging adolescents in literacy skills and scholarship in English, and not overtly on assessment. Yet, assessment is a critical part of the instructional process that measures a number of literacy skills, so we must keep it in mind as we move forward in our work.

In order to make the case for moving toward a critical literacy approach in English classrooms, we examine three literacy frameworks, Stephen Kucer's "dimensions of literacy" (2001), Colin Lankshear and Michele Knobel's "new literacies" (2006), and the New London Group's "pedagogy of multiliteracies"(2000). In so doing, we aim to show the multifaceted nature of what it means to be literate and how, in an English classroom, the goals of teaching literacy and the content of English studies can sometimes complement and sometimes be at odds with one another. In turn, this leads us to a revised vignette from Mrs. Smith's classroom that, we argue, could serve as a model for a more robust approach to teaching both literacy skills and ways for our students to become better scholars of the English language arts.

THREE LITERACY FRAMEWORKS

In this section, we outline current perspectives on literacy by leading scholars in our field, which inform our thinking about teaching literacy skills in the broad sense as well as preparing our students to become scholars of English studies. We focus on three here, beginning with a multilayered look at literacy offered by Stephen Kucer. First published in 2001 and now in its third edition, Kucer's *Dimensions of Literacy* begins with the argument that "if literacy education is to be effective, it is important that literacy be conceived as dynamic and multidimensional in nature" (p. 4). Kucer then goes on to describe four dimensions of literacy:

- Cognitive: concerning our perception of texts and how we make meaning with and from them.
- Linguistic: concerning the nature and construction of texts.
- Sociocultural: concerning the literacy events and practices in indivduals' lives.
- Developmental: concerning the ways in which individuals understand the patterns and principles of language.

Cutting across these dimensions are "literacy events," originally conceived by Heath as "any action sequence involving one or more persons, in which the production and/or comprehension of print plays a role" (as cited in Kucer, p. 7). These literacy events provide the basis from which Kucer discusses the four dimensions and reminds us that individuals use language for a variety of purposes across various contexts and situations. Literacy, in this sense, is not just about learning to decode letters and words, yet those components of literacy are crucial in order for other dimensions to have meaning in the overall context of learning to become literate.

Given this complex definition of literacy offered by Kucer, we are faced with at least two overlapping and, at times, competing visions of what it is that we are supposed to accomplish with our students in English classrooms. On one hand, as English teachers, we are both expected and required to teach the foundational skills of literacy: reading, at its most basic form of comprehension; the basics of grammar and usage; and the acts of listening and speaking, as well as viewing and producing visual texts that convey messages. On the other hand, we also have content to teach: literature, including classic and contemporary works; the art of writing, including genre and rhetoric; and, the impact of digital media on both. This duality of purpose is what sets English language arts apart from other disciplines. While it can be argued that other disciplines are also skills based and content based, it is this focus on the broad skills of reading and writing (which undergird all learning and, at the same time, are the focus of more detailed study) and the need to focus on content (Steinbeck as the author, the Great Depression, the characters and plot of the book) that set English apart. We are learning to read and write while we are learning to read and write in the service of academic goals in the study of English; we build the plane while flying.

Kucer's dimensions of literacy allow us to take a stand, to enact a critical literacy that engages us in both reading the text and the context surrounding the text. Because we are constantly in the process of comprehending texts and constructing meaning, often by looking at them through social, cultural, and political lenses, we are better able to understand ourselves as being literate and to view literacy as an act of agency. This stance toward literacy allows us to both teach students active literacy skills as well as to become more proficient as scholars of English.

In addition to Kucer's perspective on literacy we also recognize that we enter the conversation on content-area literacy outlined in this book in an era of ever-shifting literacy practices, as so clearly laid out in Miles Myers's classic article "Shifting Standards of Literacy—The Teacher's Catch-22" (1984). Myers documents the changes, what they were and the reasons for them, and we cannot help but recognize that these changes are occurring at an even more rapid pace now, making our literacy needs even more important, most notably as we consider the effects of digital media and networked computing. These are, indeed, strange days, as we feel constrained by school policies that tell us to take away our students' cell phones even when we know that they have just downloaded a new book for today's sustained silent reading. As English teachers, we question whether a message in 140 characters or less can have any value, even when we see these messages topple the regimes of dictators. We acknowledge and agree with Myers (1984), who described the sociopolitical contexts that influenced the definition of literacy at any given moment in history, and also argued that "proposals for curing the ills of America's schools should recognize that the present literacy crisis is a new challenge for America's school teachers, not a rehash of past failures" (p. 31).

In some ways, then, teaching a digital generation presents the same set of challenges as might be encountered at any other moment in history, and we should heed Myers's advice as we consider what our "present literacy crisis" really is (or what it really is *not*). At the same time, we recognize that, in this historical moment, there really are some fundamental changes in what it means for people to be literate, not just in the sense of layering on additional requirements for what it means to read and write print-based texts. Instead, there are a whole new set of technical skills such as searching for and filtering information, designing digital documents with images and hyperlinks, and creating multimedia with the addition of images, videos, and sounds.

These are more than just technical changes in literacy practices; they present us with an opportunity to rethink what we mean when we define "literacy practices." In the second literacy framework we want to explore, Lankshear and Knobel (2006) describe "new literacies" in ways that share some similarities with traditional literacies, such as the ability to read and write, yet also involve key changes that require "different (new) ways of thinking about the world and responding to it" (p. 30). Lankshear and Knobel describe these as different "mindsets" about the world that require an evolution in thinking, about the technologies we use to communicate as well as about the social practices that surround those technologies. In particular, they elaborate on the two mindsets that guide our approaches to literacy practices, which have significant effects on us as teachers of English.

First, Lankshear and Knobel describe an "industrial" mindset that values, among other elements, linear production of texts and singular expertise held by authoritative producers. Similar to a functional/cultural approach to literacy, this first mindset aligns closely to the ways in which we have produced, distributed, and consumed texts for many centuries and, in contrast to "new literacies," is somewhat outdated due to the fact that mobile phones, push-button publishing, and a remix culture have drastically changed the ways in which texts are produced and consumed. Mindset one, for Lankshear and Knobel, "assumes the contemporary world is essentially the way it has been throughout the modern-industrial period, only now it is more technologized, or alternatively, technologized in a new and very sophisticated way" (pp. 33–34). This mindset suggests that we have a number of new tools to use, yet our basic literacy practices remain the same.

In the second mindset, one that embraces a postindustrial ethos involving collaborative, distributed thinking from a range of participants, Lankshear and Knobel argue that teachers and students have the opportunity to embrace the "new" component of the "new literacies." They make the case that this new mindset—one that values multiple modes and media for production, distribution, and consumption of texts—is only powerful in the sense that we use the tools for broader and different social and communicative purposes. They argue:

> The world is being changed in some fairly fundamental ways as a result of people imagining and exploring how using new technologies can become

part of making the world (more) different from how it presently is (second mindset), rather than using new technologies to do familiar things in more "technologized" ways (first mindset). (p. 34)

The manner in which we enact these new literacy practices matters a great deal in the sense that teachers and students may approach literacy—both the skills they need and the larger ideas of what comprises the study of English—in various ways. As we consider the implications of a "new literacies" perspective, we recognize how this challenges the authority of canonical texts, the model of teacher as expert, and what it means for students to be readers and writers.

Lankshear and Knobel's conception of "new literacies," in the sense that it requires a change in mindset, connects well with the third framework for literacy we wish to explore: the "pedagogy of multiliteracies." "As curriculum is a design for social futures," the New London Group argues, "we need to introduce the notion of pedagogy as Design" (2000, p. 19). By inviting us to think about both the "what" and "how" of literacy pedagogy, they also ask us to rethink how we conceptualize meaning making by focusing on the concept of "design." In this sense, designs offer us ways to talk about the situational and complex nature of literacy. For the New London Group, the process of design is a process of meaning making.

They go on to describe six types of design: linguistic, visual, audio, gestural, spatial, and (as an overarching design) multimodal. Each one consists of different elements that constitute ways in which meaning can be made. For instance, in linguistic meaning, the use of specialized vocabulary, the structure of the information, and the ways in which the information is delivered all contribute to an overall sense of meaning. Similarly, visual design, the use of colors, perspective, fonts, and other visual components, also contributes to meaning. "Texts are designed using the range of historically available choices among different modes of meaning" (p. 29).

This then leads to a description of the pedagogy, the ways in which literacy is taught, through four recursive components: situated practice, overt instruction, critical framing, and transformed practice:

- Situated practice is an immersion in the experience of a particular design of meaning.
- Overt instruction is the systematic understanding of the design process.
- Critical framing is interpreting the social context of the design of meaning.
- Transformed practice is where meaning making is taken into other contexts.

As teachers and scholars who are interested in English language arts, we have to look at the ways in which we invite students to design meaning for themselves. Of course, this involves many of the skills that we've outlined above, but at the same time we cannot ignore the fact that students have to participate in meaning making at higher levels. For instance, it is not simply enough for students to understand what the word *start* means in a sentence that they are reading, and whether or not it is being used as a noun or verb. Instead, students need to understand the multiple layers of meaning that go into the use of the word *start*, why and how a reader might interpret that word in different ways, and how the concept could be represented through writing, talking, or visual representation. In this sense, the skills of being literate and the content of teaching English are constantly overlapping, providing writing students with opportunities to make rich meaning of the language that they encounter and the language that they use.

We have given only brief attention to three literacy frameworks here, each of which fills up an entire book on its own and is indicative of many discussions and debates that surround the question "What is literacy?" With all three of these frameworks, these scholars push up not only against the notion of what it has always meant to be defined as literate, but also up against what it means to teach and learn literate skills and habits of mind in school. Rethinking our ideas of what it means to be literate as well as how we define reading and writing presents challenges for teachers and students, challenges we elaborate on briefly below.

CHALLENGES

As we think about how and why we want to move toward a more integrated and critical approach to teaching English, we must acknowledge some of the challenges within and beyond our classrooms that could hinder such an approach.

As a service, literacy can be shown to have multiple goals for preparing students as citizens and workers. Throughout history, according to Gere, Fairbanks, Howes, Roop, & Schaafsma (1992), there have been a number of purposes for the teaching of English language arts: "to improve morality, to prepare good workers, to create an elite, to produce good citizens, to foster personal growth, and to offset inequity" (p. 24). These goals, of course, can be traced back to the turn of the 20th century, when large-scale schooling efforts were under way in the United States. Despite the very pleasant visions that many architects of the system may have presented on the surface, one could argue that the real function of such a system was to produce citizens who would not question authority and, in turn, become good workers. But as the work environment and the complexity of skills needed for that work increases, the understanding of what it means to be literate expands, pushing the previous curriculum to include higher-level thinking skills such as creativity, problem solving, and various rhetorical skills.

The service function has become even more complicated in the latter part of the 20th century and the first decade of the 21st. Of course, one could still argue that schools serve the function of making people only barely functionally literate, so that some of the ulterior motives pursued by the early harbingers of school reform can still be achieved. Proponents of the recent Common Core Curriculum, for instance, base their argument on functional and cultural literacies as described above. Even then, there are new types of functional literacy that Mrs. Smith's students are expected to have. Using what is often referred to as "21st-century" or "digital" literacies, students are now expected to do a variety of other tasks including problem solving, collaborating, and presenting information through multimedia. The concept of text has expanded from the paper and pencil that most of us are familiar with to include all the new technologies by which texts are also published. Not only must students be able to read and discern content online, they must also be able to navigate and use new technologies such as websites, blogs, Twitter feeds, wikis, e-readers, and more.

While there are assuredly more than the three we can account for here, we see the challenges to our vision for language-arts education in the three core areas of (1) reading/literature, (2) writing/composition, and (3) more broadly in the study of teaching and learning. In doing so, we hope to address both how and why we need to take on these challenges, which could keep us from adopting a more robust and integrated vision of teaching English, both essential literacy skills and the processes students need to become scholars of English.

Challenges for Teaching Reading and Literature

First, in terms of teaching literature, there still exists a tension between our desire to engage students with contemporary texts, as well as engaging them critically with canonical texts. Layered with this, we also face the challenge of censorship, both the outright (and often public) censorship of texts for moral or ideological reasons and the tacit censorship of failing to include authors outside of the mainstream, including women and minorities, or those from other cultures. Outright censorship is the lesser of our concerns, for when that occurs, teachers, and schools, and communities are able to address it directly. Of greater concern is the more insidious and often unnoticed self-censorship where teachers avoid using what they know to be effective and powerful literature for fear of possible challenges. Likewise, librarians can also add to this by not making these books available.

We have to ask ourselves: Do we teach the classic, canonical texts or do we introduce our students to the many wonderful examples of young adult literature that are available? In making that decision, we must also take into consideration the fact that our students are reluctant readers who will further avoid reading if what we select for them to read is something they cannot relate to. Young adult literature would definitely meet the needs and interests of the students, but the controversial issues dealt with in young adult literature raise other concerns.

Beyond the issue of text selection, there are also various considerations involving how to approach the texts, what the purpose of teaching the literature is, what kinds of activities to choose, and so on. What we ask the students to do during and after reading directly affects the extent to which they are able to engage with it. How do we align all of our goals with the current mandated standards and the standardized tests that may or may not measure what we hope to teach? Asked to address all of these variables and more, teachers perceive themselves to have less and less actual autonomy in making decisions about their own classrooms. As a result, they must perpetually fight this sense of being overwhelmed by competing demands and their own tendency to resort to the traditional model of simply covering the text a few chapters, quizzes, and essay responses at a time.

Challenges for Teaching Writing

In thinking about how and why to teach writing, we face a number of challenges, including the constraints of standardized testing and the question of how we approach writing as a subject worthy of study. First, we know that there is a myopic focus in some classrooms on preparing students to pass writing tests without truly preparing them to become better writers. We certainly know and understand the real pressures that teachers and students face in light of these standardized assessments, and how important it is for them to pass not only personally, but for their entire school. Yet, as many cases in the news have shown, along with our own experiences and those of our colleagues, this focus on how to form an essay with the discrete purpose of passing a test is truly limiting. Students do not study rhetorical aspects of persuasive, informational, or narrative texts beyond what they need to know in order to write a basic essay. Moreover, they do not engage in any of the rich multimedia composition that many scholars in our field are now advocating for as a part of instruction (Kajder, 2010; Yancey, 2009).

This connects directly to the second major challenge we face: how we approach writing as a subject. Despite decades of research and numerous articles, books, and workshops that encourage us to take a writing workshop approach, invite students to explore writing in different genres and for different audiences, and assess writing in terms of both process and product, we find that writing is still very often assigned only as a way to synthesize texts or create formulaic arguments. In looking at the types of skills and processes that have a positive effect on students' writing, such as the ones outlined in the *Writing Next* report (Graham & Perin, 2007), we realize that strategies alone do not comprise a writing curriculum. The teaching of recommended strategies does not, in and of itself, assure that we will create better writers. Instead we need to think about how these strategies can be used in an overall approach to teaching writing that invites students to explore different genres and present their work to a variety of audiences, effectively soliciting peer and teacher response in order to move that work forward as writers, as outlined by teacher-researchers and scholars such as Dean (2008), Kittle (2008), and Fleischer and Andrew-Vaughn (2009). In short, we need to teach students how to write, not simply assign them writing.

Challenges for Students and Teachers

One final set of challenges becomes evident when we begin to look at school culture and the effect it has on teacher and student morale and motivation. First, we have a culture that is becoming increasingly digital and interactive, and school spaces that cling to traditional modes of literacy instruction. Second, because of these changes both inside and outside of school, we encounter students who choose to be "aliterate" in the sense that they can read and write, but choose not to. Because they have been limited to learning from the traditional, teacher-led model where they learn how to read and write and learn about literature, they often remain distanced from its effects. Seldom allowed to engage or interact with language and literature as real readers and writers, they are unmoved and uninspired to continue the activity.

Moreover, they perceive their own social literacies (often Web and technology related: e-mail, blogs, wikis, tweets, and texting) to be something far apart from the stuff occupying the English language arts classroom—and who can blame them? Although scholars in the fields of educational psychology and technology are studying and describing ways in which teachers can effectively blend their content knowledge, teaching practice, and technology use in an effective manner (see, for instance, the line of work on "technological pedagogical content knowledge" or "TPACK" initiated by Mishra & Koehler, 2006), this remains a distinct challenge for teachers who grew up knowing and understanding what it means to be literate in a vastly different context than the world their students inhabit.

All of these challenges come together in our day-to-day interactions with students and in the ways we frame our curriculum (the broad set of texts, activities, and experiences we hope to provide) as well as the skills and processes that students are supposed to learn.

With our previous discussion of literacy in mind, we remind ourselves and our readers of the challenges that await us in this task of redefining curriculum and instruction to include functional approaches to literacy that move beyond simple strategies as well as approaches appropriate to fully engaging in the study of English, including reading, writing, listening, speaking, viewing, and producing visual texts. Kucer's "dimensions of literacy," Lankshear and Knobel's "new literacies," and the New London Group's "pedagogy of multiliteracies" help us understand how literacy is framed, as well as how it is changing, in our time. We review our opening scenario and discuss how a canonical text like *Of Mice and Men* is most likely to be taught, even in the most progressive classrooms around the country, such as Mrs. Smith's. We then offer a second scenario, one in which the very distinct literacy skills needed for basic comprehension of the story are intricately interwoven with the broader types of content-area literacy that we would hope to share with our students.

ENVISIONING A NEW ENGLISH CLASSROOM: AN INTEGRATION OF LITERACY SKILLS AND THE SUBJECT(S) OF ENGLISH

At the risk of oversimplifying, we might describe the ways the debate has been framed in the past about how we teach our students both literacy skills and how to become scholars of English it in the following way: you can't write an effective essay until you learn how to use a comma; or, in the case of reading, you can't enjoy a poem until you understand how allusions function. You need to have all the parts before you can build the whole.

In this era of common standards, it is easy to bemoan this latest of educational reforms and to say that we are, quite simply, teaching and learning English well enough. In fact, the type of teaching we describe in the opening of this chapter could, in many ways, be considered an ideal way to approach the standards and prepare students to take on, and not simply take, standardized tests. To the degree that this approach to teaching *could* be considered an ideal way to approach the task, we agree. Yet, as we argued early on, we do not feel that it should be considered an ideal way to approach the task of integrating literacy skills and the scholarship of English in a thoughtful, productive, and contemporary manner. As Jetton and Lee (chapters 1 and 4, this volume) suggest, we need to look at not only the instructional strategy we are choosing to employ, but also at the cognitive approaches we want students to employ as a result of our teaching strategy. We ask teachers to consider teaching this way—connecting their own instructional strategies to explicit cognitive processes that enable literacy growth as well as connecting to the scholarship of English—because there are so many more benefits: students are more engaged, they have more meaningful learning, it's more intellectually stimulating for us, and we know our students will perform better on assessments that are used to measure them.

Strategic instruction in the classroom happens in many ways. In Table 5.1, we describe a number of strategies that we have culled from our own experience in teaching and from many of the researchers and texts that we cite above. This list, while not comprehensive, does offer teachers a variety of techniques for engaging adolescents as readers and writers who are becoming equally facile with print and digital texts, as well as shifting social norms surrounding the ways we produce and consume those texts. In offering this list, we aim to show that literacy skills, in the broadest sense, are tied closely to the ways that students can learn about and from literature, as well as how to compose texts for a variety of purposes and audiences.

In thinking about how and why to employ these instructional strategies in the service of helping our students become more literate and engage in the scholarship of English, we now offer a revised version of Mrs. Smith's unit on *Of Mice and Men*.

RETHINKING A UNIT OF STUDY: *OF MICE AND MEN*

In the opening vignette, we outlined a course of study chosen by Mrs. Smith for her students. Our discussion of how particular instructional approaches can lead to particular cognitive processes and enable different literacies will be further clarified by contrasting the approach to teaching the novel *Of Mice and Men* described above, a progressive yet still traditional approach to literature, with a more expansive vision.

The old approach relies on the lens of New Criticism: lessons operate on the premise that the focus should be on the literature and that meaning resides in the text. Meaning is something that the author intended, that a body of criticism has agreed on, and is, therefore, not generally up

TABLE 5.1. Integrative Strategies for Improving Literacy and Understanding Content in the English Language Arts

Strategy	Processes for reading	Processes for writing	Processes for language	Processes for listening and speaking
		Reading		
Whole-class unit on a specific text	Reading (decoding, questioning, comprehension, reflection) and direct instruction to help guide their reading toward certain aspects of the text	Employ writing-to-learn strategies before, during, and after reading in order to activate prior knowledge, make connections, and summarize the text	Close study of the text that usually focuses on specific vocabulary words and dialectal features of characters' language	Reading aloud by the teacher models fluency and expression, allowing students to visualize scenery, characters, etc.; student discussion of text in the process of reading
Literature circles	Collaborative learning and modeling of reading (decoding, questioning, comprehension, reflection); sharing insights, building meaning, interpreting texts	Taking the original text and either creatively representing it using a different genre or modality, or transforming it in genre, voice, etc. This involves analyzing the original and the ability to understand the impact of the new changes.	Close study to look carefully at a particular aspect of the literature through the assigning of roles, including meaning, vocabulary, literary devices, the finding of connections, comparisons, etc.	Discussion for sharing insights, building meaning, contrasting interpretations. Collaborative learning and discussion skills are also explicitly learned/taught.
Sustained silent reading/ self-selected reading	Allows for practice in reading fluency through uninterrupted engagement with the text; encourages personal engagement with reading for pleasure	Write formal or informal reading response logs that capture connections, questions, and other thoughts related to or inspired by the text	Through sustained interaction with a text, readers are exposed to a variety of language uses and organizational styles employed by authors; understanding of syntax and grammar	Reflect on reading practices through brief book talks and sharing reactions to reading in small or large groups

Examining fiction and nonfiction thematically	Recognizing the ways in which themes are constructed through various text types; draw examples and similarities from various texts to further support knowledge about a topic	Compare and contrast author's techniques depending on genre and purpose; invite students to write about a topic using multiple genres	Examining techniques used to construct fiction (character development, plot, setting) and nonfiction (main idea, ordering, supporting details), recognizing the ways in which the theme is developed in each	Discussion and debate about particular topics evident in the reading, citing examples from fiction and nonfiction texts

Writing

Examining mentor texts/ genres	Selecting texts that lead to exposure to a variety of authors, topics, and genres	Examining rhetorical techniques employed by authors for different genres, audiences, and purposes	Through this examination, engage in close study of transitional words and signaling phrases, compound and complex sentence patterns, grammatical choices that affect voice and overall meaning	Reading mentor texts aloud to practice speaking fluency and to hear how-to techniques of other authors
Inquiry-based research and organization of information	Reading a variety of texts, both print and nonprint, that are related to a research topic; while in the process of research, actively citing and managing sources and examining texts for bias	In the process of researching, students take notes, summarize, evaluate the quality of information, transcribe quotations, and synthesize information; transform information into the form of a research report or multigenre research project	Understand and employ conventions related to specific citation formats and the expected discourse of an academic research paper such as headings, clear transitions, in-text citations, and inclusion of charts and tables	In the process of researching, interview sources; be able to articulate research findings and compare quality of sources; prepare for final presentation of research materials

(*continued*)

TABLE 5.1. (continued)

Strategy	Processes for reading	Processes for writing	Processes for language	Processes for listening and speaking
Writing workshop/peer response groups	By reading like a writer, students examine their own writing and the writing of others for the purpose of improving those texts; students choose mentor texts that allow them to see author's craft in a model.	Engage in the entire recursive writing process on different pieces of writing from prewriting, to drafting, sharing, revising, editing, and publishing	In the context of writing, employ a variety of grammatical and rhetorical techniques to develop meaning and add a unique voice and tone to the text	By talking about their own writing as well as the writing of others, students develop language for describing effective writing and are able to make changes to their compositions; helps them develop their own thoughts and opinions
Listening/Speaking and Viewing/Producing Visual Texts				
Reading and Composing Multimedia	Recognizing similarities and differences between print and nonprint sources; setting a purpose for reading and searching for information online; determining bias and authenticity	Employing multiple forms of text—written, oral, visual, or any combination thereof—to create effective compositions that are intended for particular audiences and purposes, distributed via the Internet	Understanding similarities and differences between traditional forms of writing and multimedia including effective use of transitions, organizing information, choosing appropriate media, and employing fair use of copyrighted materials	Evaluating various sources and presentations for effectiveness and accuracy; as an audience member, offer specific and useful feedback that recognizes the complexity of composing multimedia
Project/Portfolio-Based Assessment	Rather than measuring discrete information about a text, students approach the task holistically and apply what they have learned about the topic or theme to a related task.	Over the course of a unit of study, employ writing-to-learn (note taking, summarizing, questioning) and discipline-specific writing strategies (creating a thesis, supporting with evidence) to develop written pieces and reflect on learning	Recognizing the different ways in which word choice, conventions, and fluency affect the overall purpose and design of written and spoken texts; choosing particular grammatical conventions and rhetorical approaches to convey meaning appropriately	Present findings to various audiences (peers, teachers, outside experts) and incorporate feedback into future work; offer thoughtful feedback on the work of others

for debate. Meaning can be discovered by unlocking the symbols, metaphors, and other literary devices used in the piece. Author biography and purpose, historical significance, and other information can aid in this discovery. However, meaning remains a static entity, uninfluenced by the reader, and this suggests a vision of literacy that adheres to the following ideologies:

- This method becomes a lesson in studying the particular text rather than an overall reading experience (content is absorbed, but there is no opportunity for students to engage with the text).
- The meaning of the text is prescribed, directly or indirectly, through the types of questions that are asked.
- This method skips over the role and contribution of the reader; it doesn't allow for participation of the reader, subverting the critical and creative thinking we want to inspire.

Our approach, as we have argued throughout this chapter, is one that moves toward a critical literacy (as enacted through the different frameworks of literacy described above), which offers both teachers and students new ways to think about what it means to be literate and to engage in the study of English. Here, in light of our discussion about various frameworks for understanding literacy and instructional strategies in English classrooms, we present a different approach to teaching *Of Mice and Men*.

Before Reading

The teacher may begin by reminding students of the purpose of literature and solicit from them some titles of the book that have been most meaningful to them. "Do you have a book that you've read and reread? One that is/was really special to you? What makes these books so special to us?" Eventually, this discussion gets back to the concept of the purpose of literature in that literature is written by people through the ages in an effort to share with readers a glimpse into the human condition at that one place and time. Why do we read literature? To share in the stories that connect us through the ages, across cultures, and around the world. Hopefully, this will all be just a reminder of the mindset about literature that was established at the beginning of the semester.

Before even passing out books, the teacher may introduce certain themes or concepts for discussion. Questions might include: "To what degree are we responsible for one another? Are you responsible for anyone else? Pets or other animals? When do you feel most lonely? What do you do to cope with it? What is the difference between lonely and alone? What makes people feel powerful?" Instead of using posed questions, this discussion might begin by having students fill out a Likert scale questionnaire with similar statements about loneliness, power, sense of weakness or strength, and so forth. Although there are many themes in this novel, teachers should select only a handful to focus on—ones that allow students at a particular grade level or age can connect with specifically. Some themes to consider include: having a sustaining myth that gives us direction and hope while dealing with the daily grind; discrimination; feeling connected to people and the importance of family and/or friendship, including sharing responsibility for the care of others; striking out at others when we feel ignored, powerless, and so on. The themes in *Of Mice and Men* are exceptionally dark, adult, and misogynistic, so focusing on the more universal themes that high school students can already connect with is recommended.

Introduce the book without too much background about the author or the period. Too much information influences the reading and limits the readers' experience with the text and the ability to make sense of the reading for themselves. Rather, give a minimal overview of the characters and plot, pointing out how they connect with the basic issue(s) you used in the prereading exercise. For example, tell students, "George and Lennie are traveling to a new job as ranch hands. It's a new location and they don't know anyone. Both have been left alone, but George has promised to take care of Lennie, hence their connection to each other. This is both exciting and scary as they leave behind what they've known and head to the unknown." Direct them to think about both the comprehension skills and as the larger thematic and literary elements. Start with some sort of discussion introducing the themes in the book and making explicit the objectives that you have for teaching it to your students, then engage students in a similar manner, inviting them to share their thinking about a particular question via poll, quick writing, or through a pair-and-share.

Next, begin to read the first few chapters aloud to the entire class and then stop to discuss some of the particulars. "What do we know about the two men? Why are they traveling to this new ranch? Why are they together? What's the significance of Lennie and the dead animals? How would you characterize each of the two characters? What are their concerns?" Further teacher considerations include: getting into the voice and tone of the book; discussing relationships, setting, and attitudes toward life and other people, including their hopes and dreams; making sure that students are not having any problems with basic comprehension and noting that they are following along.

Teachers should clarify students' basic comprehension of plot as they continue to read aloud. They should not pay a lot of attention at this time to literary features but should encourage students to read on their own and try to relate to the story as readers. At this point, depending on the students' past experience with reader-response theory, the teacher will need to model appropriate connections that readers might make with the story so far. For example, she might share how she related to leaving her hometown for the first time to begin her first teaching job, leaving all friends, family, and so on, behind. Another connection might be made with the relationship between Lennie and George and either how the students might be responsible for someone else or might know someone else who is. Here the teacher might lead the students to discuss what might necessitate taking responsibility and might also discuss the fact that it's rather obvious George has mixed feelings about his promise to Aunt Clara to take care of Lennie—it complicates his life, and Lennie's actions embarrass and frustrate him.

During Reading

Students are directed to keep a response log where they pause periodically in their reading to record their thoughts and feelings about the text and pose any questions they might have about it. The teacher might direct them by providing generic writing prompts that initially help students generate their responses. Once students come to understand how response logs work, the teacher will be able to stop prompting. Explaining that these response logs will form the basis for future class discussions and writing assignments, the teacher must emphasize that most important will be the students' honest thoughts and connections made through reading. These reading logs are not meant to record discussions of symbolism, analysis, or other elements; rather, they are meant to be a place for the reader to connect with the book.

Students may be directed to read on their own within the framework of literature circles. The entire class may have been given a reading schedule, or they may have been told to have the book finished by a certain date. If the latter is the case, then the literature circles will decide for themselves how the group wishes to read—chunking the text or reading until finished. There are arguments for either method, but it is imperative that students have plenty of uninterrupted class time to read, and to discuss what they have read to share with each other what they responded to, noticed, or questioned. Again, this presumes that students have already been trained in the use of literature circles and self-directed discussion. An option would be for the teacher to provide focus questions or activities at these stopping points for all students to consider. This ensures that certain topics are covered but does not make the teacher the director of the reading once again.

At the end of the reading or periodically throughout the reading, students will pause to discuss the text with each other. It is in these discussions that literary devices can be pointed out—within the context of the reading—and students can then be asked to offer thoughts on how a particular device adds to the reading, what other occurrences of that device they can find or have noticed, and other questions that focus on the author's craft. Mentioning these techniques is important to them as readers, to gain meaning, and as writers, so that they understand how they could use similar techniques in their own writing. Perhaps one of the first to bring up in *Of Mice and Men* would be Steinbeck's use of setting description. The teacher could share with students a couple of particular sections with strong descriptions and ask them to visualize. "How do those settings support the idea of loneliness or hope? Can you think of any other settings that were used similarly?" Another mini-lesson might be on symbols with a discussion of when and how the animals are mentioned, the fact that Lennie continues to unintentionally kill them, and how animals are being used and what they might symbolize. Finally, the students could predict how the use of animals might add to the story through foreshadowing.

This book could also be paired with or preceded by a young adult novel that includes similar themes. One often used is Pam Munoz-Ryan's *Esperanza Rising* (2000). Other authors and titles to consider that would reinforce the theme of relationships and responsibility to one another include Nikki Grimes's *Bronx Masquerade* (2003); Kaye Gibbons's *Ellen Foster* (1990); Rodman Philbrick's *Freak, the Mighty* (1993); Julie Ann Peters's *Luna* (2004); Terry Trueman's *Stuck in Neutral* (2000); and Laurie Halse Anderson's *Catalyst* (2003). In each of these novels, a character is somehow dependent on someone or responsible for another. For any comparison, students would be expected recognize similarities across the texts among characters, themes, voice, the use of symbolism, plot, setting, and other literary elements.

Formative assessment with this approach to literature would be ongoing throughout the reading. Each day the teacher is able to assess students' understanding through their response logs, participation in literature circles, periodic class discussions, and other in-class assignments and activities. Throughout the lesson, students are asked to reflect, analyze, connect, and extend beyond the reading. When used consistently, formative assessments reinforce learning and prepare students for an eventual final assessment.

After Reading

If the goal of teaching literature is to get students to connect with the characters or themes, then for a summative assessment they should be asked to complete a task or activity that would demonstrate how their connections developed throughout in the novel. This project/activity might just be the culmination and compilation of the individual activities completed throughout the lesson. Selecting an assessment method is a very complex activity and one that, unfortunately, is often given the least amount of thought. Most important in the selection of assessment activities is to make sure that the method selected represents and measures what the goals of the study of literature actually are. For instance, does a multiple-choice comprehension-level test really measure whether or not students have substantively engaged in discussions about responsibility for others or fairness, or would that goal be better served through a different kind of assessment?

The assessment method(s) should allow for some student choice, and for multiple learning styles. The assessment should measure comprehension and understanding of the text, critical analysis, and use of literary devices in the text. Moreover, the assessments should also ask students to go beyond the text and make those extensions that Morris and Tchudi (1996) refer to as "dynamic readings." In addition, the assessments should allow students to incorporate multiple genres, purposes, and audiences, as well as multiple representations of literacy including writing, speaking, and performance. We want to think about moving students toward the creation of digital texts, too. For instance, might they use creative writing to extend their understanding and rewrite George and Lenny's story as a series of blog posts or Facebook updates from one or both of the characters or from the perspective of a secondary character.

In comparing the two approaches to teaching *Of Mice and Men*—Mrs. Smith's unit outlined at the beginning of this chapter and the one described above—there are similarities, but there are more differences. While the first approach incorporates a number of activities that draw in the student reader and allow for engagement, most of the lesson is teacher driven and focused on the text itself —understanding, comprehending, and analyzing. Although the student might find the reading pleasurable and may even connect with it, that goal is not primary to the objectives of the lesson. Once the content of the novel has been "covered," the lesson is over. Students are then assessed on their ability to articulate their comprehension of the text and, to some degree, their analysis of it as well.

On the other hand, the second approach—one that acknowledges multiple functions of literacy and the need to apprentice students in the scholarship of English—begins with the student's own needs and interests in reading and writing and ends with the student becoming a better reader and writer. While the literature plays a prominent role, based on the careful planning of the teacher, the students are allowed to discover ideas on their own and through connections with one another as readers and writers. Furthermore, the learning does not end with the last page of the novel. Students are asked to do more than master the literature; they are encouraged and directed to project ideas forward and move beyond the interpretation of the story into a larger discussion about social and ethical issues. Since we know that adolescents seek engagement and purpose, when students understand and buy into this approach, it can be motivating. The more they are engaged, the more they learn. And, in a stroke of good fortune, the more practice they have in reading, writing, and employing higher-level thinking skills, the better they perform on standardized tests.

CONCLUSION AND RECOMMENDATIONS

In conclusion, teaching adolescent literacy in the English language arts is a complicated and messy undertaking. The variables are innumerable and demands are layered and varied. There is a divergence of thought and purpose that has always existed within the field. This tension can have the effect of overwhelming even the most seasoned and experienced teacher. While attempting to describe the process of creating a literacy lesson for the novel *Of Mice and Men*, we were struck by the enormous complexity of the task. In fact, the process of creating the lesson paralleled the processes we were trying to create for our students, beginning with understanding and comprehension and going beyond them.

We close by offering some recommendations about where we might go next as English teachers, with the goal of teaching our students to be literate and apprenticing them as scholars of English. These recommendations come from our combined experience of over 50 years in the profession as teachers, researchers, and teacher educators, as well as countless conversations with colleagues in these same roles, and in light of our continually changing literacy landscape. If we have learned anything about teaching and learning, it is that we should adhere to principles, not fads, as our many mentors have shown us. These recommendations offer principles for what it means to teach students both the basics of literacy and how to be better scholars of English.

Recommendations for Reading and Literature

- Most important, we must establish for ourselves a working theory or philosophy of teaching literature that informs the choices we make in the classroom. Here we refer to our earlier discussion of the various ideologies of literacy: functional, cultural, progressive. We need to define for ourselves our overarching vision for literacy and literacy learning.

   o In courses that are "set" with a particular curriculum and/or texts, we can more intentionally incorporate content literacy strategies that acknowledge the needs of adolescent learners.

   o Include more young adult literature, choosing to read it as the primary text and also pairing it with classic literature. In order to pull in the reluctant reader and encourage both novices and accomplished readers, we need to situate our lessons in reading material that speaks to their interests and stages of development. Seeing themselves in the literature and reading about those with whom they can relate encourages students to recognize the primary value of reading literature, which, in turn, may foster the desire for further reading.

   o Recognize that young adult literature is a major genre in its own right; there are many titles whose quality rivals that of traditionally used canonical texts.

- Combine the explicit teaching of reading strategies with the teaching of the literature, helping students become more efficient readers within the context of real reading.

   o As we have said earlier, reading is not learned in a parts-to-whole manner. Rather, we must teach the parts within the context of the whole, pausing while reading to point out features such as type size or illustrations, and literary devices, or to discuss strategies to use when confused by the text.

Recommendations for Writing and Composition

- Given the focus in the Common Core standards on argumentative and informational writing, we do need to teach students explicitly in those genres. While crafting a thesis, gathering evidence, and supporting a thesis has always been important, it is even more so now since the main focus of our standardized assessments will be on these genres.

A somewhat new rhetorical skill, at least in the realm of K–12 writing instruction, is providing and refuting a counterargument. Even with this focus, we do not sacrifice good teaching and critical thought. By taking a genre-based approach and engaging in a writing workshop where students have some choice of topic, audience, and purpose, we can invite them to compose significant work.

• Equally important, we as English teachers must recognize the changing nature of literacy—as exemplified by the work of Kucer, Lankshear and Knobel, and the New London Group—and invite our students to compose in different genres, for different audiences, with different media. An argumentative essay can easily be produced as a podcast, or transformed into a 30-second video in the form of a public service announcement. While we recognize that there is still a digital divide, and not all students have equal access to particular technologies, including high-speed Internet, we also acknowledge the fact that if we as a field do not invite students to do this kind of work in school, they may not engage in thoughtful, literate discussions about the work outside of school. It is our ethical imperative as English teachers to understand and teach with technology in smart ways.

Recommendations for Teaching and Learning

• At least once in a student's high school career, he or she should be in an English course that has no "set" curriculum (in the sense of "Brit Lit" or "Composition"), but instead is a seminar or some other kind of course that allows students the freedom to choose topics of interest to them. The idea here is that teachers employ a workshop approach in which students would develop their own inquiry, collaborate with others who have similar interests, then read, write, and research their topic and develop a project based on their own interests.

• We need to actively and thoughtfully engage students in uses of technology that support the reading and writing that we want them to do anyway. We have intentionally avoided major discussions of technology integration in this chapter despite our interest in and application of digital writing tools in our teacher education courses, choosing instead to think more about the literacy skills and what it means to be a scholar of English. Yet, as the nature of what it means to be literate continues to evolve, technologies such as mobile phones, tablet computers, and social networks will play a significant part.

As we consider the many ways in which we can take what we are doing in our classrooms, we truly do have the possibility of creating students who are literate in more ways than just understanding how to answer comprehension questions or mimic a formulaic essay. Instead, they can engage in substantive conversations, offer a critical perspective, and produce meaningful communication. Mrs. Smith is not far off in the ways that she is teaching. Yet, with a few subtle changes in her teaching practice—changes that acknowledge the complex nature of becoming literate and engaging in the scholarship of English—she could lead her students to a better understanding of how to learn with and from texts, skills that will serve them well beyond the classroom.

REFERENCES

Anderson, L.H. (2003). *Catalyst*. New York: Viking.

Barton, D., & Hamilton, M. (1998). *Local literacies: Reading and writing in one community*. New York: Routledge.

Borsheim, C., & Petrone, R. (2006). Teaching the research paper for local action. *English Journal*, 95(4), 78–83.

Brandt, D. (2001). *Literacy in American lives*. New York: Cambridge University Press.

Cadiero-Kaplan, K. (2003). Literacy ideologies: Critically engaging the language arts curriculum. *Language Arts*, 79(5), 372–381.

Common Core State Standards Initiative. (2010). "The Standards: English Language Arts Standards." Retrieved April 5, 2011, from *www.corestandards. org/the-standards/english-language-arts-standards*.

Daniels, H., & Zemelman, S. (2004). *Subjects matter: Every teacher's guide to content-area reading*. Portsmouth, NH: Heinemann.

Daniels, H., Zemelman, S., & Steineke S. (2007). *Content-area writing: Every teacher's guide*. Portsmouth, NH: Heinemann.

Dean, D. (2008). *Genre theory: Teaching, writing, and being*. Urbana, IL: National Council of Teachers of English.

Dewey, J. (2011). *Democracy and education: An introduction to the philosophy of education*. Hollywood, FL: Simon & Brown.

Fleischer, C., & Andrew-Vaughan, S. (2009). *Writing outside your comfort zone: Helping students navigate unfamiliar genres*. Portsmouth, NH: Heinemann.

Freire, P., & Macedo, D. (1987). *Literacy: Reading the word and the world*. Hadley, MA: Bergin & Garvey.

Gee, J. P. (1996). *Social linguistics and literacies: Ideology in discourses* (2nd ed.). London: Taylor & Francis.

Gere, A., Fairbanks, C., Howes, A., Roop, L., & Schaafsma, D. (1992). *Language and reflection: An integrated approach to teaching English*. New York: Macmillan.

Gibbons, K. (1990). *Ellen Foster*. New York: Vintage.

Graff, H. J. (1991). *The literacy myth: Cultural integration and social structure in the nineteenth century*. Piscataway, NJ: Transaction.

Graham, S., & Perin, D. (2007). *Writing next: Effective strategies to improve writing of adolescents in middle and high schools.* Alliance for Excellent Education. Retrieved from *www.all4ed.org/files/Writing Next.pdf.*

Grimes, N. (2003). *Bronx masquerade.* New York: Speak.

Heath, S. B. (1983). *Ways with words: Language, life, and work in communities and classrooms.* New York: Cambridge University Press.

Hirsch, E. D. (1988). *Cultural Literacy: What every American needs to know* New York: Vintage.

Kajder, S. (2010). *Adolescents and digital literacies: Learning alongside our students.* Urbana, IL: National Council of Teachers of English.

Kittle, P. (2008). *Write beside them: Risk, voice, and clarity in high school writing.* Portsmouth, NH: Heinemann.

Kucer, S. B. (2001). *Dimensions of literacy: A conceptual base for teaching reading and writing in school settings.* Psychology Press.

Langer, J. A. (2001). Beating the odds: Teaching middle and high school students to read and write well. *American Educational Research Journal, 38*(4), 837–880.

Lankshear, C., & Knobel, M. (2006). *New literacies: Everyday practices and classroom learning* (2nd ed.). New York: Open University Press/McGraw-Hill.

Mishra, P., & Koehler, M. J. (2006). Technological pedagogical content knowledge: A new framework for teacher knowledge. *Teachers College Record, 108*(6), 1017–1054.

Morris, P., & Tchudi, S. (1996). *The new literacy: Moving beyond the 3 Rs.* San Francisco: Jossey-Bass.

Munoz-Ryan, P. (2000). *Esperanza rising.* New York: Scholastic.

Myers, M. (1984). Shifting standards of literacy: The teacher's *Catch-22.* English Journal, *73*(4), 26–32.

Myers, M. (1996). *Changing our minds: Negotiating English and literacy.* Urbana, IL: National Council of Teachers of English.

National Council of Teachers of English. (1996). NCTE/IRA Standards for the English Language Arts. Retrieved April 4, 2011, from *www.ncte.org/standards*

New London Group. (2000). A pedagogy of multiliteracies: Designing social futures. In B. Cope & M. Kalantzis (Eds.), *Multiliteracies: Literacy learning and the design of social futures* (pp. 9–37). London: Routledge.

Peters, J.A. (2004). *Luna.* New York: Little, Brown.

Philbrick, R. (1993). *Freak, the Mighty.* New York: Scholastic.

Rosenblatt, L. M. (1994). *The reader, the text, the poem: The transactional theory of the literary work.* Carbondale, IL: Southern Illinois University Press.

Rosenblatt, L. M. (1995). *Literature as exploration* (5th ed.). New York, NY: Modern Language Association of America.

Steinbeck, J. (1937). *Of mice and men.* New York: Random House.

Street, B. V. (1984). *Literacy in theory and practice.* Cambridge: Cambridge University Press.

Trueman, T. (2000). *Stuck in neutral.* New York: HarperCollins.

Yancey, K. B. (2009). 2008 NCTE presidential address: The impulse to compose and the age of composition. *Research in the Teaching of English, 43*(3), 316–338.

6

Learning with Text in Science

Cynthia Shanahan

As students move through their school day, they go to English, science, social studies, and other classes such as art, music, or shop. If they approach these classes in the same way, with the same strategies for reading text, they are not likely to do very well. Paying attention to character, plot, theme, conflict, and figurative language won't really help students to understand a scientific process through a diagram and written explanation, nor will it help them to structure a scientific argument. In fact, students may not do very well if the only change they make is from one field of science to another.

Reading in science is not straightforward, because different sciences approach their fields in unique ways. For example, a chemist relying on lab experiments and chemical structures engages in very different tasks to create new knowledge than a biologist, who may rely on observation of natural phenomenon. On some level, yes, all scientists are engaged in the same enterprise; that is, they are trying to understand and manipulate the world, and they all use various forms of observation, experimentation, categorization, and so on. Yet, they often use different tools, engage in unique kinds of discourse, and emphasize one particular kind of data gathering over others. Differences don't exist only at the level of the field, but also at the level of phenomenon that is being studied. For example, studying the genetic makeup of the brown bear is different from studying the bear's behavior in the wild, even though those who do those studies are both engaged in science. Therefore, though we are treating science as one subject in this chapter, it is important that we pause here to recognize that what is being talked about here may apply to one kind of science more than another.

This chapter discusses the role of text in science classrooms, the research on expert use of text, what experts say about students' science reading, and the implications for that use on science teaching and learning. It ends with examples of general and discipline-specific strategies to teach students as they read science text so that they can respond to reading in discipline-appropriate ways.

THE ROLE OF TEXT IN SCIENCE CLASSROOMS

Students by and large have a very hard time understanding and learning from their science textbooks and other written texts, despite the seeming prevalence of these books in science classrooms (Yore, 1991). The vocabulary in science textbooks is dense; the amount of technical vocabulary is greater in science textbooks than in textbooks in any other field (Fang, 2004). Students struggle with the structure and don't know what information to pay attention to or *how* to pay attention to it. They have difficulty with the combination of graphic information and text, and so on.

To compensate for these problems, good science teachers often end up doing something quite harmful—they give up the text and instead explain the information in the text to the students orally. A common practice in science teaching is to give a science lecture accompanied by notes on the overhead. While the teacher is talking and writing notes, students are asked to copy the notes. In addition to the lecture and notes, students may engage in hands-on activities, as they need to engage in observation, hypothesis forming, measurement, and all of those activities defined as scientific method to really understand science. While students are engaged in hands-on activities, they usually also engage in some sort of reporting. That is, students are required to produce a lab report on their process, findings, and conclusions. Also, the teacher may do demonstrations of scientific phenomena for students or show a video of these phenomena. Finally, they may have students engage in discussion about scientific phenomena in order that they might learn from each other.

Are these activities harmful? They are not. In fact, they can be quite powerful learning tools, and some do even involve text comprehension and writing. However, taking away the textbook and other written materials can be problematic. When students are not taught to read these written materials, they don't get any better at reading science. They will be ill prepared to read scientific material in college science classes, on the job, or as a citizen of a scientific world. Not only that, they are not likely to learn the science as well as they could if they were proficient in learning from reading.

Why is that? There are several reasons. First, there is a memory component to watching a demonstration or a film or listening to an explanation. Students can't automatically go back and reread an explanation or rewatch a demonstration, and memory errors can creep in. This is especially true in a field in which misconceptions are common, such as in physics. Gravity, for example, is a topic about which students often have nonscientific conceptions—they believe that the weight of an object determines how fast it falls, although scientists explain that all objects fall at the same rate if not affected by air resistance, no matter what the weight. So, when students watch a demonstration, they might remember it differently from when they saw it. A misconception can take over, as memory experiments have continued to show over the years (e.g., Loftus, 1979). They will remember, instead, that the demonstration reified their original conceptions, and that will allow them to maintain their misconceptions.

Researchers have shown that text is more likely than other kinds of materials to teach students in a way that overcomes misconceptions, especially if that text is refutational; that is, it acknowledges the misconception and then refutes it, explaining why the scientific explanation is correct and the misconception is not. Other forms of learning such as discussion and demonstration do seem to be powerful but won't as often lead to learning accepted scientific explanations for phenomena. Hynd, McWhorter, Phares, and Suttles (1994) taught students a principle of projectile motion through various combinations of instructional techniques: video demonstration, discussion and hands-on activity, and reading. Students who engaged in the discussion and hands-on activity before reading generally did not learn the scientific information, but students who saw a demonstration and then read, or students who only read, were able to learn the scientific information at a higher rate. When the research team analyzed the tape-recorded conversations of the discussion, they found that students who held misconceptions often talked other students into the misconception rather than the other way around, even when they engaged in the hands-on activity.

Second, hands-on activities can lead to incorrect conclusions because classroom measurement instruments aren't as precise as those in a scientific lab, and students are not skilled in using them correctly. In one physics classroom, students were studying gravity. Their teacher had asked them to bring in a handmade carton for a raw egg that if dropped out of a three-story window at the same time as another carton would reach the ground last. One student (with a misconception) came in with a carton that he had put nails into so that it would be the heaviest and fall the fastest. Others put feathers in their carton so that the eggs would float. Two eggs were dropped at the same time using a stopwatch, and students were on the ground to stop the watch when the eggs fell. Groups of four students then compared their data and came to some conclusions about gravity. What did they find? Only a few concluded that the eggs fell essentially at the same rate unless they were in a carton that reduced air resistance. Others concluded that heavier objects fell faster—a misconception. They had not taken into account the error of measurement, so the data were not that meaningful. The student who put nails into his carton told his teammates that he didn't understand the data because his carton should have fallen fastest, so his data must be wrong.

In another class of advanced physics students, students were supposed to position a cup on the floor in the exact spot where a ball that rolled down a ramp on a table would fall. They were to calculate the cup's position using formulas about projectile motion. What did they do instead? Several of the groups found that their calculations didn't work. The ball didn't drop into the cup. So, they first got the ball to fall into the cup through trial and error, then plugged those numbers into a formula, ending up with nonsense data. Again, the students failed to take into account measurement error, and, indeed, their equipment wasn't sophisticated enough to do away with enough error to work (Hynd, McNish, Qian, Keith, and Lay, 1994).

Advanced students in another class finally cornered the teacher and asked him to help them make sense of their hands-on activities and make connections between the textbook and these experiments. Even though they were advanced students, the textbook was hard. As one student said, "It's like a house without a foundation. It's explaining something that I have no basis for understanding." The teacher had assumed that they understood the textbook and so assigned, but did not discuss, the information with them or help them to make sense of their reading. He was more concerned that they engage in experimentation. What he didn't understand is that they needed the text to help them make sense of what they were doing (Hynd et al., 1994).

What is the lesson to be learned? Certain kinds of activities—lecture, discussion, and hands-on activities—aren't necessarily learning experiences for students, especially if students can't read explanations and examples in textbooks and other scientific materials.

Another point to be made is that in the rush to ensure that students experience what it means to engage in scientific activity, teachers often discount the fact that science is, indeed, a largely literate activity. Scientists spend most of their time reading and writing: they write lab reports, proposals for research, reports of experimental findings, explanations of scientific phenomena for the popular press, and so forth, and they discuss theory and research with other experts through writing— increasingly on discussion boards and via e-mail. They read these same things, as well as reading about new procedures, methods, and equipment in trade magazines. But the types of reading and writing they do are unique to their discipline. To translate them into classroom activity, teachers need not only to teach students textbook reading, but also help them read and write in the scientific genres listed above.

EXPERT READING AND WRITING

As noted above, scientists spend their time reading and writing. In the research project my colleague and I did for the Carnegie Corporation (Shanahan & Shanahan, 2008), I asked chemists to read material they normally read and then, at predetermined stopping points, discuss their reading and writing processes. I followed up on what they said with questions, taped the entire discussion, and met with the science team to discuss our interpretations of the data. The science team consisted of two chemists, two chemistry educators, two chemistry teachers, and two literacy experts. In the team, we also read different texts together, discussed the nature of chemistry reading, and talked about strategies for learning from reading. My colleagues and I did the same things with a history team and a mathematics team and found that these three groups had very different things to say about reading in their disciplines.

What did the chemists have to say about reading? To them, there was a difference between reading something they didn't yet understand and reading material they knew something about. If they didn't understand something, they did not engage in critique. Rather, they read carefully, moving from graphic material to text and back again, so that they could understand the text in various dimensions. One chemist discussed his method of taking copious notes that he would then read over. But when they already understood the chemistry, they read critically, thinking about who the scientists were, where they did their research, when a study was completed, what kinds of materials and procedures they used, and so forth. And they noticed the details, such as units of measurement and the accuracy of equations. They engaged in this kind of critique not only with research articles but also with articles in newspapers and popular science magazines. We did not see this pattern in the historians, who always read for critique, and it was not an explicit strategy in mathematics reading; mathematicians didn't care about the author or source of information, nor the time in which a text was written, although they did pay attention to accuracy.

It turns out that a study of physicist reading (Bazerman, 1997) had the same findings: When physicists did not know the information, they read to learn. When they did know, they read for critique.

The chemists emphasized the time-sensitive nature of their reading—because of breakthroughs in methods and materials and new findings, the field of chemistry (and other sciences as well) was always in flux. A study done 20 years ago may not be accurate. This was in contrast to what historians and mathematicians said. Although time is also important to historians, they were using the time period to place a particular reading in its sociopolitical and economic context. The mathematicians did not care when something was written: something written 20 years ago could be read and reread, and it might take that many years to understand it.

Also important to the chemists was the reciprocal nature of the various representations of chemistry—textual, graphic, and formulaic. Each of these forms of representation added a dimension to the understanding of chemistry, and being able to represent concepts in each of these was a mark of full understanding.

CHALLENGES IN READING SCIENCE TEXTS

One of the things the chemistry group did was to discuss the challenges students were likely to face reading science text. They grouped these challenges using the Chicago Reading Framework, which divides literacy into four elements: word knowledge (vocabulary), fluency, comprehension, and writing. Here is what they said about the challenges in each of these dimensions.

Vocabulary

Chemists thought that vocabulary was a challenge because it included scientific terminology that had to be learned not only on the surface level but also in depth. Learning these terms was complicated, because, as in math, they often had several different meanings, including general ones that were commonly understood. These general meanings often interfered with the learning of scientific meanings. For example, to evaporate has a more general meaning of "to disappear," but one of several chemical meanings is "to change or cause to change from a liquid or solid state to a vapor." Also, technical terms were often made up of various prefixes, suffixes, and roots that carried independent meaning. Too, technical terms are so big a part of science text that the sheer number of words could be daunting, and one sometimes needs to know some words in order to understand others. Technical terms describe systems and processes, so to not know one of the terms means not understanding the relevant system or the process.

Comprehension

Chemists believed that a big part of comprehension, beyond vocabulary knowledge, was being able to think about the concepts in the various forms of representation mentioned above—graphic (or pictorial), textual, and formulaic. Most graphic and formulaic information in science textbooks restates the textual information. It represents the same concepts but in a different way. One of the challenging things for students to do is explain a graph in text form or to take the text information and convert it to a formula or diagram.

Also important for comprehension was to separate the chemistry to be learned from the motivational information. Chemists noted that most textbooks had superfluous information meant to draw students into the material, such as insets about instances of chemical disasters. Whereas educators believe these kinds of insets are vitally important, the chemists were concerned that students would be distracted from what they needed to learn. One chemistry teacher, as well, denigrated a textbook that tried to put all of the chemistry in a real-world format that involved problem solving, saying that chemistry had to be learned in a particular way if it was to be understood, and that most problem-solving situations could only be understood if the chemistry had been learned previously.

Fluency

A big part of fluency in reading is knowing how and when to move from text to graphic to formula to text. The chemists noted that students wanted to read all of the text first and perhaps even skip the graphic information, when both had to be read simultaneously for optimal understanding. Also, they mentioned that reading formulas was a problem for students. The symbols have to be understood as entities—not just symbols—and the order of the reading is sometimes different in a formula or an equation than it is in text reading. For example, in an equation with parentheses, the information in parenthesis is said before the number or figure outside the parenthesis.

Writing

Chemists emphasized that it is challenging for students to write text explaining chemical principles and to include the various representations of understanding in the explanations, such as graphs, charts, and equations. They also emphasized that precision in writing is important—that students needed to be exact in their descriptions of technical terms, units of measurement, and so forth. Getting in the ballpark is not tolerated in chemistry writing. They believed that students should be able to write not only explanations but also lab reports that included the parts of the scientific method: rationale and hypotheses, methods and materials, findings, and conclusions.

One thing that all chemists wanted to emphasize is the importance of disciplinary knowledge to reading comprehension and writing. That is, understanding the scope of science, its core beliefs, its methods, and its discourse practices facilitates learning. In that vein, Project READi—a reading comprehension project funded by the Institute of Education Sciences and aimed at understanding and teaching argumentation in the disciplines of science, English, and social studies/history—is attempting to identify disciplinary knowledge in science. In that project teams of researchers have begun fleshing out what the core constructs in science are. To date, they claim that these science core constructs include epistemologies; inquiry practices; overarching frameworks, concepts, themes; ways of representing concepts; and discourse practices (Project READi & Goldman, 2010). Regarding epistemologies, this team noted the idea that whereas the goal of science is to "build understandings of the physical and designed world through constructed models," these models must be understood as "approximations that have limitations." In other words, like the chemists in the previous study, this team knew that scientific knowledge changes as our skill at observation of phenomena changes, and that knowledge is never finite or completely accurate. They also noted that what counts as scientific knowledge should be stated in the simplest way possible and be logically cohesive. That is, explanations that are simple are better than ones that are complicated, and explanations that fit in well with others are better than ones that do not.

If one focuses on more than argumentation, one goal of science is to be able to predict what will happen in a hypothetical instance, given what we have found out through experimentation. For example, because scientists have found that acceleration due to gravity is 9.8 millimeters per second squared on earth (at sea level and in a vacuum), I can predict when something will hit the ground if dropped in similar circumstances and, taking into account error of measurement, that prediction will be borne out. It is this predictive power that accounts for whatever progress is made in applied science and engineering. The development of new medicines, new earthquake-resistant buildings, new materials—all of these have relied on prediction.

The READi team discusses the different kinds of texts that are used in science. These include:

- Raw data
- Bench notes, field notes, journals or logs
- Refereed journal articles
- Personal communications such as interviews, letters, e-mails, and conversations
- Integrative pieces: chapters in handbooks, series on advances in science, refereed review articles, popular press articles
- Press releases, news briefs, and online articles
- Textbooks
- Trade books
- Websites and blogs

Moreover, these texts include multiple representations of knowledge, not only in text form, but also in videos, graphs, flowcharts, models, equations, and so on.

How is scientific knowledge built? The READi team discusses logical explanation, model building, and argumentation based on evidence. They say that scientists advance and challenge explanations, look for convergence and corroboration of evidence, integrate across sources and representations, and evaluate sources and evidence.

All of the beliefs and practices just discussed have implications for discourse. Scientists discuss and write about scientific information in a way that reifies these beliefs and practices. Scientists, more than other disciplines, use passive voice and nominalization as discourse practices. Often, the agent is taken out of a sentence: "The result was that ..." rather than "I found ..." This gives scientific writing a sense of objectivity. In addition, verbs such as *dissolve*, explaining the action in a single occurrence, are changed to nouns, such as *dissolution*, indicating a generalized process. These discourse moves have the effect of imparting a sense of authority to the field. On the other hand, science discourse tends to signal that certainty, generalizability, and precision of claims are valid to a degree. Overclaiming is looked down on in the discipline, so that even though a goal of experimentation is generalization (so that findings can be used for the purposes of prediction), this generalization has limitations.

In summary, scientists have unique ways of representing the world, and these translate to unique discourse practices, which, in turn translate to unique challenges for students wishing to learn science.

IMPLICATIONS FOR SCIENCE TEACHING AND LEARNING

These notions of scientific belief, practice, and discourse provide a way for us to think about what students need to do to read and understand science. The Common Core Literacy Standards in Science and Technical Subjects (Common Core State Standards Initiative, 2010) are among the latest blueprints for teaching students to read science texts. These standards are unique because they specifically lay out the literacy requirements in science reading, taking into account the nature of science texts. Students in grades 6–12 are expected to not only identify key ideas and details in science text and carry out complex written scientific procedures, they are also expected to understand scientific vocabulary and understand the structural relationships among ideas, analyze an author's purpose, translate scientific representations into other representations (such as texts to graphs), evaluate scientific claims, and compare and contrast sources of scientific information. Students need to be taught strategies to do all of these things within the context of science.

In this section, I want to distinguish between those kinds of teaching that emphasize cross-disciplinary strategies and those that emphasize strategies fitting a particular discipline. Indeed, there are expository text strategies that have been touted to work in every discipline, including K-W-L (Ogle, 1986), comparison–contrast charting, and SQ3R (Robinson, 1970). These may be helpful to learning. In fact there is a good deal of research evidence (e.g., National Institute of Child Health and Human Development, 2000) that using reading strategies increases comprehension. However, they have a greater chance of working for struggling readers than they do for others. It may be that what these strategies do is help readers pay attention to what they are reading and so increase the likelihood that what is read will be understood and remembered. It is these kinds of strategies that are often looked at with skepticism by science teachers. After all, they say, teaching the strategies takes time, and science teachers have to teach science, not reading. In other words, they believe that the strategies aren't really helping students to understand the science.

Also, they are usually introduced in a workshop—after school or during inservice days. Typically, teachers of various subject areas attend the same workshop and a general strategy is taught. The context may not be science, and even if it is, it's unlikely that the topic will be one that teachers are currently engaged in teaching. So, science teachers are supposed to transfer what they learn to their own content and their own topic. In addition, they are expected to alter their lessons to incorporate the new strategy—when they had just enough time to follow the original lesson plan. Reading teachers wonder why science teachers aren't that enthusiastic about strategy teaching, and the need for transfer may be a large part of that reason. Also, strategies are often encouraged by a reading coach or teacher who has very little knowledge of science content, so they have a hard time helping the science teacher make the transfer, and may even be encouraging a strategy that just does not make sense. For example, K-W-L may not have that much applicability to a lesson in which students do not really have any background knowledge. "What do you already know about organic chemistry?" "Nothing." "What would you like to know?" "Nothing."

So, whereas I am not suggesting that general strategies be dumped, I do think we need a different model for teaching the reading of science text. First and foremost, science teachers and reading teachers need to become equal partners in figuring out how to teach science reading. Reading teachers may know more about teaching reading, but not about teaching science. Science teachers do know more about science and have a sense of the struggles their students have when they read science; together they should engage in problem solving about how to teach particular topics using particular texts. The conversation should begin with a good deal of listening on the part of the reading teacher about what needs to be learned and with what level of precision or accuracy and on the part of the science teacher about the role of reading in learning science.

Second, it is important for both science teachers and reading teachers to understand the kinds of disciplinary knowledge that are required in order to learn and think about science and to recognize the role that literacy plays in that knowledge as is being specified in the READi project related to argumentation. Reading and science teachers can then determine how best to convey disciplinary knowledge to students and the role of text in that knowledge. If students know what they are supposed to be doing and how they are supposed to be going about doing it, they are more likely to know what to pay attention to when they read and study.

Third, science and reading teachers can together formulate strategies that will actually end up helping students learn science when they read. In the Shanahan and Shanahan study (2008), the chemists were rather reluctant to take up strategies we reading experts suggested until we made the strategies specific to a particular kind of knowledge the chemists thought was important. To that end, we devised an organizing scheme that included substances, interactions of substances, and outcomes of the interaction. When we showed that to the chemists, one remarked, "Well, if they did that, they would learn chemistry."

STRATEGIES FOR LEARNING FROM SCIENCE TEXT

I present several strategies here: for vocabulary, for comprehension, and for writing. Because the sciences are different, these strategies may be more applicable to one science than others. I include some "general strategies" that have specific applications to science and some discipline-specific strategies that are applicable only to science.

Vocabulary

The chemists with whom we worked and other scientists all emphasize the importance of precise and thorough knowledge of technical terms. These terms are vital to the understanding of scientific processes. Others have already suggested vocabulary strategies that can be used in various disciplines that are also applicable to science, such as the Frayer Model (Frayer, Frederick, & Klausmeier, 1969). The strategy I suggest here comes from the scientists' insistence that multiple representations are important. The strategy consists of a vocabulary notebook with a separate page for each word, divided into six sections for the scientific definition, the general definition (if there is one), an explanation of the process in which the term is involved, a diagram or picture illustrating the process, a formula or numeric representation of the word (if applicable), and related words. The example in Figure 6.1 uses the term *osmosis*. Note that the definition relies on several terms whose meaning students may not know. That is often true in scientific definitions, so students should write the meaning of those words into the definition itself.

Students who engage in this vocabulary activity will end up with a deeper understanding of the word *osmosis* than those who merely write the word and its definition into a notebook. It also provides students with practice in representing concepts in multiple ways. This activity helps students meet aspects of the Common Core Standards for Literacy in Science and Technical Subjects (Common Core State Standards Initiative, 2010). Specifically, students are required to "determine the meaning of symbols, key terms, and other domain-specific words and phrases as they are used in a specific scientific or technical context" (grades 6–12, p. 62). In addition, if more than one text is used, students are required to "synthesize information from a range of sources into a coherent understanding of a process, phenomenon or concept" (grades 11–12, p. 62).

Comprehension

Comprehension of science texts is interrelated with an understanding of the technical vocabulary. So, the student who successfully engaged

Osmosis	
Definition	Process where *solvent* (liquid in which something is dissolved, such as water) molecules move through a *semipermeable membrane* (letting some molecules through and not others) from a dilute solution (a solution that has less of a solute or substance dissolved in a solution, such as salt) into a more concentrated solution (with more solute, like salt), making it more dilute (watery).
General definition	A gradual process of absorption: "I learned it through osmosis."
Explanation/ example of the process	Two parts of a container separated by a semipermeable membrane are filled with water. In one side, there is also a lot of salt. In the other, there is less salt. The water will move from the less salty side to the salty side.
Illustration/diagram	
Formula	(V2–V1) ÷ (T2–T1) = Rate of osmosis (per minute)
Related terms	Solvent, solute, molecule, semipermeable, dilute

FIGURE 6.1. Example of a vocabulary notebook entry for *osmosis*.

in the vocabulary exercise shown in Figure 6.1 has also understood the process involved. Some science learning has to do with being able to classify characteristics of particular phenomena. Reading teachers often suggest to science teachers that they use a feature analysis (Anders & Bos, 1986) for this purpose, and that does make sense if used with the right kind of material. It is a general strategy but has specific applications to science. Another strategy I suggest using after reading is List–Group–Label (Taba, 1967). Students list what they have learned from the information they just read (as a group, in small groups). They then group the information in meaningful ways. For example, in learning about sea turtles, students may have said they learned that sea turtles weigh a certain amount, eat fish, are endangered, lay eggs in the sand, ward off predators with their flippers, are mated for life, and so on. They have discussed physical characteristics, mating and birthing habits, and their reactions to predators. These groups help students to think more systematically about their observations, something that is important to scientists. The activity helps students meet the Common Core Standards (Common Core State Standards Initiative, 2010) in that it requires them to "analyze the structure of the relationships among concepts in a text" (Grades 9–10, p. 62).

In subject matter where naïve conceptions abound, such as in physics, I recommend a four-step strategy of prediction, test of prediction, reading, and discussion. This strategy involves before, during, and after reading. Before reading, students engage in a prediction activity. They then see a demonstration or test out their predictions and record what they saw. Next, they read a text containing the scientific explanation of the phenomena being predicted. While they read, they mark the text for the information that matches their prediction with a plus sign (+) and circle or mark the text differently for the information that goes against their predictions. After reading, they talk about the similarities and differences between their predictions and what the text said, and they revisit the demonstration or experiment. In the absence of a refutational text that directly names and then refutes common erroneous conceptions, the teacher plays a role in helping students to understand that, if they predicted wrong, they are not alone, and the difference between explanations based upon what seems reasonable and explanations based upon experimentation and systematic observation is what science is all about. The need for precise measurement is also applicable as a discussion topic. The discussion is last (and teacher led) in this strategy because of the tendency for students to talk others into non-scientific concepts. After the discussion, students should practice explaining the phenomena using scientific explanation. In one class a colleague of mine observed, the teacher used a "shill" to facilitate this discussion. That is, as students were discussing the phenomenon, the shill would mention a common misconception in his or her explanation. The students knew that this was likely, and their job was to catch the misconception and refute it (Guzzetti, Hynd, Skeels, & Williams, 1995). This activity also addresses the Common Core Standards (Common Core State Standards Initiative, 2010). Specifically, it helps students "integrate and evaluate multiple sources of information presented in diverse formats" (Grades 11–12, p. 62) and "compare and contrast findings presented in a text to those from other sources (including their own experiments, noting when the findings support or contradict previous explanations or accounts" (Grades 9–10, p. 62).

Students should also be asked to read multiple sources and representations of information, including texts, experiments, simulations, qualitative data, video, and multimedia. These multiple sources provide opportunities for students to engage in sourcing and contextualization. Students should be led to consider the author of what they are reading and to make determinations of credibility based on who that author is, where the material appears (in a scientific journal or on a website known for a political stance, for instance), who the audience is, and what the author's purpose for writing is. They should look at the time period in which the material was produced and consider how up-to-date the information is. They should also engage in corroboration—looking at whether or not the various representations agree or disagree. From these activities, they learn more about the nature of scientific investigation, in that what is known changes as scientific materials and questions become more refined. They also learn that scientists write for different audiences, and the purpose and structure of the text changes as the audience changes. Activities such as these help students meet the Common Core Standards (Common Core State Standards Initiative, 2010), in that they must "integrate and evaluate multiple sources of information presented in diverse formats and media," and "to analyze the author's purpose in providing explanation, describing a procedure, or discussing an experiment in a text, identifying issues the remain unresolved" (Grades 11–12, p. 62).

Writing

The Common Core Writing Standards for Literacy in History/Social Studies, Science, and Technical Subjects (Common Core State Standards Initiative, 2010) are all about making arguments. In grades 6–12, students are expected to be able to make claims, distinguish them from opposing claims, organize reasons and evidence in a logical way to support the claim(s), provide a conclusion, and use language to make the reasoning coherent and understandable. In science, arguments contain particular grammatical structures (nominalizations and passive voice), technical and specialized expressions, and a signaling of the degree of precision and certainty of findings. Evidence is used to support claims.

One general strategy that gets at the different purposes for science writing might be RAFT (Role/Audience/Format/Topic; Santa, 1988). In this strategy students take on a role, an audience, a format, and a topic. The role might be scientist, the audience might be a source of funding, another scientist, a journal article, or a popular science magazine, for example. The format would change depending on the audience—from a proposal to conduct an experiment (source of funding), to a log of lab results and an informal discussion of findings (another scientist), to the formal reporting of an experiment (journal article), to an accessible explanation of findings (popular science magazine). In science class, students could take on a different audience at various stages of scientific activity. In each case scientific conventions for writing would need to be learned, and students would need to be assessed on these expectations using appropriate rubrics or other ways of measuring performance.

The way I described RAFT is very different from descriptions on various websites where its use in science is seen as a way to understand the material. For instance, in one such example, the student is supposed to take on the role of a root writing a letter (format) to stems, leaves, seeds, and flowers (audience) for the purpose of convincing them they need the root (topic). Both of these descriptions of RAFT involve writing and even argumentation and explanation in one form or another. The second description is not indicative of real scientific activity but might be useful for younger students.

A discipline-specific activity for science writing is writing a paper describing an experiment after engaging in hypothesis testing and recording results. Students would have to take their lab results and construct a paper that includes the various parts of a scientific paper—review of relevant literature, explanation of hypothesis, methods, and results, and discussion—using the discussion to integrate what they found with explanations from their textbooks and other sources. Students could be given procedural facilitators for carrying out this rather complex task, and as they gain experience, these facilitators can be removed. For example, students may not know how to formulate a hypothesis, so the paper is structured with blank spaces for students to write in their specific information. In the same vein, the structure of the literature review, explanation of findings, and discussions could be laid bare by section and paragraph starters. This structure may seem formulaic to teachers, but it may be needed in order for students to be inducted into the process of scientific writing.

In sharing these strategies and activities, I want to emphasize that I took into account several things—my work and consultation with scientists and science educators, my familiarity with the disciplinary knowledge in science and literacy, and my review of the standards to which students will be held accountable. These strategies have worked in various science class contexts. However, that doesn't mean that these strategies will work with all science topics, texts, and classrooms. That is why teachers need to work together to determine what strategies and practices they will use to teach their students their subject matter.

CONCLUSION

This chapter has discussed reading in science classrooms, how experts read and what they think is challenging for students, and the implications for science reading. I have emphasized the need to teach students disciplinary knowledge—what it is that scientists do, why they do it, what methods they use, how they talk about it, and how they are evaluated. If students don't understand these things, they won't understand very well how they are to approach the reading they are doing in science classes. They won't know why some information is more important than other information, what to critique, and what to try to learn in depth. A colleague of mine tells the story of his daughter who came to him after doing poorly on tests in her science class, even though she did well on the lab work and participated in class. He asked what she did to learn what was in the textbook and she told him that she "read for the gist," a strategy that she had learned in English class. Of course, this strategy wasn't at all appropriate for reading science. He taught her to read carefully and to make cards on each of the technical terms she came across, then to practice explaining what she read. Those adjustments in her reading were enough to move her from failing to excelling. The fact that nobody had bothered to help her understand the difference between reading science and reading literature is an indictment of a system of education in which it is assumed that reading in any subject matter proceeds in the same way, and that if students know how to pronounce the words and understand a simple story, they can read anything. More and more, we are discovering that this is not the case.

REFERENCES

Anders, P., & Bos, C. (1986). Semantic feature analysis: An interactive strategy for vocabulary development and text comprehension. *Journal of Reading, 29*(7), 610–660.

Bazerman, C. (1997). Discursively structured activities. *Mind, Culture, and Activity, 4*(4), 296–308.

Common Core State Standards Initiative. (2010). Common core standards for English language arts and literacy in history/social studies, science, and technical subjects. Retrieved from *www.corestandards.org*.

Fang, Z. (2004). Scientific literacy: A functional systemic linguistic perspective. *Wiley Interscience.* Retrieved from *www.interscience.wiley.com.*

Frayer, D., Frederick, W. C., Klausmeier, H. J. (1969). *A schema for testing the level of cognitive mastery.* Madison, WI: Wisconsin Center for Education Research.

Guzzetti, B., Hynd, C., Skeels, S., & Williams, W. (1995). Improving science texts: Students speak out. *Journal of Reading, 38,* 656–665.

Hynd, C., McNish, M., Qian, G., Keith M., and Lay, K. (1994). When science contradicts intuition: How students learn scientific concepts. *Reading Today.*

Hynd, C., McWhorter, Y., Phares, V., & Suttles, W. (1994). The role of instructional variables in conceptual change in high school physics students. *Journal of Research in Science Teaching, 3 31,* 933–946.

Loftus, E. (1979). *Eyewitness testimony.* Boston: Harvard University Press.

National Institute of Child Health and Human Development. (2000). *Report of the National Reading Panel. Teaching children to read: An evidence-based assessment of the scientific research literature on reading and its implications for reading instruction: Reports of the subgroups* (NIH Publication No. 00-4754). Washington, DC: U.S. Government Printing Office. Available at *www.nichd.nih.gov/publications/nrp/report.htm.*

Ogle, D.M. (1986). K-W-L: A teaching model that develops active reading of expository text. *Reading Teacher, 39,* 564–570.

Project READi, & Goldman, S. (2010 October). Comprehending multiple documents on the Internet: The road to the public engagement with science in the 21st century. Workshop presentation, Muenster, Germany.

Robinson, F. P. (1970). *Effective study* (4th ed.). New York: Harper & Row.

Santa, C. (1988). *Content reading including study systems.* Dubuque, IA: Kendall/Hunt Publishing.

Shanahan, T., & Shanahan, C. (2008). Teaching disciplinary literacy to adolescents: Re-thinking content-area literacy. *Harvard Educational Review, 78*(1), 40–59.

Taba, H. (1967). *Teachers' handbook for elementary social studies.* Reading, MA: Addison-Wesley.

Yore, L.D. (1991). Secondary science teachers' attitudes toward and beliefs about science reading and science textbooks. *Journal of Research in Science Teaching, 28*(1), 55–72.

Yore, L D., Florence, M. K., Pearson, T. W., and Weaver, A. J. (2006). Written discourse in scientific communities: A conversation with two scientists about their views of science, use of language, role of writing in doing science, and compatibility between their epistemic views and language. *International Journal of Science Education, 28*(2), 109–141.

7

Reconceptualizing Literacy and Instruction for Mathematics Classrooms

Daniel Siebert *and* Roni Jo Draper

Proper literacy instruction is crucial for learning and doing mathematics. Indeed, we believe it is impossible for an individual to confront mathematical problems, create sound mathematical solutions, and communicate mathematical ideas without facility in using the texts central to mathematics. We appreciate literacy educators' dedication to working with mathematics educators to improve the learning and literacies of adolescent students. However, we believe that misconceptions about literacy for mathematics classrooms have hindered collaborative attempts between literacy specialists and mathematics teachers and have at times led to recommendations for literacy instruction in the mathematics classroom that are at odds with the norms and practices of the discipline of mathematics (Siebert & Draper, 2008). Our purpose in writing this chapter is to help literacy educators reconceptualize literacy for mathematics classrooms and provide them with ideas for how to collaborate with mathematics teachers to design instruction that strengthens adolescents' mathematical understanding, practices, and literacies.

We have divided the chapter into three sections. First, we review and critique current perspectives and approaches to literacy instruction in the mathematics classroom. Although we acknowledge that there is a growing literature describing literacy instruction for mathematics classrooms, we are critical of much of this literature because we fear that it promotes conceptions about literacy instruction for mathematics classrooms that do not acknowledge the unique literacy needs of students as they engage in learning and doing mathematics (Siebert & Hendrickson, 2010). Therefore, in the first section of the chapter we problematize some of these conceptions about literacy and the nature of literacy instruction for mathematics classrooms.

In the second section of the chapter, we work to replace the misconceptions about literacy for mathematics classrooms with conceptions that, if taken up by literacy and mathematics educators, hold potential to help adolescents learn mathematics and acquire accompanying literacies. The conceptions of literacy we promote in this chapter are built on broad definitions of *text, reading, writing,* and *literacy* and their centrality to learning and doing mathematics (Draper & Siebert, 2004). Our goal in this section is to demonstrate the inextricable link between literacy and content and to describe mathematics instruction that simultaneously supports content and literacy learning. This is a departure from the literacy–content dualism, which suggests that teachers must decide to teach either literacy or content in any instructional moment (Draper, Hall, Smith, & Siebert, 2005). By describing mathematics instruction based on these broad notions of text, we hope to help literacy and mathematics educators see how instruction can simultaneously promote both mathematics and literacy.

The kind of literacy and mathematics instruction we propose in this chapter requires a commitment from both literacy and mathematics educators. Indeed, because descriptions of literacy instruction suitable for mathematics classrooms do not exist, literacy specialists and mathematics teachers must form collaborations to identify the texts and literacies present in mathematics classrooms and design instruction to promote these literacies. Therefore, we end the chapter with a section in which we describe how literacy specialists can create and sustain fruitful collaborations with mathematics educators.

PROBLEMATIZING CONCEPTIONS OF LITERACY FOR MATHEMATICS CLASSROOMS

Before we provide a description of how we have reconceptualized literacy for mathematics classrooms, we must demonstrate how current conceptions of literacy are problematic for supporting literacy and mathematics learning. We focus our discussion on three particular problematic conceptions of literacy. The first is that mathematics teachers should devote time in mathematics classrooms to help adolescents develop general print literacies. We fear that literacy educators, in their zeal to promote general literacy, lose sight of the primary goal of content-area classrooms—to develop disciplinary expertise. We argue that a focus on general print literacy in a mathematics classroom, paradoxically, actually undermines this type of literacy because it inhibits students' learning of the mathematical content they need to read and write the texts that involve mathematical ideas. We conclude, therefore, that the primary goal of literacy instruction in the mathematics classroom must be to support students' learning of mathematics. The second problematic conception we address has to do with the nature of mathematics as a discipline. Many people, especially literacy educators, assume that being knowledgeable or skilled in mathematics amounts exclusively to computational fluency. However, computational fluency represents only a portion of mathematical knowledge and competency. Thus, we describe the nature of mathematics that should be promoted in mathematics classrooms. The final problematic conception we address is the belief that reading any print text or incorporating any general literacy instructional strategy is appropriate for mathematics classrooms. Because educators have not always been clear on the purpose of literacy for content-area instruction (the first problematic conception) or the nature of the discipline under study (the second problematic conception), they have made recommendations for literacy instruction that neither support literacy nor the discipline. In this last section, we address many of common recommendations for literacy instruction in the mathematics classroom and show why they are problematic.

The Need for Mathematics Instruction to Support General Print Literacy

Much has been written and discussed about how to improve adolescent literacy. While the arguments vary somewhat, the general point is that adolescents' literacy would improve if all teachers, not just language arts teachers, would provide adolescents with access to and support for the print texts associated with the discipline (see Carnegie Council on Advancing Adolescent Literacy, 2010). Therefore, advocates for advancing adolescent literacy have suggested that content-area teachers, including mathematics teachers, use children's picture books and other popular texts to motivate student engagement, engage students in more writing about the content under study, and provide support with texts used or created as a part of learning such as textbooks and note taking. The message is clear and simple: adolescent literacy will flourish when "all content area classes are permeated by a strong literacy focus" (Carnegie Council on Advancing Adolescent Literacy, 2010, p. 36). However, we wonder if the difficulty that adolescents face with the print texts they confront is not with the print, per se, but with a lack of content knowledge.

Consider what is needed to make sense of the following statement found on a poster in a shoe-store window: Buy two pairs of shoes and get the third pair half off. Relatively few people beyond fourth grade have difficulty decoding the words that make up this sentence, and most people know what each word or phrase means. Indeed, according to the scale used by Microsoft Word to calculate readability (Flesch-Kincaid grade level), the sentence is written at the first-grade level. Likely it scored low because all the words consist of a single syllable and none of them represent low-frequency words. However, a smaller number of readers (particularly first-grade readers) may understand what kind of discount is really being offered. Indeed, the marketers are relying on consumers' lack of mathematical understanding to sell shoes. The authors hope that readers will see the "half off" and think, "This is a great deal—I only pay half!" However, a reader with sufficient mathematical understanding realizes that what the offer is really saying is something like this: "If you buy three pairs of shoes, we will give you almost a sixth or almost 17% off the total transaction, but you must buy three pairs of shoes and they must be of equal cost; the discount is smaller if the shoes are not of equal cost." This may still be a great sale, but not as great as the sale going on across the street advertising 20% off all shoes in the store. Indeed, it may not be better than a store offering 10% off all shoes for a consumer who only needs one pair of shoes. This example illustrates that the difficulty in reading many mathematics-related texts may not be facility with print, but facility with the underlying mathematical ideas.

Despite the centrality of content knowledge in reading, writing, comprehending, and critiquing texts, literacy educators have not explicitly acknowledged the importance of disciplinary knowledge to improve adolescent literacy. Certainly, this is implicitly acknowledged during discussions of the importance of background knowledge as part of preparing learners to read or write a text. Indeed, activating background knowledge is central to many of the literacy instructional activities shared and demonstrated as part of teacher inservice activities (e.g, K-W-L, anticipation guides, graphic organizers). However, the fervor surrounding the need to improve adolescent literacy has resulted in an examination of school policies and initiatives that would increase adolescents' time and support with texts but has not resulted in a serious discussion of the need to improve content instruction. For example, teachers and policymakers who argue for longer literacy blocks in secondary schools at the expense of content courses such as social studies, science, and the arts are not attending to the improvement of content knowledge.

While not addressing the need for improved content knowledge directly, some literacy educators argue that providing adolescents with increased exposure to texts will result in a dual benefit for adolescents: (1) an increase of their literacy development, and (2) an increase in their content knowledge (see Fisher & Ivey, 2005). This argument goes something like this: providing adolescents with opportunities to read and write in content-area classrooms provides another opportunity for them to engage in the content, thus strengthening both their literacy and content knowledge. This argument may be valid for learning in the disciplines where traditional print text consisting of words, sentences, and paragraphs is the medium through which most of the ideas and meanings of the discipline are communicated. However, in mathematics, experts often use objects other than traditional print text (e.g., graphs, equations, diagrams) to create, convey, and negotiate meaning, because traditional print texts cannot convey mathematical ideas and meanings as well as these other objects. We fear that many of the texts that adolescents read and write under the auspices of literacy instruction in a mathematics classroom are only tangentially associated with the discipline (e.g., children's picture books, rap songs, descriptions of the discipline). These materials are not cost-effective in terms of the amount of instructional time they take up compared to the amount of content learning they promote. Furthermore, using these materials in a mathematics classroom can actually undermine students' general literacy, because their use can prevent students from developing the content knowledge they need for future literacy events.

Rather than argue for an infusion of print texts in mathematics classrooms to improve literacy instruction, we argue for improved mathematics instruction to prepare adolescents to interact with a variety of texts they will confront as part of daily living and through their occupations. However, this should not be interpreted as an argument against literacy instruction in mathematics classrooms. On the contrary, we argue for a particular kind of literacy instruction in mathematics classrooms that enables adolescents to participate in a full range of mathematical activities.

The Nature of Mathematics

While many of the literacy educators who have made recommendations for literacy instruction in mathematics classrooms have not explicitly declared their understanding of the nature of mathematics, we can infer their understanding by the recommendations they have made for mathematics teachers. For example, the promotion of algorithms and the focus on describing steps used to determine answers, which are promoted in much of the literacy literature (Siebert & Draper, 2008), suggest that many literacy educators believe mathematics is a collection of rules and procedures and that mathematical activity consists mostly of performing computations. However, this is not a view of mathematics held by mathematics educators.

To better understand how mathematics educators define mathematics and mathematical expertise, we turn to the *Principles and Standards for School Mathematics* (National Council of Teachers of Mathematics, 2000), the national standards for the teaching and learning of mathematics. In this document, expertise in mathematics is described using two sets of standards. The first set, typically referred to as the content standards, describes what students should know and understand in various topic areas such as algebra or geometry. Much of what is found in these standards can be categorized either as computational fluency or conceptual understanding. The second set of standards, often called the process standards, describes important mathematical processes that are required for participation in mathematical activity. While others have made important additions to the list of what constitutes mathematical expertise (e.g., National Research Council, 2001), these three constructs—computational fluency, conceptual understanding, and mathematical processes—are the most widely recognized across the field. Each is described in greater detail below.

Computational fluency refers to "having and using efficient and accurate methods for computing" (National Council of Teachers of Mathematics, 2000, p. 32). Because of the important role that computation plays in understanding, learning, and doing mathematics, computational fluency is an essential component of mathematical expertise. However, computational fluency does not necessarily imply that students are proficient at traditional, standard paper-and-pencil procedures, because these procedures are often not the most efficient or accurate (National Council of Teachers of Mathematics, 1989). For example, some mathematics teachers no longer teach the standard long-division algorithm because it takes too long to learn, obscures meaning, and often leads to errors of large magnitude. Instead, they teach alternative algorithms for division that are only marginally more time consuming to perform but that are more quickly learned and easily remembered by children because the meanings of the operations and numbers are more readily apparent. Furthermore, when students make errors using these algorithms, they often catch errors of large magnitude because they understand what the numbers and operations mean. Given the widespread availability of calculators, these alternative division algorithms, which require less time to teach and often lead to more accurate results, seem an appropriate choice for students to learn. As this example illustrates, computational fluency does not necessarily refer to competence with standard algorithms. Instead, it refers to knowing and being proficient at using a set of procedures that meet students' mathematical needs both in and out of school.

While computational fluency is important, by itself it is insufficient. Mathematics educators recognize that students also need conceptual understanding. Skemp (1978) noted that conceptual understanding includes at the very least knowledge of why the procedures work, when they can be applied, and their relationship to other important procedures and mathematical ideas. Considered more broadly, conceptual understanding refers to any type of knowledge that is related to making sense of mathematical objects, operations, and processes. Mathematics educators believe that conceptual understanding has many benefits. It helps students to remember and flexibly use what they have learned; it motivates students to learn mathematics; and it serves as a foundation on which students can construct new mathematical meanings and understandings (Hiebert et al., 1997; Skemp. 1978). Given all of the benefits of conceptual understanding, it is not surprising that many mathematics educators feel that "understanding should be the most fundamental goal of mathematics instruction" (Hiebert et al., 1997, p. 2).

In addition to computational fluency and conceptual understanding, mathematics educators also recognize that students need to be adept at participating in mathematical processes—the activities essential to doing and learning mathematics. These processes include, but are not limited to, forming and testing conjectures, solving problems, constructing proofs and justifications, communicating reasoning and mathematical thinking, creating and interpreting mathematical representations, and modeling real-world situations (National Council of Teachers of Mathematics, 2000). Because of the essential role these processes play in doing and learning mathematics, students cannot be said to have expertise in mathematics unless they are adept at engaging in them. Furthermore, it is important that students learn to participate in these processes because it is often through this participation that they develop computational fluency and conceptual understanding.

Uses of Texts in Mathematics Classrooms

For literacy instruction in the mathematics classroom to support content learning in mathematics, and thus enable students to develop the mathematical knowledge they need for general literacy, it must help students develop computational proficiency, conceptual understanding, and fluency in mathematical processes. Past suggestions for literacy instruction in the mathematics classroom have focused largely on helping students read and write the common print texts in mathematics classrooms or importing additional print texts or print genres for students to read and write. Unfortunately, both of these approaches seldom lead to gains in mathematical expertise. We explore these approaches in detail below and explain their shortcomings.

Perhaps the most common focus of literacy instruction in mathematics classrooms is on reading textbooks and word problems and writing descriptions of solution methods, the commonly perceived texts and literacies of mathematics. The main problem with this focus is that these texts and literacies receive only limited use in authentic mathematical activities, which mathematics educators employ for students to develop all three components of mathematical expertise. For example, rather than reading about mathematical ideas in their textbooks, students who are participating in authentic mathematical activities are typically engaged in exploring mathematical ideas, solving problems for which they do not already have a prescribed solution method, forming and testing conjectures, and sharing their reasoning with others. In this setting, the textbook becomes a secondary source, rather than a primary source, for mathematical knowledge and understanding. Likewise, reading and answering the highly stylized word problems often found toward the end of a problem set does not fit well with authentic mathematical activity; the contextualized problems are merely used as an excuse for practicing the procedures the students have just learned, typically without providing the students with any greater insight into the conditions under which the procedures might be appropriately applied. Lastly, the recording of steps taken to produce a correct answer is not authentic mathematical writing; to be authentic, students would also have to explain why the steps are appropriate and why they work.

A second common approach to literacy instruction in the mathematics classroom is to import texts and genres into the classroom so that students have something to read and write. For example, students may be given popular written accounts of mathematical topics or biographies of famous mathematicians. They may be asked to write poems or rap songs about mathematical concepts or ideas. As mentioned above, while students can have valuable experiences with these texts, they often do so without learning very much mathematics, because these texts and genres can't communicate rich mathematical content. Furthermore, spending class time helping students read and write these texts and genres does not help prepare them to read the texts and genres that are most common for learning and participating in mathematics. Thus, they provide limited benefit to mathematics students.

For example, consider the recommendation to read the classic short story *The Lottery* (Jackson, 1948/2007) as part of a unit on probability. The plot of the story certainly provides an interesting, albeit gruesome, context in which to consider conditional probability. In the story, villagers choose an individual each year to stone to death. The individual is chosen by first having a lottery to determine which family the individual will come from. Once the family is determined, a second lottery is conducted to determine the individual. This context, however disturbing it may be, opens up interesting mathematical questions like the following: If there are 150 families in the village and Sarah's family includes herself, her husband, and their three children, what is the probability of Sarah being chosen for the lottery? How might a family work to minimize the probability of a family member being chosen in the lottery? Despite the opportunity for the story to engage learners in a mathematics classroom with subsequent questions that require probability content, it still is not worth the time it would require to read the story because the story itself does not contribute to students' development of computational fluency, conceptual understanding, or fluency in mathematical processes. As such, given the density of mathematics curricula, devoting large amounts of instructional time to the reading of one short story that does not contribute to students' mathematical expertise may be derelict on the part of a mathematics teacher.

What we are arguing is that general print texts consisting of words, sentences, and paragraphs do not play a prominent role in learning and doing mathematics. Furthermore, a focus on helping adolescents develop fluency with general print texts is not likely to help them develop expertise in mathematics. We conclude, therefore, that content-area literacy instruction that focuses on supporting adolescents' reading and writing of general print text has limited relevance in mathematics classrooms and does not warrant the allocation of significant amounts of instructional time. The question remains, then, as to whether content-area literacy can be reconceptualized so that it is relevant to the learning of mathematics. In the next section, we present our reconceptualization of content-area literacy and show how it can support mathematics learning.

RECONCEPTUALIZING LITERACY INSTRUCTION FOR MATHEMATICS CLASSROOMS

One of the major flaws in the current conception of content-area literacy instruction is that instruction is focused almost entirely on supporting students' literacy with general print texts. The reconceptualization of content-area literacy offered below is based on broad definitions of the terms *text, reading, writing,* and *literacy.* First we explain how this reconceptualization makes literacy instruction relevant to and necessary for mathematics learning. We then present a general approach to designing literacy instruction that acknowledges and addresses the discipline-specific texts and literacies found in the mathematics classroom. Last, we offer two vignettes that exemplify the kind of literacy instruction we believe is possible when literacy and mathematics educators work together to design literacy instruction appropriate for mathematics classrooms.

Mathematical Texts and Literacies

Several years ago when we first began collaboratively thinking about literacy instruction that supports mathematics learning, we struggled with the issue of whether there was a legitimate place for content-area literacy instruction in the mathematics classroom (Draper & Siebert, 2004). At that time, Draper, a literacy educator, had arranged with Siebert, a mathematics educator, to regularly attend his university mathematics course for preservice elementary teachers. Draper was particularly interested in observing how Siebert addressed his students' literacy needs. She noticed immediately that Siebert's students were not reading and writing traditional print texts consisting of words, sentences, and paragraphs. In particular, Siebert did not use a textbook, and his students were not solving word problems. Despite this, the students seemed to be developing rich understandings of mathematics and were becoming adept at many important mathematical processes. Draper wondered if there was any need for content-area literacy instruction in this class, and if so, how it could be used to enhance rather than detract from what Siebert was accomplishing with his students. In particular, she did not want to suggest literacy activities if such suggestions were not likely to improve on the efficiency and quality of ongoing student learning.

As Draper continued to attend Siebert's mathematics class, she became increasing aware that despite the general lack of traditional print text, there were nonetheless many objects in Siebert's class that were being created and interpreted—one might even say "written" and "read"—by both teacher and students as they collaboratively constructed, shared, and negotiated meaning. These objects included pictures, symbols, hand gestures, written explanations, and verbal discussions, to name just a few. Furthermore, she noticed that students' learning of mathematics depended on their ability to create and interpret these objects in appropriate ways. Through extended conversations, we both came to see these and other similar objects as the "texts" in Siebert's mathematics class. Because of the predominance of these objects in the mathematics being taught, and because of the need for students to interact with them in ways similar to their interaction with traditional print text, we chose to broaden our definition for the term *text* to include all objects created or interpreted for the purpose of constructing, sharing, and negotiating meaning.

We feel there are several reasons why this broadened definition of *text* is necessary for reconceptualizing content-area literacy in the mathematics classroom. First, it acknowledges and validates the essential role that these "text-like" objects play in constructing and learning in mathematics. Mathematics is a human creation, not something that exists in the universe waiting to be discovered. Furthermore, the initial stage in creating a mathematical idea is invariably an attempt to represent the idea in the form of an object imbued with meaning, which we call text. These texts include a pattern of symbols, a drawing, a spoken word or phrase, a graph, or a series of gestures. From this point on, the development of the mathematical idea and the evolution of the texts used to represent it are inextricably connected. In fact, Sfard (2000) argues that there is a coevolution between a person's understanding of a mathematical idea and the way the person uses the texts associated with the idea. On the one hand, refined meanings and increased understanding of the mathematical idea lead to more expert uses of the texts associated with the idea; on the other, inventions of more sophisticated ways of using text lead to refinement of the mathematical idea. Simply stated, the construction of mathematical knowledge is not possible without text creation and use. Similarly, texts play an essential role in learning mathematics. Because mathematical knowledge cannot be transmitted directly from mind to mind, people rely on text creation and interpretation to communicate and negotiate mathematical meaning. Students who cannot interpret these texts in appropriate ways or respond by creating texts in acceptable ways will not be successful in learning and, ultimately, doing mathematics.

Second, a broadened definition of text uncovers the essential role that literacy plays in mathematical expertise. When the term *text* is broadened to include all of the objects that people create and interpret during meaning-making activities, text interpretation and creation—reading and writing—take on new importance, because without the ability to read and write mathematical texts, it is not possible to have computational fluency, conceptual understanding, or fluency in mathematical processes. Computational fluency relies heavily upon reading and writing mathematical expressions to know what steps to perform, how to perform them, how to record and make sense of intermediate results, and how to review a series of computations for accuracy. Conceptual understanding, as Sfard (2000) suggested, is inextricably tied to text use, because it is through increasingly sophisticated ways of creating and interpreting texts that mathematical ideas are refined and understood. Fluency in mathematical processes is not possible without knowledge of how to appropriately create and interpret mathematical texts, because all mathematical processes are mediated through text use. Without literacy in mathematical texts, mathematical expertise is not possible.

Third, a broadened definition of text suggests a direction for content-area literacy instruction that makes it relevant to mathematics teaching and learning. The immediate effect of a broadened definition of text is that the mathematics classroom is suddenly recognized as a text-rich environment teeming with literacy events. In fact, every action taken by the teacher or student involves some kind of text creation or interpretation. For students to develop mathematical expertise, they must become adept at reading and writing mathematical texts in discipline-appropriate ways. Furthermore, because students do not naturally know how to read and write mathematical texts, they will need support in learning how to do so. Literacy instruction is needed to help students identify mathematical texts and learn to interpret and create them appropriately. Moreover, because of the profusion of texts in every mathematics lesson, there is a legitimate need for regular and frequent literacy instruction in the mathematics classroom.

The adoption of a broader definition of text is only the first step in reconceptualizing content-area literacy to make it relevant to mathematics teaching. Because we have chosen to use a different definition for *text*, we must also redefine what is meant by the terms *reading, writing*, and *literacy*. *Reading* refers to the interpretation of texts, including such acts as listening to and understanding a verbal explanation, looking at and making sense of a graph, and reading and critiquing a mathematical proof. In contrast, *writing* refers to acts of text creation, including arranging a set of manipulatives into a particular configuration, providing a verbal description of the proportional relationship between two quantities, and writing down an equation to model a real-world context. Note that for each type of text in a mathematics classroom, there are particular discipline-appropriate ways of reading and writing that text. These ways of reading and writing comprise the multiple literacies of the discipline of mathematics. Furthermore, these literacies, and not general print literacy, should be the focus of literacy instruction in the mathematics classroom, because they are the literacies that are crucial for learning and doing mathematics.

A General Approach to Designing Literacy Instruction for the Mathematics Classroom

Unfortunately, there is very little in the literature on adolescent or content-area literacy that takes seriously the task of developing students' fluencies with mathematical texts (see Thompson, Kersaint, Richards, Hunsader, & Rubenstein, 2008, for a notable exception). No master list exists that describes the wide variety of mathematical texts and literacies that students must become fluent with if they are to be successful in learning and doing mathematics. Given the vast assortment of mathematical texts, such a list may in fact be impossible, or at least very impractical, to create. Also missing are comprehensive resources for teaching all of these texts and literacies, such as lists of literacy instructional strategies for mathematical texts or resources containing descriptions of how to take literacy strategies for general print text and adapt them for teaching the reading and writing of mathematical texts. Once again, compiling such resources would be very difficult given the wide variety of general print literacy strategies and the many different mathematical texts.

It would be nice if these lists of texts with their accompanying literacies and instructional strategies existed. Then literacy specialists could simply help mathematics teachers match the texts with their literacies and design instruction based on the suggested instructional strategies. Without these resources, it is unlikely that literacy specialists can design and model appropriate literacy instruction for the mathematics classroom on their own. Because literacy specialists usually have limited experience in mathematical text creation and interpretation, they are not fluent with the literacies in mathematics. Furthermore, literacy educators cannot draw on their vast knowledge of general print literacy strategies to suggest appropriate literacy instruction, because mathematical texts do not typically consist of traditional print in the form of words, sentences, and paragraphs. Recommendations based on general print literacy strategies without regard to particular mathematical literacies may not help students learn to read and write mathematical texts and may actually lead students to read and write mathematical texts in inappropriate and nonsensical ways.

Given that there are currently inadequate resources available to help literacy specialists design literacy instruction for mathematics classrooms on their own, we propose that they collaborate with mathematics teachers to design instruction that supports students' reading and writing of mathematical texts. Through this collaboration, literacy specialists can draw upon mathematics teachers' expertise with mathematical texts, literacies, and content to target specific texts and literacies and to protect against instruction that promotes ways of using text that violate the norms and practices of the discipline. At the same time, literacy specialists can contribute to the collaboration by helping mathematics teachers notice the mathematical texts and literacies that are present in their classrooms and by encouraging them to consider ways to support students' fluency with these texts and literacies. We describe below a three-step process (Draper, Nokes, & Siebert, 2010) that literacy specialists and mathematics teachers might follow while collaborating to design appropriate mathematics literacy instruction.

- *Step 1: Identify the texts that are to be read and written during the lesson.* Because it is not possible to communicate mathematics or engage in mathematical activity without the use of texts, every lesson will require students to read and write texts. Literacy specialists can help mathematics teachers understand the broad definition of text we have described here and then work with them to identify what objects are being created and interpreted to negotiate and convey meaning. To identify the texts that students must read, teachers can ask themselves what objects students will have to attend to, make sense of, listen to, or identify in particular ways as they participate in the lesson. To identify the texts that students must write, teachers can ask themselves what objects students will have to write down, speak, gesture, act out, or configure as they record or convey meaning during the lesson. Additional texts that were overlooked during the planning stage may become apparent during the lesson when students struggle to read or write a particular mathematical text.

- *Step 2: Identify the literacies—the specific ways that texts are to be read and written—that are required during the lesson.* Mathematical texts can often be read in multiple correct ways. For each text identified in the previous step, literacy specialists and mathematics teachers can work together to clarify which ways of reading and writing are appropriate for the lesson. This may be difficult to do, because much of this knowledge may be tacit for the mathematics teacher and nonexistent for the literacy specialist. Teachers can start by thinking about the various contexts and activities in which a particular form of text is used (both in this lesson and in other areas of mathematics), and then identify the ways the text is read or written differently in those situations. Often, however, a more fruitful method is to observe how students read and write a particular type of text during the lesson and compare it to how the teacher reads and writes the same type of text. Through comparison of the way the text is read and written in different contexts or by different people, literacy and mathematics teachers can become aware of the multiple literacies for a particular text and the particular literacy that is required for the lesson.

• *Step 3: Develop an instructional plan that makes explicit the texts and literacies and allows students to develop these literacies through participation in mathematical processes.* Although good mathematics instruction will often implicitly address students' literacy needs (Draper & Siebert, 2004), students can nonetheless benefit from explicit literacy instruction. This instruction should help students to recognize a particular object as a text—something that needs to be made sense of or that is created to convey meaning—and learn to interpret and create that text in particular ways. Often it is helpful for teachers to expose students to multiple readings of the same text. Through this experience, students become aware that the object is a text, because it can be interpreted in multiple ways. They also realize that there are literacies—specific, appropriate ways of creating and interpreting the text—associated with the text. After students learn about the specific ways of reading or writing a text that characterize a particular literacy, they should be encouraged to practice that literacy while engaged in a mathematical process, such as problem solving, modeling a real-world context, or justifying a solution method. The use of a mathematical process is essential to ensuring that students learn an authentic mathematical literacy rather than a way of reading and writing that is used and valued only in the classroom.

Note that throughout this design process, the literacy specialist and mathematics teacher play very different roles. The literacy specialist's predominant role is that of questioner. By asking the appropriate questions, the literacy specialist can help the mathematics teacher identify texts, literacies, and instructional settings for exposing students to multiple literacies and practicing particular literacies. These questions should focus on helping the mathematics teacher reflect on what objects are used as texts in the classroom, how these texts should be read and written, and what contexts involving mathematical processes are appropriate for practicing particular literacies. Mathematics teachers will need this prompting because they are not accustomed to acknowledging and addressing the essential role that texts and literacies play in mathematics learning. In contrast, mathematics teachers will largely play the role of answer provider. This is because the mathematics teacher, not the literacy specialist, is the expert regarding mathematical texts and literacies. In fact, literacy specialists need to be careful not to impose their own views about the nature of mathematics, mathematical activity, and mathematics texts and literacies during the design process, because such an imposition could lead to literacy instruction that does not help students read and write mathematical texts in discipline-appropriate ways.

Another important implication of this general approach to designing literacy instruction is the underlying assumption that literacy instruction needs to take place regularly in the classroom and be closely related to the ongoing content instruction. The development of literacy and the learning of content are inextricably intertwined (Bean, 2000). Students' struggles to develop new understanding or competence are invariably linked to their struggles to interpret or create texts that are new to them in discipline-appropriate ways. Advances in content knowledge can lead to more sophisticated text creation and interpretation, and vice versa. We believe that the most profound need for literacy instruction occurs when a student is struggling with a text to learn something new. Thus, the most beneficial literacy instruction consists of literacy support that is offered as close to this moment of struggle as possible. The general approach we suggest is designed to attend to and address these critical in-the-moment literacy needs. The resulting literacy instruction should enhance, support, and blend in with ongoing content instruction.

Examples of Literacy Instruction in the Mathematics Classroom

To help illustrate the three steps to designing literacy instruction, we present two vignettes of literacy instruction in the mathematics classroom. The first vignette is situated in a junior high school Algebra 1 class and demonstrates how literacy instruction can be used to help students understand the multiple ways that the equal sign is used to write mathematical expressions (Carpenter, Franke, & Levi, 2003; Matz, 1982). The first vignette also illustrates how the need for literacy instruction is sometimes not anticipated before the lesson; instead, the need becomes apparent only after observing students' inappropriate reading or writing of mathematical texts. The second vignette is situated in a high school Algebra 2 class and illustrates how literacy instruction can be planned in advance to help students read graphs in a way that enables them to make sense of what is happening in the situations being modeled by the graphs (Dugdale, 1993; Roth & Bowen, 2001). After each vignette, we describe how the general three-step approach was followed to create appropriate literacy instruction.

VIGNETTE 1

Mr. Gonzalez is teaching his students how to evaluate algebraic expressions. They are working on evaluating the expression $ab + b + 7$ for $a = 2$ and $b = 4$. Marissa volunteers to show how she computed the answer and then writes the following expression on the board: $2 \times 4 = 8 + 4 = 12 + 7 = 19$. She explains, "*ab* means *a* times *b*, and *a* is 2 and *b* is 4, so I multiplied 2 times 4 and got 8. Then I had to add on *b*, so I added 4 onto the 8 and got 12. And then I had to add 7, and 12 and 7 is 19." Heads nod across the classroom as Marissa waits at the board for students to ask questions or make comments, a common practice in Mr. Gonzalez's classroom. Mr. Gonzalez hopes that some of the students will comment about how Marissa used the equal signs incorrectly in her solution and point out that the amounts on the right- and left-hand sides of some of the equal signs are not actually equal. After several seconds of silence, Marissa, smiling, looks at Mr. Gonzalez for the signal to return to her seat. Mr. Gonzalez is not sure what to do. It bothers him that students do not notice that the equal signs were used incorrectly, but he wonders if he is just being picky. After all, Marissa's solution suggests that she understands that letter symbols can be used as placeholders for numbers, that two letters written side by side implies multiplication, that numbers can be substituted for the letters in the expression, and that the resulting computations can be performed to find a numeric answer. These are the important ideas he wants students to understand during today's lesson. After a few seconds of deliberation, he decides to move to the next problem and waves Marissa back to her seat.

Marissa's error stays with him, though, and he continues to think about it throughout the day. It gradually occurs to him that he and Marissa have very different understandings of the equal sign. Marissa seems to have a "compute" meaning for the equal sign—it signals that a numeric operation needs to be performed. A correct use of the equal sign from this perspective seems to be to write the operation on the left side of the equal sign and to record the answer on the right. In contrast, Mr. Gonzalez has a "balance" meaning for the equal sign—it signals that the two numbers or expressions on the two sides of the equal sign have the same numeric value. Furthermore, Mr. Gonzalez realizes that this balance meaning for the equal sign is essential for being able to understand and solve algebraic equations, an important upcoming topic for his algebra students. Thus, he decides that he will devote some instructional time during the next class period to helping his students develop a balance meaning for the equal sign and teach them how to use the sign correctly.

The next morning, Mr. Gonzalez tells his department chair about his experience with Marissa. She recommends that he read a chapter on equality in a book written by Carpenter, Franke, and Levi (2003). This gives Mr. Gonzalez ideas for helping his students develop a richer understanding of the equal sign. He begins the next class by asking the students to predict what number goes in the blank in the equation $7 + 9 = \underline{} + 6$. Both 10 and 16 are given as possible answers. Mr. Gonzalez leads the students in a discussion about which answer is correct. As they talk, he helps students to identify the meanings for the equal sign that are associated with each answer. Mr. Gonzalez then writes the equation $7 + 9 = \underline{}$ under the first equation and asks the students which conception of the equal sign will lead to the correct answer. After some debate, the students realize that both conceptions lead to the right answer for the second equation, but not for the first. Mr. Gonzalez then asks the students to come up with as many situations as they can where the balance meaning, and not the computation meaning, results in the correct answer. As they discuss these situations, Mr. Gonzalez writes Marissa's solution on the board. They talk about why her solution worked, and then discuss which meaning for the equal sign she used. Mr. Gonzalez has students work together in pairs to rewrite the solution in a way that does not violate the balance meaning for equality but still remains true to Marissa's original ideas. Students share their ideas in a whole class discussion. Two students' solutions are shown in Figure 7.1.

Before this lesson, Mr. Gonzalez may not have been aware that there are multiple ways of using the equal sign in writing mathematical expressions. Consequently, he was unable to anticipate that students might need support with this type of mathematical text. However, by allowing his students to share their solution methods, he was able to identify their misuse of the equal sign. Moreover, by comparing how he would have used the equal sign with how the students used the equal sign, he was able to identify two different ways of writing mathematical expressions with this symbol. To help his students see that there are multiple ways of using the equal sign, he proposed a context for which the computation meaning for the equal sign produced a result different from the balance meaning of the equal sign. This helped the students see that the equal sign might have multiple meanings and uses, some of which are not always appropriate. To help the students practice a new way of writing with the equal sign, Mr. Gonzalez returned to an ongoing mathematical process—communicating a mathematical solution—and asked students to critically read and revise the solution, preserving Marissa's original meaning.

VIGNETTE 2

This year at Mrs. Jackson's high school, Mrs. Shapiro, the school literacy specialist, has been encouraging teachers to think about the discipline-specific texts and literacies that their students must negotiate to learn content. Mrs. Jackson is surprised to find out that literacy in a mathematics class involves more than reading the textbook and books about mathemati-

Solution 1:	Solution 2:
$2 \times 4 = 8$	$2 \times 4 + 4 + 7 = 8 + 4 + 7 = 12 + 7 = 19$
$8 + 4 = 12$	
$12 + 7 = 19$	

FIGURE 7.1. Two student-generated ways of rewriting Marissa's solution ($2 \times 4 = 8 + 4 = 12 + 7 = 19$) so that the solution does not violate the balance meaning for the equal sign.

cians or the history of mathematics. Mrs. Shapiro has introduced them to a broad definition of text and literacy, and Mrs. Jackson is becoming aware of the many different texts students must read and write as they are learning in her classroom. Mrs. Jackson is currently teaching a unit on functions, and her class has been modeling real-world contexts using tables, equations, and graphs. She has been working to help her students make connections between these three different representations of functions. She has talked with Mrs. Shapiro about the different ways that students must read each representation to better understand the other two. However, in their discussion, she realizes that she has not been teaching the students to read each representation in a way that helps them better understand what is happening in the real-world situation the representations are supposed to model. With the encouragement of Mrs. Shapiro, she decides to teach her students how to read speed–time graphs.

Mrs. Jackson begins her lesson by showing her students the graph in Figure 7.2, which she claims depicts the speed of a person on a roller coaster over a period of time. She asks them if they can tell anything about the shape of the roller coaster—whether there are any hills or flat stretches that the person is traveling over during this time period. The students discuss the graph in small groups for a few minutes. As they develop explanations of what is happening, Mrs. Jackson travels from group to group, listening carefully to understand what the students are thinking. When it appears that most groups have come up with an explanation, Mrs. Jackson purposefully chooses one of the groups with an incorrect solution to share their reasoning with the class. She knows from listening to the groups that this incorrect explanation stems from an error that is common to many of the groups, namely the mistake of interpreting the graph as the actual shape of the roller coaster.

Jason is chosen by his group to present their explanation. He comes to the front of the classroom and grabs a meter stick to point at parts of the graph, which is projected onto the white board. Pointing to the first half of the graph, he suggests that the roller coaster is traveling up and over a very steep hill, probably steeper than any roller coaster he has ever been on. Then the roller coaster bottoms out and travels over a low, level section of track.

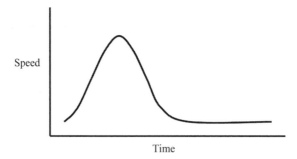

FIGURE 7.2. A graph of the speed of a roller coaster over a period of time.

Mrs. Jackson asks for a show of hands for those who agree with Jason, and a majority of the students raise their hands. Marie, a student at the front of the class, spontaneously comments that her group couldn't figure out what was happening, and that Jason's story makes sense. Mrs. Jackson comments that a lot of people think Jason's explanation is reasonable. She then points out that not all of the hands went up, which means that some people might have a different explanation. She tells the class that she heard a different explanation from a group in the back, and asks the group if they would be willing to share their ideas. Tanya reluctantly agrees to represent her group.

Tanya comes to the board and starts by admitting that her group originally thought the same way as Jason when they first looked at the graph. But then they noticed that the top of the "hill" wasn't actually a hill at all, but was a "spike" in speed. She points to the top of the spike with the meter stick and says that at this time the roller coaster has reached top speed. Since this happens at the bottom of a hill instead of the top, her group concluded that the roller coaster has reached the bottom of a hill at this point in time. She then notes that the speed decreases rapidly, which means that the roller coaster is probably climbing up another hill. She points to the level part at the end of the graph and wonders out loud if perhaps the roller coaster has leveled out at this point and is making a turn on a high section of the track so that it can go down another hill and travel back the way it had come. Mrs. Jackson thanks Tanya and asks the groups to discuss the two different interpretations of the graph and decide whether they are both right, both wrong, or one is right and one is wrong.

When the class comes back together to discuss the students' thinking, it quickly becomes clear that Tanya's interpretation is considered the best. Through a whole-class discussion about why Tanya's story is better, students note that her explanation is better because it takes into account what quantities are being represented in the graph and how the changes in the quantities are related. Mrs. Jackson asks if there are different quantities they could write on the axes so that Jason's interpretation was correct. Chris suggests that if the vertical axis had been labeled height instead of speed, then Jason's explanation would makes sense. Sandra quickly disagrees, saying that the graph would then mean that the roller coaster had traveled over the hill very quickly, which would not be possible if the hill was so big. She suggests that for Jason's interpretation to make sense, the horizontal axis would have to be changed to distance along the bottom of the track. After a few more minutes of discussion, Mrs. Jackson asks the groups to draw a picture of a small roller coaster of their own design, make a speed–time graph for the roller coaster, and then exchange graphs with another group to see if the other group can guess the shape of the coaster. The groups eagerly set to work.

In this vignette, Mrs. Jackson begins her instructional design by first becoming aware of the common types of texts in her current unit, namely equations, tables, and graphs. By reflecting on the many different purposes for reading and writing these texts, she notes a particular literacy that has been neglected in her teaching. This literacy is reading graphs that model real-world contexts to determine what is happening in those contexts. Note that Mrs. Shapiro, the literacy specialist, plays a key role in helping Mrs. Jackson recognize this neglected literacy by providing broadened definitions of text and literacy and encouraging her to look for texts and literacies in her classroom. When Mrs. Jackson teaches her students to read graphs, she engages them in a mathematical process they have been engaged in throughout the unit—the modeling of real-world situations with functions. She presents them with a text that she anticipates will lead to multiple readings, and then has them share and discuss these readings to identify how they are different and which one makes more sense. Students learn that in order for their reading to be correct, it must take into account how the quantities in the graph are related. To practice this new literacy, students continue in the ongoing mathematical process of modeling real-world contexts and write and read graphs of roller coasters.

CREATING AND SUSTAINING COLLABORATIONS BETWEEN LITERACY AND MATHEMATICS EDUCATORS

Stories abound about the resistance of mathematics teachers to engaging in discussions about literacy with literacy specialists. Despite these stories, we believe that collaborations between literacy and mathematics educators are possible. We also believe these collaborations are necessary, as they hold the potential to help educators transform mathematics classrooms and improve adolescents' learning. Much has been written recently about how to create and sustain collaborations in schools (Hargreaves, 2007; Roberts, 2007). Rather than summarize the general literature on teacher collaboration, we choose instead to draw upon our own work with literacy and content-area educators (Draper, Nokes, et al., in press) to suggest ways to create and sustain collaborations between literacy specialists and mathematics teachers.

Creating Collaborations

School literacy specialists are often charged with improving instruction within the school. Publications like *Standards for Middle and High School Literacy Coaches* (International Reading Association, 2006) suggest that literacy specialists adopt a coaching model of professional development. Because they have approached their work as coaches, literacy specialists generally enter the classrooms as experts or professionals with ideas to offer teachers to improve instruction. That is, they have taken up the responsibility to teach teachers and help them teach better. Moreover, literacy specialists have often focused their attention on the teachers most in need of assistance (e.g., novice teachers, teachers who struggle to teach well). However, the model of collaboration based on the expertise of literacy specialists as individuals with ideas to share with content-area teachers, especially struggling teachers, may need to be reconsidered, because literacy specialists may not have the requisite expertise with discipline-specific texts and literacies. Instead, we recommend that literacy educators enter into collaboration as learners rather than instructors, and that they seek out collaborations with competent, enthusiastic mathematics teachers.

First and foremost, literacy educators must enter any collaboration with mathematics teachers with a desire to learn. This requires a level of humility and curiosity on the part of literacy specialists. We suggest that literacy educators learn more about the texts and literacies of the discipline by asking mathematics teachers some of the questions that we discussed earlier in the chapter: What are the texts to be read and written during the lesson? What are the literacies—the specific ways that texts are to be read and written—that are required during the lesson? How might instruction be designed that would make explicit the texts and literacies and allow students to develop these literacies through participation in mathematical processes? Moreover, literacy educators must ask these questions with a genuine desire to learn rather than simply as teaching tools to aid the learning of the mathematics teachers with whom they are collaborating.

Our second recommendation for creating collaborations is for literacy specialists to collaborate with experienced, knowledgeable, and enthusiastic mathematics teachers. Rather than seek out the mathematics teacher who is struggling the most (e.g., novice teachers or teachers who find it difficult to work with adolescents who struggle), we suggest that literacy specialists seek out the best mathematics teacher in the building. Working with the best mathematics teachers they can find, literacy specialists will have the best source of information about literacy for mathematics classrooms. Moreover, once the collaboration is under way, both the literacy specialist and the collaborating mathematics teacher are in better positions to help struggling mathematics teachers. Literacy specialists should seek out mathematics teachers who engage regularly in professional development activities and strive to create mathematics classrooms in which students can construct computational fluency, conceptual understanding, and expertise in mathematical processes. These mathematics teachers are best prepared to help literacy educators identify the texts central to learning and doing mathematics and to describe the accompanying literacies. Ideally, these mathematics teachers are incorporating the recommendations from the national standards in their teaching practices. However, if not, part of the collaboration might include reading and discussing *Standards* documents (e.g., National Council of Teachers of Mathematics, 2000). Essentially, because literacy educators should be entering the collaboration as learners, they should seek out mathematics teachers who are prepared to teach.

Sustaining Collaborations

Once collaborations have begun, effort will be required to sustain them. Again, lists abound regarding the characteristics of enduring collaborations. We offer three ideas based on collaborations in which we have participated (Draper, Broomhead, Jensen, & Siebert, 2010). First, collaborators must work from a shared purpose. Second, collaborators must work from their individual strengths. Third, collaborators must seek ways to evaluate their work together.

Develop a Shared Purpose

Mathematics teachers and literacy educators may have goals for adolescent learners that seem at odds. For example, mathematics teachers want adolescents to learn mathematics and literacy specialists want adolescents to acquire a range of sophisticated literacies. In fact, mathematics teachers may often ignore literacy educators' recommendations because they perceive that literacy educators are interested in achieving literacy goals at the expense of content goals. When a broad definition of text is used to define literacy goals, however, these goals become compatible with the goals of mathematics educators. Consequently, we suggest starting off the collaboration with discussions of the broad definitions of text and literacy that we have offered in this chapter. Literacy and mathematics educators can then work from these definitions to get clear on their instructional goals and to find ways that their goals are complementary. As we have demonstrated in this chapter, achieving literacy goals has the potential to help adolescents achieve the mathematics learning goals and vice versa. Commitment and work to achieve these goals is difficult and crucial given the multiple, often high-stakes, demands placed on teachers and students.

Work from Collaborators' Strengths

Mathematics teachers and literacy educators must work from their own strengths and honor the strengths of their collaborators. Mathematics teachers have knowledge of mathematics and a knowledge, albeit often only tacit, of how to read and write the texts used to learn, communicate, and do mathematics. Moreover, mathematics teachers have expertise in teaching mathematics to adolescents. They often know what concepts will give adolescents difficulty and they have a sense of the typical misconceptions that adolescents develop when striving to learn mathematics. Literacy educators understand that each discipline, including mathematics, relies on its own texts and literacies. While literacy educators may have difficulty listing the texts and literacies particular to mathematics, they are in a position to work with mathematics teachers and help them identify the texts and literacies found in their mathematics classrooms by tapping into mathematics teachers' tacit literacy understanding. Moreover, literacy educators have knowledge of literacy instructional frameworks (e.g., before/during/after; critical literacy frameworks, etc.) and can offer these frameworks as starting points for designing literacy instruction for mathematical texts.

Evaluate Work Together

Finally, as literacy and mathematics teachers work together and design instruction to help adolescents learn and grow, they must take measures to ensure that the ideas they develop together are sound. There is a risk that the work of collaborators will fall short of collaboration. This happens when collaborators simply compromise with one another rather than do the hard work of talking themselves toward a solution that satisfies all the conditions specified by all the collaborators. It also happens when collaborators deceive themselves, and through a kind of collusion, accept ideas that fall short of the ideals they held to going into the collaboration. To prevent the possibility that literacy instruction for mathematics classrooms developed through collaborations between mathematics and literacy educators does not result from compromise or collusion, collaborators must evaluate their work together. Literacy and mathematics educators can ensure their work together is sound if they check it against *Standards* documents (e.g., National Council of Teachers of Mathematics, 2000) or make their work available to other mathematics education and literacy experts for review and feedback.

Ultimately, when literacy and mathematics educators work together to identify texts and literacies associated with learning and doing mathematics and design instruction that allows adolescents to learn mathematics and corresponding literacies, adolescents will be prepared to confront the wide range of texts they will encounter in their daily lives and throughout their careers. Indeed, we, like others, realize that adolescents face an increasingly complex world. We understand that in order for individuals to confront pressing social and technological problems and to devise solutions that promote human well-being, they will need to be armed with a wide range of knowledge and skills—including literacy and mathematics. Preparing adolescents to live in and make contributions to their neighborhoods, communities, and the greater society requires the commitment of teachers who are knowledgeable about their content (whether mathematics or literacy) who are willing to work together to create opportunities for adolescents to learn and grow, and who are willing to both listen to and question each other. The process of designing literacy instruction for mathematics classrooms through collaboration represents a great deal of work for both literacy specialists and mathematics teachers. We understand that literacy educators and mathematics teachers may be hesitant to invest time and energy in this endeavor. However, we believe the potential benefits to adolescents' mathematics and literacy learning make the effort worthwhile.

AUTHORS' NOTE

The authors contributed equally to the authorship of this chapter.

REFERENCES

Bean, T. W. (2000). Reading in the content areas: Social constructivist dimensions. In M. L. Kamil, P. B. Mosenthal, P. D. Pearson, & R. Barr (Eds.), *Handbook of reading research* (Vol. 3, pp. 629–654). Mahwah, NJ: Erlbaum.

Carnegie Council on Advancing Adolescent Literacy. (2010). *Time to act: An agenda for advancing adolescent literacy for college and career success.* New York: Carnegie Corporation of New York.

Carpenter, T. P., Franke, M. L., & Levi, L. (2003). *Thinking mathematically: Integrating arithmetic and algebra in elementary school.* Portsmouth, NH: Heinemann.

Draper, R. J., Broomhead, P., Jensen, A. P., & Siebert, D. (2010). Aims and criteria for collaboration in content-area classrooms. In R. J. Draper, P. Broomhead, A. P. Jensen, J. Nokes, & D. Siebert (Eds.), *(Re)imagining literacies for content-area classrooms* (pp. 1–19). New York: Teachers College Press.

Draper, R. J., Hall, K. M., Smith, L. K., & Siebert, D. (2005). What's more important—literacy or content? Confronting the literacy–content dualism. *Action in Teacher Education, 27*(2), 12–21.

Draper, R. J., Nokes, J., & Siebert, D. (2010). (Re)imagining collaborations for content-area literacy. In R. J. Draper, P. Broomhead, A. P. Jensen, J. Nokes,

& D. Siebert (Eds.), *(Re)imagining literacies for content-area classrooms* (pp. 159–171). New York: Teachers College Press.

Draper, R. J., & Siebert, D. (2004). Different goals, similar practices: Making sense of the mathematics and literacy instruction in a standards-based mathematics classroom. *American Educational Research Journal, 41*(4), 927–962.

Dugdale, S. (1993). Functions and graphs—Perspectives on student thinking. In T. A. Romberg, E. Fennema, & T. P. Carpenter (Eds.), *Integrating research on the graphical representation of functions* (pp. 101–130). Hillsdale, NJ: Erlbaum.

Fisher, D., & Ivey, G. (2005). Literacy and language as learning in content-area classes: A departure from "every teacher a teacher of reading." *Action in Teacher Education, 277*(2), 3–11.

Hargreaves, A. (2007). Sustainable professional learning communities. In L. Stoll & K. S. Louis (Eds.), *Professional learning communities: Divergence, depth and dilemmas* (pp. 181–195). London: Open University Press.

Hiebert, J., Carpenter, T. P., Fennema, E., Fuson, K. C., Wearne, D., Murray, H., et al. (1997). *Making sense: Teaching and learning mathematics with understanding.* Portsmouth, NH: Heinemann.

International Reading Association. (2006). Standards for middle and high school literacy coaches. Newark, DE: Author.

Jackson, S. (1948/2007). *The Lottery.* Logan, IA: Perfection Learning.

Matz, M. (1982). Towards a process model for high school algebra errors. In D. Sleeman & J. S. Brown (Eds.), *Intelligent tutoring systems* (pp. 25–50). New York: Academic Press.

National Council of Teachers of Mathematics. (1989). *Curriculum and evaluation standards for school mathematics.* Reston, VA: Author.

National Council of Teachers of Mathematics. (2000). *Principles and standards for school mathematics.* Reston, VA: Author.

National Research Council. (2001). *Adding it up: Helping children learn mathematics.* Washington, DC: National Academy Press.

Roberts, S. M. (2007). *Schools as professional learning communities: Collaborative activities and strategies for professional development.* Thousand Oaks, CA: Corwin Press.

Roth, W. M., & Bowen, G. M. (2001). Professionals read graphs: A semiotic analysis. *Journal for Research in Mathematics Education, 32*(2), 159–194.

Sfard, A. (2000). Symbolizing mathematical reality into being—Or how mathematical discourse and mathematical objects create each other. In P. Cobb, E. Yackel, & K. McClain (Eds.), *Symbolizing and communicating in mathematics classrooms: Perspectives on discourse, tools, and instructional design* (pp. 37–98). Mahwah, NJ: Erlbaum.

Siebert, D., & Draper, R. J. (2008). Why content-area literacy messages do not speak to mathematics teachers: A critical review of the literature. *Literacy Research and Instruction, 47*, 229–245.

Siebert, D., & Hendrickson, S. (2010). (Re)imagining literacies for mathematics classrooms. In R. J. Draper, P. Broomhead, A. P. Jensen, J. D. Nokes, & D. Siebert (Eds.), *(Re)imagining literacies for content-area classrooms* (pp. 40–53). New York: Teachers College Press.

Skemp, R. (1978). Relational understanding and instrumental understanding. *Arithmetic Teacher, 26*(3), 9–15.

Thompson, D. R., Kersaint, G., Richards, J. C., Hunsader, P. D., & Rubenstein, R. N. (2008). *Mathematical literacy: Helping students make meaning in the middle grades*. Portsmouth, NH: Heinemann.

8

Learning with Texts in History

Protocols for Reading and Practical Strategies

Bruce VanSledright

At their teacher's request, two eighth graders, Ayesha and Brad, sat poring over accounts of shootings in Boston in March of 1770. In reading these accounts, they were trying to figure out what had happened on that fateful day when a melee between British soldiers and Boston citizens resulted in the death of five of those citizens. It was early in the school year, and Ayesha and Brad had not studied the American Revolution period since fifth grade. Neither remembered much about what colonial separatists led by Samuel Adams called the Boston Massacre. In fact they did not remember much about the revolutionary period at all other than that the colonists won a war and gained independence from Great Britain. A review of the historical period was therefore important to their eighth-grade history studies.

In front of them lay four accounts. The first was a brief textbook rendition, three short paragraphs, in which an omnisciently voiced narrator explained that the melee erupted when a group of agitated Boston residents approached the Customs House, a repository of the king's tax receipts, and began demonstrating against British occupation of the colonial city. A group of red-coated British regulars, led by their Captain Thomas Preston, were dispatched from their barracks nearby to protect the Customs House and put down the demonstration. At some point, rocks and chunks of ice were hurled at the soldiers. The soldiers responded by raising their muskets and firing at the angry citizenry. Five of them lay dead or mortally wounded. The textbook's narrator portrayed the incident as a key flashpoint that would galvanize the American revolutionaries' cause and later help ignite the war between the colonists and the British, one in which the Americans eventually prevailed.

A second account came from Captain Preston himself. It was drawn from testimony he gave at a trial of the British soldiers following the incident. He insisted under oath that he had not given the order to fire, but rather he said just the opposite, commanding his troops not to fire their weapons. He pointed out how rowdy and taunting the Bostonians were, how dangerous and confusing the situation became, and how his troops were attacked with clubs and spoke shaves by the crowd while they were doing their duty protecting the Customs House.

The last two accounts of the incident were brief. They came from eyewitnesses. The first claimed to have been standing close by and distinctly heard Preston give the order to fire weapons. The second, also from a close observer, claimed that Preston had clearly said, "Do not fire." Both accounts also represented testimony offered at the trial of the British soldiers.

This mixed accounting both intrigued and puzzled Ayesha and Brad. Ayesha found it more intriguing than puzzling. Brad reacted the opposite way, repeatedly signaling his interest in answering the teacher's question about what happened, so that they could simply move on to the next activity. Ayesha wanted to ruminate, study, and press against the accounts as she searched for what she thought should be their best response. A quiet but somewhat heated discussion ensued between the two about how to proceed. It caused their teacher, Ms. White, to wander over to their clustered desks and sit beside them to listen in.

Brad insisted that the textbook account should trump the other accounts. That account contained all they needed to know. Besides, the text's main ideas were clear, he comprehended them rather easily, and the account was balanced and impartial and explained what happened without unhelpful sidebars or digressions. As Ms. White walked up, she could hear him saying to Ayesha that it was best to go with the textbook account because it offered the best explanation. He then read the textbook account aloud to Ayesha, emphasizing each word and stressing the straightforwardness of each explanatory sentence. He told Ayesha that he really did not read the other accounts very carefully because Preston's account in particular was too complicated and biased. Once he read the textbook version, he figured that that was all he needed to accomplish the task. Clear, concise, authoritative, easy to read, and correct. It was *the textbook* after all, and history textbooks were supposed to be correct. That's what his fifth-grade teacher had told him. Ms. White waited for Ayesha's response.

Ayesha refused to give in to Brad's textbook-as-authority argument. She began pointing out and reading lines from the other accounts that contradicted one another. She then pointed back to the textbook, again reading aloud and noting how the account there failed to fully answer the question "What happened?" She argued that it simply glossed over the significant problem of whether or not the troops were ordered to fire. She thought it significant because, from a historical point of view, if Preston had ordered his soldiers to fire, then, in effect, it was as if "they were like trying to start the war or something." On the other hand, if the citizens were the aggressors, the responsibility was on them.

She pointed out to Brad that, in Preston's testimony, he described how the Bostonians had taunted the soldiers, hit them with clubs, and challenged the soldiers to fire at them. Reading his detailed account enabled her to imagine the scene, the shouts, the pushing and shoving, the confusion, and the sound of musket fire. She was not at all sure that the soldiers were acting in more than simple self-defense when they shot into the unruly crowd. The other eyewitness accounts, she explained, were tricky too because they had not explained exactly how close they were to Captain Preston, nor had the witnesses revealed their sentiments—loyalist, patriot, or indifferent— toward British–American relations. She wanted to know before she trusted what each had claimed. In the end, her reading led her away from the textbook account and toward the detail of Preston's description. She was siding with his account. The shootings could be understood as self-defense. The angry crowd more than likely encouraged their unfortunate fate, perhaps as a sacrifice to further enflame colonial opinion against the British. She wasn't certain, but it seemed like a plausible story and she was sticking to it. Ms. White smiled wryly, got up, and told Ayesha and Brad to prepare to offer their interpretations to the class.

PROTOCOLS FOR READING HISTORY

Here we have two different protocols for reading history texts.[1] Of course, there are many different reading protocols possible in history. But these can suffice for the moment because they represent two rather distant and distinct poles on a continuum of ways of reading in history. They also represent a couple of fairly common adolescent reading practices, Brad's probably far more so than Ayesha's. I want to explore these two protocols for what they tell us about literacy practices both outside and inside a discipline (if I can put it that way) and what they can teach us about more or less satisfactory ones. I am working from an assumption that reading history texts is a pathway toward building deeper and more powerful understandings of the past. Such understandings, in turn, enable readers to make better sense of themselves because that knowing of the past helps at least partially situates identity within a historicized context. Situating sense of self (a text) within history (many texts) holds the potential to elide parochial tendencies and extend and sharpen one's self in relation to the world—an important accomplishment. Historical learning and the reading that enables it is good at that, perhaps more so than most subjects studied in school with the possible exception of the humanities, of which history might be thought of as one. Several other assumptions I am working from here also bear mentioning at the outset, for they help frame my analysis of Ayesha's and Brad's protocols and the lessons we can derive from it.

Following Robert Scholes (1989), I will maintain implicitly or explicitly throughout that all reading is intertextual (see also RAND Reading Study Group. 2002). Our text/story about the world and the single text that we may be reading at a given moment involves a trans-actional process. We cannot make sense of, say, a history text we are actually reading without already holding a text about the world and ourselves in that world in our head. The more unrelated the text in our head is to the history text we are reading at a given moment, the more challenging the reading process. Nonetheless, the text/story about the world and how it hangs together with the one we tell about and to our-selves regarding our place in that world (however nascent or limited) serves as a core building block for our encounters with other texts. It is all signs and signifiers, a transactional process that depends on language learned at an early, prereading stage. There, words (signs) begin to form and stand in for other things (signifieds) to which they purportedly refer. Words as stand-ins allow prereaders to build a story about the world and their place in it that later is augmented, changed, or modified as they begin to map words in spoken language to words on a page. Reading therefore is always already intertextual. Protocols for reading in history form out of this intertextuality. It can be loud, noisy, difficult, cumbersome, and challenging because the relationship of signs to signifieds (words to what they stand for) is a slippery, elusive one at best.

All texts can be construed as hypertexts at some level. Texts of whatever sort—Internet-based historical accounts, a teacher's lecture, a historical film or painting, Captain Thomas Preston's account of the Boston shootings—all invoke/display/note/refer to other texts as they proceed. Sometimes this occurs visibly and directly and other times more invisibly and indirectly. What demarcates some texts from others is their degree of hypertextuality. There are simply different levels of access to the other texts that a present text invokes (immediate or distal, direct or more indirect, both on a continuum). It is a matter of degree, not kind. The more immediate and/or direct the access, the more challenging the load because the reader has to engage in increased monitoring to attend to the task and ward off possible distractions the increased hypertex-tuality presents. This assumption is important for understanding that protocols of reading in history all depend to one degree or another on this hypertextuality, and more of it may not necessarily be better than less, but sometimes can be. In these senses, hypertextuality is a subspe-cies of intertextuality.

Finally, in history I am assuming that virtually all types of sign–signifier media need to be read to develop a deeper historical understanding. For example, a student needs to read a teacher's history lecture even if it is delivered only orally (i.e., sans the ubiquitous PowerPoint presentation, but if the lecture does include one, it is simply another text to be read). A historical painting and a pottery shard must be read, as well as photographs, Internet iconography, and mass culture symbols on billboards or boxes, wrappers or Web pages. A film with historical content also needs to be read, even if it is a silent film. In short, I am assuming here that reading in history involves a very broad definition, perhaps one bordering more on the idea of a multimodal literacy when we think of all the different types of texts that can be read for historical understanding to grow and deepen.

Brad's Protocol for History Reading

Brad is not happy with the cognitive noise that the four texts on the Boston shootings provoke. He seeks to reduce that noise by silencing three of the four texts he encounters. In a sense he is trying to escape the play of intertextuality because it makes him uncomfortable. To answer the historical question his teacher poses, he pursues the shortest route that he believes he can defend. We can surmise that the text in Brad's head about the nature of task indicates that the best solution to the question is a simple, clean, and straightforward one. That's one of the criteria Brad appears to possess that contributes to his reading protocol. But it is not the only one. He holds other texts in his head that serve to provide relational criteria that frame his protocol. One of the more obvious criteria is that history textbook texts are epistemologically superior to other types of history texts, allowing him to argue that the former should therefore trump and silence the latter. Based on his account, this criterion stems from a text in his head a former teacher helped him to create, one that declares—at least on Brad's reading of it—that all textbooks get the story right and therefore are the most believable. They are to be trusted on occasions such as this. They synthesize, organize, and convey the past better.

Brad also works from a text in his head that tells him a more easily comprehended text is preferable to one that is complex and more difficult to decipher. A history text that requires less comprehension monitoring, less onerous strategy use, is superior. And then there is the issue of reporting bias. For Brad, the textbook text remains superlative on this matter, the omniscient author accomplishing the feat of eliminating bias, appearing detached, and operating as a mere chronicler of what actually happened might, all while providing an ostensibly unmediated conduit between past and present. Brad appreciates this. Preston's text (as well as the others) fails on this criterion, one that functions quite powerfully within his protocol for reading history.

A less visible set of criteria is embedded in who Brad thinks he is, the story he tells himself about who he has become. To the extent that Brad is a white American of European immigrant stock, of Anglo origin in particular, born of upper-middle-class parents, he is predisposed to develop certain protocols for reading history, and their concomitant evaluative criteria, that would not necessarily be fully shared by African American Ayesha, who descends from southern slaves and was born of working-class parents. The textbook's text of America, a nation-building commemorative of constant progress toward achieving its founding (Anglo fathers') ideals, with a subtext that suggests it has come very, very close, coheres nicely with the story Brad likely tells about himself, one learned at home and in his community, and reinforced in school and by the many texts of mass culture.

Preston's account of the Boston shootings tends to lay blame at the feet of an angry mob of Bostonians who initiated an assault and created a massively complex and threatening scenario on those Boston streets. His text could be construed by Brad to be anti-American and so therefore too deeply biased to be believable. If Brad is to choose bias (i.e., present versus absent) as a key criterion in his reading protocol (and he does), he wants to select one that aligns with his own text of what it means to be an American. That the bias of his selection (the textbook's text) also comes replete with an omniscient author's ostensibly transparent, easily comprehendible sign–signified relationships means that two protocol criteria can be wedded. This wedding provides Brad with a powerful protocol for reading in history, one that leads him directly from the textbook's account to his answer to Ms. White's question. But is his answer good enough? Does it allow him to deepen his historical understanding, to stretch the text he tells about himself, to develop a less parochial reading protocol, and to learn better management of the relentless bombardment of the hypertextual, intertextual noise? I will return to these questions in a moment.

Ayesha's Protocol

Ayesha appears to be more welcome to the intertextual noise she encounters in this historical exercise. She embraces the texts, close to the full intertextual field available to her. She seems to enjoy the play of ideas and accountings. This play increases the comprehension and monitoring load and challenges her to extend the range of reading strategies at her disposal. Whereas Brad works from a criterion that calls for accepting the account that sounds the most authoritative, Ayesha opts for a criterion that centers on accepting what makes most sense given her analysis of all the accounts within her reading range. Brad tries to block out the noise. Ayesha uses it to her advantage. She digs in; Brad tries to avoid doing so. Ayesha draws on the noise to get greater purchase on a range of ways of thinking about how this confusing episode in American history could get sorted out if one wanted to better understand what happened. Without ever saying so, she appears to be working from a text in her head that says that confusing incidents will, by definition, generate confusing and ultimately contradictory accountings. To get to the bottom of the matter—if there is a bottom—a reading protocol ought to plumb the depths of the available accounts.

Ayesha's protocol then appears to work off a criterion that effectively says, "Wait to form a final judgment until you have read all the relevant historical stuff you can attend to with your eyes. Each new reading might surprise you." She welcomes the investigative challenge. It piques her interest and her engagement propels her forward. She finds the accounts perplexing and difficult to read, but she engages them nonetheless. Ayesha refuses to give in to the seductive desire to declare the textbook account the one authoritative source that arbitrates against all other types of texts.

We can surmise that Ayesha's protocol operates with additional criteria. One of these could be framed as evidence, or perhaps more accurately, preponderance of evidence. That is, her protocol contains the idea that in order to answer a historical question, a reader needs to assess the status of the array of accounts for the evidence they might contain that can actually address that question. A reader cannot assume that if a text sounds authoritative it should therefore rise to the top epistemologically. Put a different way, authoritative-sounding texts do not necessarily get it right. Words are slippery and can be used in different ways to say very different things. Accounts all need to be read carefully for the evidence they might contain, evidence that can be brought to bear on the question one is asking. And they need to be read intertextually, up against other texts. One arrives at an answer to a historical question by evaluating all the textual accountings and begins assembling the evidence in a way that addresses a further question: what does the preponderance of evidence say across accounts (texts)? She chooses Preston's account for just this reason. It best explains the circumstances, context, and actors' behaviors once all other accounts are so assessed.

Ayesha also appears to be working from the idea that, given the complex and confusing context, readers could expect accounts to disagree and be more or less coherent. Perhaps experiences with disagreeable friends and/or on a school playground have helped her to see that when something compelling happens, such as a schoolyard fight, everyone seems to have a different way of explaining who started it, why, and who was at fault. Partisanship (or Brad's idea of bias) can enter in because people hold different affinities for the parties involved (a subtext). But that's simply to be expected. Good readers need to be able to sort through the effect of those different affinities on how people arrive at the stories they tell about what happened. Account bias is not something that can be eliminated. People hold different perspectives for a host of different reasons. Even the authoritative-sounding textbook harbors its own sets of biases or perspectives. Ayesha seems to be saying that protocols for reading history need to operate with that in mind, to establish these perspectives and sort their influences as one builds up an idea of evidence preponderance. Accounts rise or fall in epistemological status by virtue of what (partisan) perspectives they contain and how they are wielded in the face of other (partisan) accountings. It may be the case that Ayesha is working from the criterion that eyewitness accounts are better than, say, secondary accounts, because eyewitnesses were there. However, we cannot say for sure; she doesn't tell us.

Some protocols for reading history contain a criterion that works off the idea that a reader can arrive at an answer to a question such as "What happened here?" by resorting to a type of cut-and-paste operation. That is, the reader assembles an interpretation by fitting together "the best elements" of multiple accounts. Ayesha shows little interest in doing this. We might assume that she's learned somewhere that "the best elements" are difficult to divine. Arriving at a defensible answer to a question by this means requires possessing more solid criteria for determining those elements than she apparently has been able to find. She prefers to rely on the criterion of evidence preponderance vis-à-vis situational context, which does not involve quite the same reading protocol as simple cutting and pasting.

Ayesha's protocol for history reading contains at least a rudimentary sense of another criterion—the incident's significance. Understanding better why and by whose orders (if any) the soldiers fired on the Bostonians helps readers make sense of the larger, more significant issue of the role the incident played in fueling increased animosity between colonists and their red-coated British occupiers, animosity that contributed to the onset of the American Revolutionary War. The broader sociopolitical context is important to historical understanding. At a minimum, Ayesha appears to sense this and it forms a part of her protocol for reading. Significance functions as yet another criterion that guides her protocol. It works in her effort to challenge Brad's reading protocol and his choice of allowing the textbook account to trump the other texts. As she notes, the textbook really never fully answers the question "What happened here?" because it does not say for whether blame for the deaths of the Bostonians was justified, and, if so, on the basis of what evidence. The textbook appears to assume that the soldiers were at fault, so therefore Samuel Adams, as a revolutionary patriot, was right to use the incident to enflame public opinion against Great Britain. Ayesha seems to sense that the (partisan?) perspective of the textbook author leaks through, despite Brad's claim to its detached, objective rendering.

Finally, the story or text African American Ayesha tells about herself and carries in her head no doubt shapes her history-reading protocol. In what ways, we cannot be sure. However, we can speculate that, being a descendant of slaves and a child of an American history plagued by unfortunate ethnoracial turmoil of which her forefathers and -mothers bore the brunt, it must bear on the text she tells herself about who she is and where she comes from. Ayesha's history-reading protocol, the one shaped by this self-text, may well predispose her to be more skeptical of accepting the textbook accounting at face value. The texts of her ancestors' lives were not blessed by unalloyed progress of the sort that the textbook makes primordially thematic.

We can surmise that her self-text comes with criteria that require more careful readings of the past and more careful attention to subtexts, words that imply rather than state directly. Her self-text, understandably, appears wary of authoritative-sounding accounts because such accounts, particularly those generated by dominant white culture, seemed to contain self-interested agendas (and their subtexts) that have not always benefited people who shared her skin color, at least not in the United States. As a middle-school student, Ayesha may not be able to articulate such matters this way. But we would be remiss in not at least speculating on how her working-class African American self-text shapes her reading protocols in ways that upper-middle-class, Anglo-American Brad's do not (for more on how self-texts shape reading protocols, see Epstein, 2009, and Salinas & Sullivan, 2007, for example).

Reading Protocols in the Discipline of History

Research and theorizing over the last several decades have allowed scholars to begin mapping how disciplinary experts in the domain of history read as part of the way they practice deepening their understandings of the past.[2] For educators, among whom I count myself, this research and theoretical enterprise is fortunate. It is probably fair to ask why.

The argument might go something along these lines (for greater detail on this argument, see VanSledright, 2011): If history educators are interested in growing and deepening their students' historical understandings for all the reasons noted in the foregoing, then it would help to have some targets that they could teach their students to attain. Where to find those targets? To answer this question we need to ask: Who epitomizes those with the greatest depth of historical understanding and how did they get there? The short answer to the first half of the question would be the experts, historians in this case. Therefore, it makes good sense to study what they do, and in particular how they read, in an effort to distill their reading protocols. If those protocols help them develop deep understandings of the past, then knowing what those protocols consist of would assist educators in getting purchase on some targets for students. At this point, researchers have provided a reasonably clear initial grasp of these experts' reading protocols (for more, see Wineburg, 2001). Summarizing them here will make it possible to see how far along Brad and Ayesha are in acquiring enough expertise in their reading protocols to obtain deeper historical understandings. It will also help educators think about how to teach them more sophisticated reading protocols in order to move them forward.

Historians appear to work from some very carefully honed reading protocols. These protocols are replete with customized criteria, many of them imbued with particular epistemological anchors. That is, these experts frame their protocols with a sense that texts from the past can all contribute to understanding in different ways. There is no single, definitive text that reduces to Truth, with a capital *T*, none that anchors meaning once and for all. One cannot silence intertextual, hypertextual noise by finding one authoritative text. To believe that one can is an illusion, a chimera.

Even the synthetic texts of understanding that experts produce by engaging the past and carefully exercising deeply skilled reading protocols cannot diminish the noise. The texts that these experts construct only add to the intertextual, hypertextual racket. And on it goes. Understanding the past and the texts that emanate from it never ceases. It is an ongoing interpretive project filled with almost endless opportunities for conversation. Almost anyone who can read can participate, even middle school students like Brad and Ayesha. What distinguishes novices such as these two from those more expert is the quality and quantity of criteria for reading, understanding, and producing new conversations (new texts) that emerge from their protocols. In short, deep understanding depends on criteria for reading and producing new texts. New texts (e.g., Brad's and Ayesha's stories of what happened during the Boston shootings) rise and fall in epistemological status in direct relationship to the nature of how these criteria and understandings can be and are deployed.

Decoding and comprehending texts from the past is the sine qua non of initial understanding. Without the capacity to decode or comprehend a text, initial levels of meaning making cannot be achieved. Here, all the research work on strategies for decoding and text-comprehension success come into play. I lack the space here to review all this work, and the task ahead in laying out expert reading protocols in history requires that I push on to sort through the complex strategies and criteria that distinguish those discipline-specific protocols. Suffice it to say that if educators are confronting adolescent readers who have difficulty decoding and comprehending text, consulting the research work, say, that outlines comprehension-monitoring strategies would be quite valuable. The first several chapters of this book might also be useful.[3]

However, it is important to note that, in history at least, comprehension, say, of the main ideas in a history textbook passage on the Boston shootings is not necessarily a prerequisite for fully understanding the incident, nor is it a requirement. Historical understanding as I am describing it here results from the application of intertextual reading protocols. Contrary to common belief, understanding does not depend on *first* having comprehended the textbook. A reader such as Brad or Ayesha could be taught to understand the Boston shootings by learning to comprehend a number of eyewitness accounts and then comparing and contrasting them. The textbook would only be yet another account. To comprehend it does not guarantee understanding and, as I will labor to show, may actually impede it.

Reading protocols in history indicate considerable tolerance for inter/hypertextual noise among those who possess expertise. Understanding the past depends on the capacity to seek out and carefully consume multiple texts on a particular subject. If anything, more texts from the past are better than fewer, although in trying to understand certain periods in history or specific incidents few texts may be available, either in texts of the period itself or in synthetic texts produced by earlier investigators.

The available texts must be carefully read, synthesized, analyzed, and intertextually evaluated for the ideas they contain that can lead to deeper understanding of a historical question(s) being pursued. Accounts from the past, experts reason, are likely to be better or worse at answering questions because many, if not all, of them were never produced to answer the questions a current reader is asking. Determining worse from better requires criteria. The key criterion here is the concept of evidence and its teammate, preponderance of evidence. These criteria assume prominence only in relation to a question a reader is trying to address. Armed with a question(s), a reader can exercise a protocol that effectively says, does this text (account) provide evidence that addresses my question, and if so, what is that evidence? Once accounts that may speak to the question have all been read and the reader begins to build incident models (see Ayesha's reading of Preston), the criterion of evidence preponderance takes over. Intertextual synthesis and evaluation are crucial here. How do these accounts stack up?

To help answer that question, experts assess the perspective of the authors of the accounts. In order to facilitate that type of assessment, they identify the type of account (a newspaper article, a painting, a wiki, poster, cartoon, diary, etc.) and attribute it to one or more authors whom the expert attempts to locate in time and temporal space, thus aiding in contextualization and mental modeling.[4] Texts and contexts are inseparable. They use identifications and attributions to gauge the nature of the subtexts an account might contain (e.g., How are words used? Does the author have an agenda, and if so, what might it be?). This helps get purchase on the reliability of the accounts in addressing the question(s) an investigator is asking (VanSledright & Afflerbach, 2005). It allows her to corroborate evidence in and across accounts, to see how things stack up.

A degree of precision in exercising this type of reading protocol is a necessary criterion here. However, precision is often elusive because the accounts can present conflicting evidence. Judgment becomes crucial but, expert judgment is difficult to teach. Expert historians frequently handle the exercise of judgment through a tribunal of peers. That is, readers become authors, offering up interpretations of the past to other like-minded readers. They therefore open their reading protocols to critique by these others.[5] Critique sharpens future reading protocols in text-author-text dialectics. Many experts would likely agree that, given the fluidity characteristic of this terrain and the absence of outside texts/ authors that authoritatively trump all other texts/authors, there are only (1) more or less powerful criteria, (2) more or less satisfactory reading protocols in history, and (3) ongoing arguments about them. This is about as good as it gets.[6] Yet, history and building understandings of the past proceed every day in spite of such limitations.

Organizing ideas such as significance, causation, progress/decline, and change/continuity also serve as criteria that guide experts' reading protocols (see Lee, 2005; Seixas, 1996; VanSledright, 2011). These ideas are rooted in the expert judgments readers exercise as they read. For example, the crucial questions that frame the reading task are formed from a text (or sometimes multiple texts) that an expert holds in his or her head about what is historically significant, what constitutes progress and/or decline, change and/or continuity. These texts are formed from prior exercises of history-specific reading protocols and earlier questions and by developing synthetic understandings of the past (more texts). These ideas take time to build, and much reading and investigation. And as I just observed, experts have been known to quibble among themselves about how they are exercised (e.g., Finlay, 1988; Davis, 1988). Such is the nature of judgment. Advanced understanding, however, is typically connected to advanced judgment, which in turn depends on advanced reading and the sorts of reading protocols described in the foregoing.

Finally, expert reading protocols in history are characterized by the exercise of contextualization. Skilled history readers attempt to assess and judge the words and subtexts of an author from the past in terms of that author's temporal position in the world at the time he or she created the text. Making claims about what an author meant by judging that meaning in relationship, say, to current normative standards is a form of presentism and, as a practice, is eschewed by expert history readers. Figure 8.1 summarizes many of the characteristics, assumptions, and strategies that describe expert reading protocols in history.

Discipline-specific practice sharpens reading protocols. Without practice, reading protocols stagnate or simply do not develop in the first place. Arrested development and stagnation can create cognitive impasses for readers that keep them from deepening their understandings. Research studies in school history education have documented many instances of stagnant protocols among learners. A number of impasses appear to occur as a consequence of the way readers are taught to develop reading protocols in school (see note 3).

Assessing Brad's and Ayesha's Reading Protocols

So how do Brad's and Ayesha's reading protocols in history measure up to what the experts do? Before attending to this question, it is important to point out that Brad and Ayesha are novice readers and can hardly be held to account for their lack of expertise. They are still developing their reading-protocol repertoire. If we agree that it is deeper historical understandings that we are after in school history classes, for example, then the goal of that development would be to grow and sharpen their history-specific reading protocols. It is not to make them into little historians. Rather, it might be better to think of this in the aforementioned way: Deepened historical understanding is a gateway to (1) deeper self understanding, (2) greater tolerance for intertextual noise, (3) greater tolerance and respect for difference and ambiguity, and (4) increased capacity for reading a complex, inter/hypertextual world. History, if taught well, is a common school subject that can be pressed into the service of these goals. Brad and Ayesha deserve that much from their education.

Brad's discomfort with the intertextual noise of the multiple texts on the shootings in Boston in 1770 works against him. It constrains his efforts to deepen understanding. Attempting to silence that noise by

Epistemic Framework and Reader Assumptions

- It is all texts all the way down.
- Texts come in many different forms (paintings and pottery shards, wikis and Web pages, synthetic texts and original accounts, trial testimonies and personal diaries).
- Textual meaning making in history is slippery and elusive (e.g., a historical text's "main idea/s" can be different for different readers).
- No text is available that will anchor historical meaning once and for all.
- Texts are only more or less useful in creating meaning and enhancing historical understanding.
- Deepening understanding of the past depends on asking questions and investigating and interrogating available texts; more texts are typically better than fewer.
- Reading in history is always already intertextual and hypertextual (in varying degrees).
- The sharper the judgment criteria a reader holds (e.g., what counts as evidence in answering a question), the more powerful and skilled the reading protocol.
- Everyday judgment criteria (e.g., if it sounds convincing, it probably is; you cannot trust the text because it's biased) are often serially unproductive in making meaning in history.
- Powerful reading protocols in history, therefore, must be explicitly taught and learned; they do not simply emerge over time with age or maturation.

Organizing Concepts and Ideas (key examples)

- Historical significance
- Continuity/change
- Decline/progress
- Causation (multiple)
- Human agency
- Evidence/preponderance of evidence
- Historical contextualization

Reading Strategies

- Asking rich, significant historical questions
- Identification and attribution of texts
- Assessing author perspective (involves reading for author subtext linked to context)
- Corroboration of evidence across texts to facilitate judgments about preponderance
- Judging the reliability of different accounts in relation to addressing a historical question
- Making judgments within the confines of the historical context in question
- Exercising historical imagination to fill in evidentiary gaps (constrained by historical contextualization) through a process of mental modeling
- Building a variety of differing mental incident/thought models
- Continual refining and revising of understandings/interpretations
- Metacognitive awareness of the role a reader's text of the world (e.g., positionality) plays in making meaning from historical texts under analysis (to the extent that this is possible)

FIGURE 8.1. Characteristics of expert reading protocols in History.

disregarding additional accounts of the shootings creates a situation in which meaning making is held hostage to the textbook account. And that account appears inadequate for answering Ms. White's historical question. In effect, Brad's belief (the text in his head) that the textbook should hold the highest epistemological value creates a cognitive impasse for him. His text and the way it factors into his reading protocol block him from considering the additional evidence the extra accounts supply. He is therefore unable to manage the conflicting testimonies presented by the additional firsthand reports and turns them away.[7]

If history can be thought of as an argument about what the past means based on a perplexing array of possible evidence for making claims, Brad is unable to do history. He is stuck. History stops for him the moment he exercises this one-right-text criterion in his reading protocol. As he continues to encounter varying ways of making sense of the past via different texts and contradictory arguments, his thinking will be handcuffed by his reading protocol. His understanding of the past cannot deepen as a consequence, and what he could learn from future experiences in history class will suffer. If Ms. White is listening carefully to Brad and keenly observing his reading protocol in operation, she will find that she has much work to do with him if she wishes to unstick his cognitive impasses.

Sometimes when sharp history teachers document and then succeed in freeing up readers such as Brad, those readers move quickly to that aforementioned cut-and-paste operation. It's as though these readers discover that they now have license to use all the accounts. All are equally biased by various author opinions (Brad is quick to remark on the bias problem), so all have similar (identical?) epistemological value (i.e., are equally reliable or unreliable, as the case may be). As I noted, readers then attempt to "select out the best" of each account and paste the pieces together synthetically. Done. Understanding achieved. On closer analysis of such reading protocols, equally sharp teachers will notice that these cutters and pasters lack criteria for "selecting the best." When pressed on this point, these readers frequently say things such as "Well, everything is biased, so I just picked out what I thought worked from each account and fitted it together. And hey, if everything is just someone's opinion about what happened, I'm entitled to my opinion too. And this is it, my cut-'n-pasted text." Brad might be poised to make this his next move, especially if Ms. White continues putting him in classroom situations where he has to learn to deal with history's inter/hyertextual noisiness.

In some ways, we might argue that this is a step forward because now such readers are at least drawing on more, rather than fewer, texts. They are no longer hostage to one author's text, one author's position, one author's referential illusion that his or her account maps directly onto (signs of) the event in question (the signified) without distortion or mediation. The reader has moved closer to being able to tolerate ambiguity and difference and form the capacity to manage inter/hypertextual clamor. However, closer inspection will reveal that, absent criteria such as for reading and assessing subtext, judging reliability and gauging the sort of evidence various accounts supply on the way toward making sense of its preponderance, will lead this reader into yet another impasse. History will stop because the reader has no means of distinguishing more from less acceptable synthetic arguments about what events mean, because all accounts are equally biased and so therefore equally believable, or unbelievable. How does a reader then choose what to believe and therefore what to understand? To help them with this problem, smart teachers must provide such readers with more powerful strategies and especially criteria to add to their reading protocols.

Ayesha's reading protocol is considerably closer to achieving this more expert status, suffused with strong criteria. She also, though, has some distance to travel. She welcomes the inter/hypertextual noise and appears to desire it, cultivate it, and use some of it to her advantage. We can see the appearance of a nascent sense of the idea of evidence and evidence preponderance. She is also sensitive to perspective and, without saying so, perhaps to the idea of author subtexts that slip and slide almost invisibly through their words. She is at least starting to ask questions about subtextual possibilities. This is fueled by her perhaps inchoate capability of reading the texts in terms of the historical contexts in which they were created. She is at least less apt to wrench the texts she reads out of their historical context. She wants to read those words on their own historical terms because she is using all the texts to contemplate possible incident models.

Given the illustration, much of what Ayesha is thinking about as she exercises her reading protocol is unavailable to us. However, we can speculate nonetheless, much as a history teacher might do on hearing Ayesha talk about the consequences of deploying her reading protocol. Moving Ayesha forward would likely first entail questioning exactly how she got to her faith in the Preston account (is she working from an evidence-based mental model of what happened in Boston in 1770?), how she dealt with the evidence the other accounts supplied, and what she did with the "disconfirming" evidence. These sorts of questions might open up elements of her reading protocol for her to examine. She could then gauge their power. If she recognized some limits in her protocol, Ms. White could assist her in sharpening her judgment criteria. To that end, Ayesha could begin growing her own metacognitive awareness about the relationships among the text(s) in her head, those she reads, and the reading protocols on which she draws.

Figure 8.2 sketches out some judgment-criteria comparisons that appear to be at work in Brad's, Ayesha's, and the experts' reading protocols. Effectively, they form a continuum from less to more powerful (left to right). The exercise requires some conjectural logic concerning Brad and Ayesha because they are not present to fully confirm or deny the existence of these criteria in their protocols. In that sense, the depiction operates as illustrative rather than definitive. As Figure 8.2 suggests even at a cursory glance, the criteria that suffuse experts' reading protocols are far more well developed than those of Brad and Ayesha. This points to the important role history teachers must play in growing their adolescents' reading protocols and the criteria that give them power, assuming of course that the goal is to tilt in the direction of reading expertise as a means of deepening historical understanding.

WEAK READING PROTOCOLS AND JUDGMENT CRITERIA IN HISTORY AND THEIR CONSEQUENCES

A key point here is realizing the wisdom of Ms. White in her design of this investigative exercise into the shootings in Boston. By providing students with cooperative opportunities to read multiple history texts, some of which are in conflict with one another (more often than not the case in history), she creates a classroom context in which she can hear her students' reading protocols at work. Such exercises are nothing like conducting round-robin exercises in reading paragraphs from the textbook for example. More subtly, by structuring this reading task as she has, Ms. White conveys the idea that history is about a struggle to make meaning from the *residua* of the past, that it's about crafting new interpretive texts, and making evidenced-based and judgment-rationalized arguments to defend those new texts. Ms. White therefore aligns her classroom learning opportunities more tightly with the sort of practices that make historians more expert readers. If she continues to push on this approach and has success reshaping her students' history-reading protocols and unsticking impasses that challenge readers like Brad (as slow and gradual a process as that might be), her students will reap the powerful rewards mentioned earlier.

In school, we simply do not teach history as Ms. White does very much (see Cuban, 1991). Studies of history teaching repeatedly indicate that textbooks and the narratives they relay are intentionally or otherwise given aerial epistemological status. Teacher talk often serves to reify the textbook account. The questions teachers frequently ask already have predetermined, correct answers that are arbitrated by the textbook's story line. Supplemental materials such as films, reading guides,

Brad	Ayesha	Experts
• Textual realism • Seeing is believing, or the more authoritative it sounds, the more believable it is • Words in an authoritative-sounding text map directly onto the world without mediation • Authoritative texts trump all others (they are bias free) • Simplicity and directness is best • Detachment and an omniscient tone signal truth • Texts that display bias are untrustworthy and must be discarded • Conflicting texts indicate presence of bias • Fact can be easily separated from opinion; facts are best—opinions are to be discarded as untrustworthy • Read for facts; a text that contains the most facts is best	• Nascent textual skepticism • More texts help create a better picture/mental model • Available texts must all be considered • Firsthand accounts are likely the best for answering questions; the author was there • Texts help present evidence for answering historical questions; the more evidence the better • Expect texts/authors to disagree; people read things differently • Perhaps solve the perspective–conflict problem through a cut-paste process, and/or … • Empathize with authors to understand perspective and create a possible mental model of "what happened" • Base interpretation (understanding) on what makes most sense after exercising empathy and evidence gathering; use the process to figure out believability	• Textual skepticism (texts do not necessarily mean what they say) • Historical texts all contain perspectives that must be assessed; authors will disagree • Assessment depends on (1) questions being asked, (2) author positionality, (3) investigator positionality, (4) context in which texts were created, (5) subtext • Determining the reliability of texts for developing interpretations depends on (1) assessing them (as above), (2) amassing a sense of evidence they contain (or do not), (3) assembling evidence preponderance by reading intertextually, (4) attempting to fill in gaps in evidence through context-constrained imagination • Texts cannot be removed from the context in which they were produced without creating a presentism threat • Judgments are always more or less defensible, even based on careful exercise of the foregoing criteria • Criteria are necessary but perhaps never sufficient to ground interpretations once and for all—be prepared to revise understanding

FIGURE 8.2. Comparisons of judgment criteria in reading protocols.

and worksheets are designed to do the same. If additional accounts are used, they are employed to provide additional information to support the official story (Hicks, Doolittle, & Lee, 2004). School history curricula and history tests—standardized and otherwise, high stakes or low—typically reinforce and sanction that story (see the opening chapters in Grant, 2006).

The textbook narrative serves fundamentally as a socializing agent (e.g., VanSledright, 2008). Ostensibly, it schools children and adolescents (and immigrants) into the one right story of America. It inculcates in recipients what it means to correctly say "we" when referring to being an American. That narrative symbolically carries what Gunnar Myrdal once called the American creed (see Schlesinger, 1991). To recite the creed, to believe it and own it, is to claim membership in America. Therefore, pledging allegiance to the creed and being able to cite at least the rough contours of the narrative that gives that creed substance constitute powerful cultural capital. Or so the argument goes.

Some have claimed that American history classrooms operate on the principle of indoctrination rather than education (see different scholars' analyses in VanSledright, 2008). Ms. White appears to be opting more for the latter. Doing so challenges the reading protocol privileged and sanctioned by the typical American history curriculum. It would be fair to wonder why she does this, especially in the face of powerful policy pressures that bless the reading protocols of students such as Brad and use it as a corrective for Ayesha's.

Teaching Powerful History-Reading Protocols

Ms. White has read the research in history education (e.g., Barton, 2008; VanSledright & Limon, 2006; Voss, 1998; Wineburg, 2001). Gradually, she became convinced that the goal of socializing the young into command of the quintessential story of America in order to shape their budding national identities may be necessary, but it was hardly sufficient to declare that her charges had obtained an education in American history. She came to believe that she could help her students understand the official nation-state story line while simultaneously deepening that understanding through the cultivation of more powerful history-specific reading protocols. She was convinced that, in a complex inter/hypertextual world, her students would inevitably encounter challenges to the official story line from any number of angles. She wanted them to be prepared to meet those challenges head on. She could not countenance letting students leave her classroom with the impression that it was acceptable to be slaves to a single text.

Ms. White also knew that because her socioeconomically and ethnoracially diverse students arrived in her classroom already possessing competing versions (texts in their heads) of what it means to be an American that would intersect with the official version (recall again the differences between Brad and Ayesha), the best pedagogical strategy was to confront that terrain openly. She took to heart something she once read by historian Michael Frisch (1989), who had studied the degree to which his college freshmen had appropriated the official nation-state story line and the roles of its putative heroes and heroines. After 10 years of data collection from which he discovered that his students remembered a few things from their K–12 history-course experiences but forgot many others, Frisch concluded that "[history] students cannot be bullied into attention or retention; that [type of] authoritarian cultural intimidation is likely to be met with further and more rapid retreat" (p. 1154). Ms. White's own teaching experiences had proven Frisch quite astute.

What to do? Ms. White reframed her approach. She began teaching American history less as a collection of facts and details wrapped up in a narrative bound between hard covers and more as a running argument about what those details meant. She gave up the idea that she could use the textbook account to silence the inter/hypertextual noise surrounding different conceptions about how to define what it is to be an American. For her classroom, understanding American history—making sense of it deeply—became an exercise in reading the multitude of varying arguments (texts) that served as inter/hypertextual underbelly of those conceptions, and noting how they were built up and brought down and changed over time. Instead of focusing on preconceived answers, Ms. White began pursuing questions with her students: What happened in Boston on that fateful evening in early March 1770. What did it mean? Why did American colonist Samuel Adams call it the "Boston Massacre"? Was it a massacre? If not, what did he hope to gain by spinning it that way? How did the British view the incident? Did Captain Preston give the order to fire? If not, why did his troops fire anyway?

In keeping with the way she understood what often happens among the historian experts, she provided her students with many texts, many different accounts that would allow them to puzzle over those questions and learn to sharpen their own sense-making capabilities, construct their own texts—ones that might temper, contextualize, leaven, expand—and reframe the ones they already held in their heads. By her lights, that was deepening their historical understanding, and in turn their self-understanding.

Of course, doing so required that if she was turning over a good measure of interpretive judgment and license to her students, she had to exercise her pedagogical responsibility by arming them with reading strategies and judgment criteria that would be sufficient to enable sound reasoning and result in carefully considered conclusions. She drew from the research literature on expertise to shape her approach to enhancing her charges' history-specific reading protocols (Figure 8.2, right column). She stopped insisting on having her students find the text's one main idea, pursuing the circular exercise of separating fact from opinion, and using the terms *bias* and *biased texts* to dismiss accounts that differed from the official version. She stopped intentionally or inadvertently encouraging her students to think that the textbook could trump other texts, as well as necessarily the one in their own heads. She ended talk of getting the correct answer. And she ceased asking questions for which she thought she already held the best answer.

Instead, she began exemplifying what it means to be a more expert reader in history. She modeled what she was after: reading closely with a historical question in mind; suspending judgment until as many texts as were available could be considered;[8] building ideas gradually; using organizing concepts to stitch those ideas together; identifying, attributing, and assessing the perspective of each text's author(s); (as opposed to bias because as it turned out, all texts are biased) reading for subtext while evaluating a text's reliability; building a sense of the evidence based on the way it preponderates; and the like. As she went, she began to shape her students' judgment criteria. For example, she taught them that an interpretation is justified on the basis of how evidence is employed in defending it, that some interpretations are better supported and so therefore are more justified (believable) than others. But just because a history text sounds authoritative does not mean that it is. It is all texts all the way down, and readers need to be constantly vigilant in the way they read and assess them. A little textual skepticism is a good thing. It aids the process of deepening historical understanding and helps prevent cognitive impasses that arise from weak reading protocols (for more on teaching history as Ms. White does, see VanSledright, 2011).

Does Ms. White get it right? Is this how reading in history needs to be taught? At this point, we might say yes. However, additional research work is needed to provide Ms. White with even greater purchase on the pedagogical moves she could make that would propel her students even farther forward in making sense not only of history, but also of themselves and the complex worlds they inhabit. So what might this additional research entail?

NEW HISTORY-READING RESEARCH PROTOCOLS

One of the key difficulties researchers face is finding ways to adequately map the landscape that separates the history-reading protocols of novices such as Brad and Ayesha and the experts whose protocols enhance their understandings. It is one thing to study how Brad and Ayesha read and then descriptively compare it to what experts do. Some of this work has been done, and of course, Brad and Ayesha are found wanting by the comparison. It is quite another to figure out why, say, Brad reads the ways he does to trace the sources of his reading protocols, and then figure out what pedagogical strategies and moves are necessary to shift him, first, away from what he is comfortable doing, and second, toward more powerful protocols that will more deeply cultivate his historical understandings. As I have noted, we have learned a number of things from the research on what it means to learn history and on the reading protocols that may assist in it. However, to date, the landscape from novice approaches to expertise has not been fully mapped.

British researchers have attempted to build such a map (see Lee, 2005). They have studied groups of children ages 7 to 14 in an effort to, among other things, understand how they read history and how it influences their understandings. This work is complex, difficult, and expensive. But it has yielded some powerful dividends. We now know more about how students in England compared to American students progress in their ideas about what an account is and how to think about and use evidence drawn from accounts. Despite this work's importance, these researchers have focused more specifically on how learners make sense of key organizing concepts in history rather than on the nuances of specific reading protocols. Reading researchers must read between the lines of these studies to sort out inferentially how the student readers sampled are reading. As a result, specific reading strategies and protocols that aid deeper understandings must likewise be inferred from the work.

We could use additional studies—longitudinal ones in particular—that attempted to sort out which strategies and protocols work best when, and under what circumstances, in order to move students such as Brad and Ayesha forward. Studies that make clearer which elements of students' reading protocols serve to consistently block progress would also help, especially if the results of such studies could help us develop a clearer picture of a range of protocol impediments that slow novices' growth toward greater expertise over time. Conversely, studies that occurred in contexts in which novices made reasonably swift forward progress in their developing history-specific reading protocols would also help us more concisely plot the developmental trajectory from less to more powerful protocols. This would require, of course, a teaching–learning context that consistently provided opportunities for students to read more expertly (e.g., the one Ms. White has developed). However, such contexts are difficult to come by in naturalistic settings, particularly since American history courses typically taught in school are less about building deep understandings and cultivating reading expertise than about inculcating correct ideas and story lines (the American creed) and assessing their ability to be recalled at will.[9]

Some researchers have tried to solve this naturalistic-setting problem by studying students in laboratory contexts. Doing so has allowed them to create reading tasks for their participants that produce outcomes that can be adequately measured and analyzed. However, it is difficult to be sure that these reading tasks are ones that students would encounter in actual schooling contexts. As a result and without more specific studies, it becomes a relatively high-inference adventure to map findings onto classroom activities and the range of reading protocols possibly taught there. Put a different way, reading protocols and learning processes observed in laboratory contexts are not necessarily ones cultivated in schools. Therefore, what one context produces from and reinforces in readers may not be akin to the other, leaving unresolved questions about the relationships between the two and their influences on reading development. This is a gap that also needs filling.

A key challenge for research programs, then, is to link the history-reading protocols novices typically learn in school and rely on in classroom contexts to both the impediments they create and the growth in historical understanding they might promote. Such linkages need to be researched across the K–12 experience and, as I have noted, in a longitudinal manner if possible. Related to this challenge is an equally important one: the need to connect pedagogical practices pursued and curricular opportunities provided in history classrooms to the types of student reading protocols that either retard or cultivate growth. Consequently, it would help to have studies that compared and contrasted history-specific reading protocols occurring in classes taught more traditionally (as I have defined them in the foregoing) with ones taught in an investigative manner, such as the way Ms. White proceeds. Since the latter settings are relatively rare, researchers may need to adopt a series of researcher-teacher design experiments to create the opportunities necessary to provide students with experiences that promote the types of reading-protocol expertise that previous studies indicate might advance historical understanding. Given the constraints of traditional pedagogical and curriculum practices in history classrooms, this could entail no small feat of research engineering.

If, however, we are to map the landscape of movement in reading protocols from novice approaches to that of those with greater expertise, we need such studies. Without them, we continue to guess at what steps to take and which strategies to employ when pedagogically. If we care about the benefits a sound history *education* can produce, Brad, Ayesha, and Ms. White deserve better.

NOTES

1. In using the term *protocols*, I am referring to the work of Robert Scholes (1989), who in turn is referencing Jacques Derrida (1967). When referring to protocols for reading, I take both Scholes and Derrida to mean ways of reading texts. Generally speaking, these include strategies and skills for making sense of texts, as well as criteria for judging those texts to be more or less adequate for accomplishing tasks readers set for themselves (or have set for them in the case of adolescent readers in school). These ways of reading are underpinned by an epistemology of text and shaped by a reader's ontological framework. Power is also always in play in reading and shapes and impinges on protocols. There are perhaps an infinite number of protocols for reading. Because of the nature of my task here, I comparatively examine only a few of them in the domain of history. When I refer to texts throughout, as I will note, I am using a very broad definition. I am thinking of texts as written, painted, spoken, narrated, lectured, cartooned, and so on. As a result, I use the term *authors* as broadly, including, for example, obliquely referring to a painter or a cartoonist as an author of a painting or cartoon that can be read. I believe, with both Scholes and Derrida, that strong reading protocols are necessary, but elusive. It is difficult to find fully satisfactory ones, including the ones I will describe here—even those that I will characterize as expert.

2. The seminal work on experts' reading protocols in history was done by Wineburg. See the collection of article reprints and essays on the subject in *Historical Thinking and Other Unnatural Acts* (2001). Working from theoretical and idealized forms of history-specific reading described by scholars such as Collingwood (1994), British history-education researchers have also attempted to map such types of reading protocols onto the students (ages 7–14) they studied in Great Britain. See, for example, Lee (2005), Lee and Ashby (2000), and Lee and Shemilt (2003). In North America, history education researchers have studied the reading protocols of elementary-age students (e.g., VanSledright, 2002; VanSledright & Afflerbach, 2005; VanSledright & Kelly, 1998), adolescents (e.g., Seixas, 1994), and college students (e.g., Yeager & Davis, 1996) by comparing them to what research has taught us about experts' protocols. Some researchers have done cross-national comparative studies (e.g., Barton & Levstik, 1998; Barton & McCully, 2010). Much of this work can be construed as an effort to understand where novices (both young and older, intelligent ones) are relative to experts and thereby begin sketching a trajectory that suggests how to move learners from less to more powerful history-reading protocols. My story lines of Brad, Ayesha, and the unnamed experts are structured around and draw from this line of research work. In the specific cases of Brad, Ayesha, and Ms. White, they derive from my own classroom-based empirical work on reading and understanding history.

3. See also Pressley and Afflerbach (1995), Afflerbach and Cho (2009), and RAND Reading Study Group (2002). A note of caution is in order here. As I will note, some features of generic reading-comprehension strategies, such

as those often observed being taught in history classrooms (e.g., identifying and summarizing the text's main idea, separating fact from opinion, spotting and discounting author bias, disregarding texts that cannot be made to fit an interpretation, searching for the correct answer to a question), frequently result in cognitive impasses in reading in history. They may initially seem important and perhaps even necessary. However, as unexamined strategies within reading protocols, they can block readers from deepening their historical understandings. In short, such reading strategies can take readers only so far and then they must be dislodged and replaced with more powerful strategies that are described in what follows.

4. In the case of synthetic wikis, for example, doing so can be exceptionally problematic. As a result, wikis could be judged as quite unreliable as sources because a reader cannot sufficiently identify and make sense of the multiple authors' possible agendas and subtexts. In some ways, analog/print texts, such as textbooks and encyclopedia articles, present readers with the same problem (see Paxton, 1999), not to mention the fact that they typically strip out the evidentiary trails they drew from in order to create their synthetic accounts. Readers with powerful history reading protocols, such as experts, typically put such texts near the bottom on lists of reliable sources of evidence (Wineburg, 2001). Adolescents (e.g., Brad) tend to put them near the top, suggesting inherent weaknesses in the reading protocols they often acquire in school (see the cautionary observations in notes 3 and 7).

5. In historical accounts written by historians and other skilled investigators, signals of their reading protocols can often most clearly be found in the footnotes. It is here that these investigators put on display how they read the past and the residue that emanates from it. Footnotes reflect how investigators have drawn from the past and organized its texts in ways that permit the "new" text they are generating. Among other things, peers use these footnotes to judge the adequacy of the "new" text's argument.

6. An astute historian, James Kloppenberg (1989), once summed up the problem this way: "Beyond the noble dream of scientific objectivity and the nightmare of complete relativism lies the terrain of pragmatic truth, which provides us with hypotheses, provisional syntheses, imaginative but warranted interpretations, which then provide the basis for continuing inquiry and experimentation. Such historical [reading and] writing can provide knowledge that is useful even if it must be tentative. ... As [investigators], we cannot aspire to more than a pragmatic hermeneutics that relies on methods of science and the interpretation of meanings. But we should not aspire to less" (p. 1030).

7. Scholes (1989) might be tempted to refer to Brad's reading protocol as textual fundamentalism. Scholes describes the protocol this way: "Textual fundamentalism is the belief that texts always say just what they mean, so that any honest or decent person ought to be able to understand this perfectly clear meaning without making any fuss about it. The problem with this position is that it requires an infallible author, a perfect language, and a timeless context in order to work" (p. 52). Unfortunately for students like Brad, these three conditions cannot be established. To the extent that, in school

history (e.g., Brad's fifth-grade teacher), we tilt in the direction of teaching textual fundamentalism, teachers make pedagogical moves that cognitively handcuff readers in history. And it turns out to be pedagogically difficult to circumvent the limitations of this sort of reading protocol once it takes hold (see VanSledright, 2002, on this point).

8. In the interests of time, Ms. White had to make a practice of artificially limiting the number of texts she makes available to her students as she invites them to conduct ongoing investigations into the past. The exercise on the Boston shootings was a case in point (only four texts). Ms. White recognizes that she and her students are not historians who can spend months in the archives reading everything they can lay their hands on. She samples with her students. She chooses to focus on illustrating a process of coming to understand, of learning to read more expertly, of sharpening reading protocols. Frequently, though, she points out to her students that she has partially truncated the textual space (e.g., number of accounts she invites students to read) to get through the curriculum she is required to cover. She is well aware of the irony of doing so. She does, however, come far closer to modeling the practices inhering in expertise than what typically goes on in history classes.

9. For an interesting case example of how this has played out in the state of Virginia, see van Hover and Heinecke (2005).

REFERENCES

Afflerbach, P., & Cho, B. (2009). Identifying and describing constructively responsive comprehension strategies in new and traditional forms of reading. In S. E. Israel & G. G. Duffy (Eds.), *Handbook of research on reading comprehension* (pp. 69–90). London: Routledge.

Barton, K. (2008). Research on students' ideas about history. In L. Levstik & C. Tyson, *Handbook of research in social studies education* (pp. 239–258). New York: Routledge.

Barton, K., & Levstik, L. (1998). "It wasn't a good part of history": National identity and ambiguity in students' explanations of historical significance. *Teachers College Record, 99*, 478–513.

Barton, K., & McCully, A. (2010). "You can form your own point of view": Internally persuasive discourse in Northern Ireland students' encounters with history. *Teachers College Record, 112*, 142–181.

Collingwood, R. G. (1994). *The idea of history.* Oxford, UK: Oxford University Press. (Original was published 1946).

Cuban, L. (1991). History of teaching in social studies. In J. Shaver (Ed.), *Handbook of research on social studies teaching and learning* (pp. 197–209). New York: Macmillan.

Davis, N.Z. (1988). "On the lame." *American Historical Review, 93*, 572–603.

Derrida, J. (1967). *Of grammatology.* Baltimore: Johns Hopkins University Press.

Epstein, T. (2009). *Interpreting national history: Race, identity, and pedagogy in classrooms and communities*. New York: Routledge.

Finlay, R. (1988). The refashioning of Martin Guerre. *American Historical Review, 93*, 553–571.

Frisch, M. (1989). American history and the structures of collective memory: A modest exercise in empirical iconography. *Journal of American History, 75*, 1130–1155.

Grant, S. G. (Ed.) (2006). *Measuring history: Cases of state-level testing across the United States*. Greenwich, CT: Information Age Publishing.

Hicks, D., Doolittle, P., & Lee, J. (2004). Social studies teachers' use of classroom-based and web-based historical primary sources. *Theory and Research in Social Education, 32*, 213–247.

Kloppenberg, J. T. (1989). Objectivity and historicism: A century of historical writing. *American Historical Review, 94*, 1011–1030.

Lee, P. J. (2005). Putting principles into practice: Understanding history. In S. Donovan & J. Bransford (Eds.), *How students learn: History in the classroom* (pp. 31–78). Washington, DC: National Academies Press.

Lee, P. J., & Ashby, R. (2000). Progression in historical understanding among students ages 7–14. In P. Stearns, P. Seixas, & S. Wineburg (Eds.), *Knowing, teaching, and learning history* (pp. 199–222). New York: New York University Press.

Lee, P. J., & Shemilt, D. (2003). A scaffold not a cage: Progression and progression models in history. *Teaching History, 113*, 13–24.

Paxton, R. (1999). A deafening silence: History textbooks and the students who read them. *Review of Educational Research, 69*, 315–339.

Pressley, M., & Afflerbach, P. (1995). *Verbal protocols of reading: The nature of constructively responsive reading*. Mahweh, NJ: Erlbaum.

RAND Reading Study Group. (2002). *Reading for understanding: Toward an R&D program in reading comprehension*. Santa Monica, CA: RAND.

Salinas, C., & Sullivan, C. C. (2007). Latino/a preservice teachers' positionality: Challenging the construction of official knowledge through historical thinking. *Journal of Curriculum and Pedagogy, 4*, 178–199.

Schlesinger, A. M., Jr. (1991). *The disuniting of America: Reflections on a multicultural society*. New York: W.W. Norton.

Scholes, R. (1989). *Protocols of reading*. New Haven, CT: Yale University Press.

Seixas, P. (1994). Confronting the moral frames of popular film: Young people respond to historical revisionism. *American Journal of Education, 102*, 261–285.

Seixas, P. (1996). Conceptualizing the growth of historical understanding. In D. Olson & N. Torrance (Eds.), *The handbook of psychology in education* (pp. 765–783). Oxford, UK: Blackwell.

van Hover, S., & Heinecke, W. (2005). The impact of accountability reform on the "wise practice" of secondary history teachers: The Virginia experience. In E. A. Yeager & O. L. Davis, Jr. (Eds.), *Wise social studies teaching in an age of high-stakes testing: Essays on classroom practices and possibilities* (pp. 89–116). Greenwich, CT: Information Age Publishing.

VanSledright, B. A. (2002). *In search of America's past: Learning to read history in elementary school.* New York: Teachers College Press.

VanSledright, B. A. (2008). Narratives of nation-state, historical knowledge, and school history education. *Review of Research in Education, 32,* 109–146.

VanSledright, B. A. (2011). *The challenge of rethinking history education: On practices, theory, and policy.* New York: Routledge.

VanSledright, B. A., & Afflerbach, P. (2005). Assessing the status of historical sources: An exploratory study of eight elementary students reading documents. In P. Lee (Ed.), *Children and teachers' ideas about history. International research in history education* Vol. 4, (pp. 1–20). London: Routledge/Falmer.

VanSledright, B. A., & Kelly, C. (1998). Reading American history: The influence of using multiple sources on six fifth graders. *Elementary School Journal, 98,* 239–265.

VanSledright, B. A., & Limon, M. (2006). Learning and teaching in social studies: Cognitive research on history and geography. In P. Alexander & P. Winne (Eds.), *The Handbook of Educational Psychology* (2nd Ed., pp. 545–570). Mahweh, NJ: Erlbaum.

Voss, J. (1998). Issues in the learning of history. *Issues in education: Contributions from educational psychology, 4,* 163–209.

Wineburg, S. (2001). *Historical thinking and other unnatural acts: Charting the future of teaching the past.* Philadelphia: Temple University Press.

Yeager, E., & Davis, O. L. (1996). Classroom teachers thinking about historical texts. *Theory and Research in Social Education, 24,* 146–166.

9

Learning with Text in the Arts

Kathleen Moxley
with James Batcheller, Larry Burditt, Sue Gamble,
Alan J. Gumm, Johanna Paas, *and* Judy Thurston

> In order to be read, a poem, an equation, a painting, a dance, a
> novel, or a contract, each requires a distinctive form of literacy,
> when literacy means, as I intend it to mean, a way of conveying
> meaning through and recovering meaning from the form of
> representation in which it appears.
> —Eisner (1997, p. 353)

There is a need for future teachers of adolescents to reconsider the
notion of literacy. Armed with a deeper understanding of literacy in
their respective disciplines, teachers can improve the meaning making of
the adolescents they will be instructing. Recently, students in Kathleen
Moxley's secondary-content literacy course were asked to nudge their
conceptual frameworks about literacy. Elliot Eisner's (1997) view of literacy was unmistakably present as these students produced projects that
reshaped their understandings of text and literacy. Consider the following scenario in which their work epitomized Eisner's views of literacy.

In preparation for carrying out these projects Kathleen grouped her
students according to specific disciplines in order to brainstorm about
how text and literacy are represented. Students recorded their ideas on

chart paper and presented the results to the class. As one can imagine, their ideas represented text that was largely print based, such as textbooks, essays, novels, manuals, rules, lab reports, and primary source documents. Students from the arts, physical education, and mathematics acknowledged that they seldom used textbooks in their own learning as adolescents. In order to challenge her students' beliefs and bring about a common understanding of the complexities of these concepts, Kathi introduced a frame for thinking about text and literacy. Borrowed from Paul Broomhead's (2010) explanation, she framed text as "what" we intend our students to create, produce, interpret, or make sense of in their learning. Literacy was framed as "how" we intend our students to interact with text, for example how they might go about creating, interpreting, and making sense of it. A discussion about print-based and nonprint text ensued; for most, thinking about and accepting nonprint objects as "text" was new and intriguing. With this common, yet multifaceted, understanding of text and literacy students brainstormed again. They engaged in determining what counts as text and how literacy is carried out with a higher level of interest and a deeper awareness of the role text and literacy play in teaching and learning their subjects. This change in thinking was evident across all disciplines, but especially noticeable with music and visual arts, where traditional print-based text is not the predominant source of learning.

These brainstorming tasks were a prelude to the crafting of discipline-specific photo essays for which students selected visual representations to signify their new understandings of the texts and literacies essential to learning in their subject areas. Within these essays students also integrated the rationale for their photo and pictorial representations. They shared rich depictions of what they counted as text and literacy through PowerPoints that incorporated links to personally created videos on YouTube and video clips of famous speeches by historical figures, as well as music and carefully selected photos and pictures. Particularly interesting were the photo essays from the arts disciplines, where nonprint texts prevail over traditional print texts as sources of subject matter learning (see Figures 9.1 and 9.2).

One music group created a video taking us on a personally guided tour of the music school, pointing out the texts and literacies-in-action along the way. On this journey we witnessed small clusters of students gathered in the common areas playing, collaborating, and discussing their art. Our tour guide stopped occasionally to interview other music students about important texts they were using and the literacies they were enacting to make meaning from text, for example, reading and interpreting music language, singing words printed in the music (English or foreign), performing memorized music, recognizing and understand-

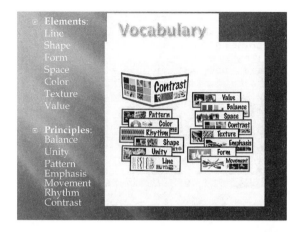

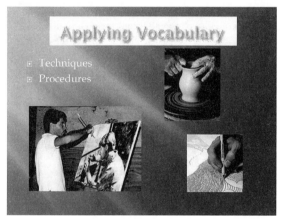

FIGURE 9.1. Art photo essay examples.

ing music symbols and terms, and listening to recordings to develop musical literacy.

Visual arts students defined their texts and literacies by the language or vocabulary they use to understand, demonstrate, or critique their artifacts. Their photo essays described text in terms of the *elements of design* (fundamentals of the artifacts you can see) such as line, space, color, shape, texture, form, and value and the *principles of design and composition* (arrangement of the fundamentals of an artifact), such as unity, contrast, variety, pattern, emphasis, movement, rhythm, and balance used to create and critique their own work and the work of others. Print-based text was exemplified in photos as textbooks, labels on jars of

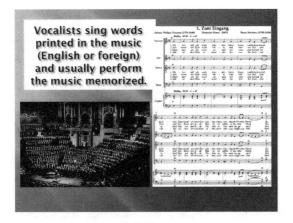

FIGURE 9.2. Music photo essay examples.

paint, washes, solvents, and chemicals used to develop film, charts like the color wheel, and the safety rules posted on the walls of the art studio. Photos of artifacts like paintings, graphic design works, photographs, sculpture pieces, and an architectural design were included as important exemplars of nonprint texts from which artists naturally draw meaning. Artists' tools also represent texts: pencils, brushes, markers, tablets, a canvas, an easel, a palette, and even an art studio were selected by students. Artists must understand how to interact with these tools before utilizing them to create artifacts.

The techniques and procedures artists use to carry out their work count as literacies. Visual arts students described these literacies in terms of understanding the elements and principles of design that afford artists the know-how to carry out a critique. In this way, an artist is exercising literacy by critiquing a painting for technical correctness (perspective, proportion, and subject matter) or the emotional response it generates.

During a debriefing discussion following the photo essay presentations students expressed several "aha's" with regard to what they learned about their own disciplines and the disciplines of their peers. First, students recognized that each discipline has idiosyncratic ways of knowing and learning their subject matter. They noted the distinctive representations of text and the literacies that are dominant in one discipline and not in another. Second, students observed that every discipline makes use of both traditional print text and nonprint text in their teaching and learning with each discipline using these print and nonprint texts in varying ways and to different degrees. Third, because of their reshaped and common view of literacy students concluded that all teachers in all disciplines could appropriately talk about text and literacy in their teaching; these students could see themselves as future teacher collaborators intent on improving literacy among the adolescents they soon will teach. Most profoundly, students in the arts disciplines, where text is more often represented by nonprint entities like sounds, symbols, acts of conducting, facial expressions, paintings, sculpture, graphic designs, and architecture, perceived their texts and how they interacted with them as literacies. Kathi helped them reconceptualize what literacy means for their respective disciplines. They now believe they can participate in the larger conversation about text and literacy. These students can be considered a microcosm for the field of adolescent literacy.

This chapter begins with a brief overview of the literature on adolescent and content literacy in relation to teaching and learning in music and visual arts. The chapter coauthors, who are music and visual arts experts, reflect on how literacy is defined and what counts as text in their fields. We examine the National Standards for the Arts as a point of reference for exploring the discipline-specific strategies that guide adolescents in their ability to learn from text in music and art. Finally, we discuss practical instructional strategies that music and visual arts teachers can use to increase adolescents' literacy learning.

ADOLESCENT LITERACY

The field of adolescent literacy offers limited research focusing specifically on how adolescents learn through the arts. Existing adolescent literacy literature connects to the arts primarily in two ways—promoting the inclusion of the arts within the teaching and learning of other disciplines (Albers, Holbrook, & Harste, 2010; Zoss, 2009) and linking the arts to how adolescents make sense of their worlds (Conley, 2008; Hinchman, Alvermann, Boyd, Brozo, & Vacca, 2004; Vacca, Vacca, & Mraz, 2011). In the last few years much talk about adolescent literacy has emphasized the literacies with which adolescents engage in their out-of-school lives. Many of their outside literacies can be attributed to the arts both at home and while interacting with peers. The adolescent literacy field has brought attention to the way adolescents define their world and their culture by what they do and how they learn outside of school (Diket, 2003; Hinchman et al., 2004). Adolescents' lives outside of school are keenly connected to the arts through performing, creating, listening to, and observing in the world around them. Many of the literacy practices in which adolescents engage in their daily lives revolve around music and visual arts and are described as uses of popular culture. Researchers have suggested that popular culture texts such as magazines, movies, music and song lyrics, photographs, drawings, TV, radio, video games, movies, CDs, Internet, wiki books, podcasts, artwork, stories, videos, and other multimodal texts be incorporated within school learning contexts and activities (Alvermann, Phelps, & Gillis, 2010; Heron-Hruby & Alvermann, 2009).

CONTENT-AREA LITERACY

Literacy educators have long assumed that knowledge of how to teach literacy reaches across all disciplines, including those where traditional print text is not the accepted mode of delivering content. Challenges to this assumption exist particularly in the area of arts education. The content-area literacy field has paid little attention to literacy as it relates to the arts disciplines.

As recent conversations among literacy experts shift away from content-area literacy toward a discussion of disciplinary-specific literacies (Shanahan & Shanahan, 2008; Draper, 2008), they continue to point specifically to the core subjects of history, science, language arts, and math. The arts disciplines remain largely ignored in the conversation. Some would even consign the arts to extracurricular programs, outside of the normal school day and excluded from the core subjects (Eisner, 2005). Under the No Child Left Behind Act (NCLB), however, music and visual arts are considered core academic subjects and should be included in meaningful ways in conversations among literacy experts.

Moreover, content-area literacy textbooks have traditionally endorsed a print-based text approach and a common set of literacy instructional strategies to improve reading and writing across all content areas. Limited attention has been afforded to the arts disciplines and how they use arts-specific texts to communicate or make meaning.

LITERACY AS DISCOURSE

We draw on the notion that literacy is a socially constructed and always-changing practice based on our beliefs in the world (Street, 2006). Further, we apply Gee's (1996) notion of literacy as "Discourse/s"—ways of using language, of thinking, and of acting that can be used to identify oneself as a member of a socially meaningful group or "social network." Therefore, being trained in music or the visual arts means one learns to speak, think, and act like a musician or visual artist and to recognize other members of the same group when they behave in similar ways. Each larger discourse has subdiscourses with different socially accepted ways of being. In this way, being a musician is the larger discourse from which specifically trained musicians are members. However, they are also members of a subdiscourse of their specific domain; flutists are identified by a particular discourse as are harpists, drummers, and the like. Adolescents who study the arts, then, would follow a set of values and viewpoints that identify them as members of a particular music or visual arts subdiscourse with certain socially constructed practices and texts that are unique.

WHAT COUNTS AS TEXT AND LITERACY IN MUSIC?

In a recent volume on content-area literacy, Paul Broomhead (2010) rethinks the meaning of text as it is represented in music education. Broomhead describes text as objects that students "negotiate and create in order to interact appropriately with music," (p. 69). He further defines music literacy as how we negotiate texts: "the ways students interact with them are your literacies," (p. 69). Even though Broomhead is specifically talking about text and literacies through a music discipline lens, clearly, his view applies to all disciplines.

Musical texts that students create or interact with might include vocal and instrumental musical scores, a conductor, sounds, and symbols (Draper & Broomhead, 2009). Other representations of musical texts include compositions, music theory texts, concert programs, professional journal articles, instrumental methods books, CD liner notes, and fingering charts (Watson, Johnson, Lesley, & Brass, 2009). These exemplars of musical text represent a range of print and nonprint texts—

"what" is negotiated when teaching and learning in the music discipline.

So, when we think about text in music education we are obliged to broaden our view beyond the traditional print-based text that often permeates the core of our educational curriculum such as written lab reports in science, essays in language arts, and time-honored textbooks that exist in many disciplines. While music students use traditional texts like the previously mentioned theory textbooks and those used in general music or music appreciation classrooms, they are more often likely to build their knowledge of music through the use of nonprint objects like symbols, sound, musical scores, or interpretation of a conductor's visible gestures.

Consider the responses from music specialists Alan Gumm, Sue Gamble, and James Batcheller when prompted with the question "What do you count as text in music?" The following commentary by these experts reflects a range of texts, including both traditional print-based and nonprint objects, from which adolescents construct meaning in music classrooms.

This description of music text spans both traditional and nontraditional exemplars. Alan describes text as

> "beginning instrumental methods books, one for each instrument, sight-reading and ear-training method books for singers (often self-designed), basal music series [K–8 music series] textbooks for general music, sheet music or music scores, nonverbal conducting, pitch hand signs for *do-re-mi-fa-so-la-ti-do* and half-steps in between, classroom board, teacher and peer modeling of music-making actions and musical sound, and nonverbal imagery, mime, and metaphors."

Sue adds:

> "Conducting, for sure," and explains how using the literacies of body movement, listening, singing, and reading helps students interact with print text:
> "A lot of times we use a basal series in music classrooms. And in general music classrooms—not performance classrooms—we would always be working on ... music reading skills. In preparation for listening to a piece of music by Beethoven, we're looking at ... how can ... we clap the rhythm? Can we read this and can we sing it?"

For thinking about music literacy we again borrow from Broomhead (2010). Broomhead describes the national standards for music in terms of four distinct interactions—*performing, listening, contemplating,* and *creating.* Draper and Broomhead (2009) extend our thinking about the performance literacies beyond reading notes and symbols to the "meaning singers make with a conductor, ... balancing volume within and between sections of the choir, locking intonation, blending tone color." They also broaden our view of the listening literacies to include listening "to other singers in an ensemble" (p. 1).

Consider the following commentary from our music experts in response to the question "How do you define music literacy?" These comments support the fundamental use of performance literacies to negotiate music text for the purpose of making meaning while singing or performing on instruments in a band or choir classroom or within a vocal or instrumental ensemble.

The process of constructing meaning from traditional print-based text is similar to constructing meaning from music literature. In both cases reading or interpretation of text happens. Understanding musical notation requires one to interpret the symbols into sound just as when reading a book the reader must interpret the message of the author by reading the words on the page. Alan describes music literacy as

> "being able to read and write music and being able to look at musical notation and interpret it. Music literacy is the ability to identify, name, and interpret into sound the basic music symbol system of clefs, staffs, time signatures, pitches and intervals, rhythms and meters, tempo, and dynamics markings, and special markings for articulations, bowings, muting, and other instrument-specific instructions."

Jim agrees: "It is the same thing as verbal literacy ... with reading ability being one level of literacy." In music instruction, the teacher and students enact literacies through reading notation—musical notes on the page. Sue, however, allows us a peek at the use of a basal series in general music classrooms with adolescents.

> "Reading is very specific with music notation ... just as it's specific with words.... If a teacher's using a text in a general music classroom, as opposed to a choir rehearsal or a band rehearsal, then they're going to have something like this (points to a music basal) and I did in fact have my students actually read ... text from the actual basal series. I would ... have them take turns just as an English teacher would."

Jim defines literacy as "an ability to read and interpret alone and with others ... and perform a broad repertoire of music ... to be able to describe and evaluate one another's performances, their own performances, performances by professionals, both recorded and live." He further describes a complicated process of music literacy—reading music notation. How students interact with music notation determines how they pick up meaning from notated text and transfer that meaning to their performance.

> "When you think about how to sing or how to play a pitch that's specified on the page, for example, the dynamics of musical expression ... just in terms of the pitch itself ... high versus low ... in terms of frequency. So it's either a really high pitch or a really low pitch. That's one basic dynamic range. Then, from loud to soft and then, in terms of duration, long to short, and then there is articulation to be considered—light versus heavy or strong. And then we get into issues of tone and color because that changes depending on the context—light versus dark."

WHAT DO THE MUSIC STANDARDS SAY ABOUT TEXT AND LITERACY?

The National Standards for Arts Education (National Association for Music Education [MENC], 1994) for adolescents in grades 5–8 and 9–12 describe music literacy in terms of creating, performing, listening to, analyzing, describing, evaluating, and thinking about music. According to Williams (2007) these standards presume students will be involved in such literacy activities as "performance, listening, composition, improvisation, analysis, notation-skill acquisition, and associations with other arts as well as fields outside the arts" (p. 18). Not only do these standards describe expectations for music literacy activities, but they also clearly encourage relationships and communication with other disciplines and cultures (see Table 9.1). This intention to support an interface with other disciplines and cultures underscores the notion that music and the arts are forms of communication literacy and extend our thinking about literacy and learning as social endeavors.

Performing Literacies

Performing literacies are reflected in four of the nine national standards for music, signifying that music is dominated by performance and that performing is crucial to the negotiation of music texts in adolescent classrooms. Much of teaching and learning in music classrooms depends on the performance literacies represented in these performance standards: *Singing, alone and with others, a varied repertoire of music*; *Perform-*

TABLE 9.1. Music Texts and Literacies as Indicated by the National Standards for Arts Education

Standards	Texts (what is negotiated)	Literacies (how text is negotiated)
Singing alone and with others, a varied repertoire of music	*Vocal music literature* of diverse genres and cultures for multiple parts; *choral ensembles*	*Performing* with expression, technical accuracy, good breath control, memorization, alone or in ensembles, with or without accompaniment
Performing on instruments, alone and with others, a varied repertoire of music	Varied repertoire of *instrumental literature* for multiple parts and ensembles	*Performing* with expression, technical accuracy; good posture, playing position, breath control, bow and stick control; alone and in ensembles; with or without accompaniment
Improvising melodies, variations, and accompaniments	Stylistically appropriate *harmonizing parts, rhythmic and melodic variations, original melodies*	*Creating and performing*— improvising a variety of styles with consistent style, meter, and tonality
Composing and arranging music within specified guidelines	*Vocal and instrumental musical scores*	*Creating*—composing and arranging music using the elements of music for expressive effect, unity and variety, tension and release, and balance, applying the principles of composition for imagination and technical skill
Reading and notating music	*Instrumental or vocal score, standard and nonstandard notation symbols, choral or instrumental ensemble*	*Performing*—describing how elements of music are used, sight-reading accurately and expressively, identifying, defining, and using standard and nonstandard notation symbols to record musical ideas
Listening to, analyzing, and describing music	*Aural examples of music*	*Listening*—analyzing uses of the elements of music of diverse genres and cultures, describing specific music events using appropriate terminology, demonstrating knowledge of basic principles of meter, rhythm, tonality, intervals, chords, and harmonic progressions
Evaluating music and music performances	*Performances, compositions, arrangements, and improvisations, musical works*	*Listening*—developing and applying criteria for evaluating the quality and effectiveness of personal and others' musical works

(*continued*)

TABLE 9.1. (*continued*)

Standards	Texts (what is negotiated)	Literacies (how text is negotiated)
Understanding relationships between music, the other Arts, and disciplines outside the arts	*Characteristic materials, products, creators, and performers* of various disciplines (sound, visual stimuli, movement, events, scenes, emotions, musical works, etc.)	*Contemplating*—comparing two or more arts, describing ways principles and subject matter of other disciplines are interrelated with music
Understanding music in relation to history and culture	*Music literature—both aural and written*	*Contemplating* —identifying, classifying, describing genre, stylistic features, musicians' roles in a variety of musical works across aesthetic traditions and historical and cultural contexts

ing on instruments, alone and with others, a varied repertoire of music; *Improvising melodies, variations, and accompaniments*; and *Reading and notating music.* Performance is the dominant literacy enacted by musicians. Musicians draw upon the following skills and strategies in a variety of ways and with a range of expertise in order to negotiate or interact with the performance of music: notation, improvisation, sight-reading, rehearsal, memorization, intonation, expression, and body movement. More time is spent on performance goals than on goals like improvising and composing (Williams, 2007).

Listening Literacies

Listening is the next dominant literacy enacted to negotiate music texts. Listening literacies require students to interact with music texts, negotiating music meaning by ear. Two of the music standards represent the listening literacies: *Listening to, analyzing, and describing music* and *Evaluating music and music performances.* In order for students to enact listening literacies they must use aural examples of music representing diverse genres and cultures. The listening literacies also require students to interact with aural music text using higher levels of thinking, for example, analyzing a variety of text genres for implementation of the elements of music and evaluating the quality and effectiveness of music, their own and that of others. The skills and strategies used to develop listening literacies include improvisation, rehearsal, memorization, intonation, expression, and body movement.

Ear training is used for developing the listening literacies among students. Indeed, it is suggested that students listen to music and reproduce it by ear and improvise before introducing musical notation—the reading and interpreting of musical notes (McPherson & Gabrielsson, 2002). Compared to reading printed text, this is analogous to the way early readers develop oral language through listening before they recognize letters and whole words in print. According to Alan, ear training "is the ability to discriminate, identify, label, and symbolize musical sound, to put sound to paper as in writing words you hear spoken." Sue agrees: "They have to hear it and then reproduce it." She clarifies that music "is time related; it is always moving." This affects the listening literacies, so students need to learn they cannot stop and *redo* in a real-time performance.

Unlike print text, which students can reread to clear up or revise mistakes, music does not stop for mistakes to be fixed. Sue describes this scenario.

> "You can't go back and fix it ... because it's still moving ... when high school students are in an ensemble situation, they have only their part, so the conductor has the entire score in front of him or her. So, if you miss that spot ... you have to have some kind of ... tools within you whether it's feeling ... counting beats ... to come back in at the right spot. You can't just stop."

Creating Literacies

The creating literacies in music education include composing and arranging of vocal and instrumental musical scores. I would also include improvisation in this category because it fits both performing and creating literacies. Therefore, two of the national standards for music represent the creating literacies: *Composing and arranging music within specified guidelines* and *Improvising melodies, variations, and accompaniments.* Creating music depends on a certain amount of understanding—a knowledge base—of music skills like the symbols and sounds and is developed through the use of composing and improvising skills and strategies.

Before students can compose and arrange music they need to understand how to use the elements of music in a way that elicits an expressive effect. They need to understand such key components as melody, harmony, rhythm, and dynamics and how they interact to create a balanced piece of music. They need to apply the principles of composition using imagination as well as technical skill. Improvising takes the creating of music to another level altogether. It requires one to spontaneously invent music in a variety of styles, within the boundaries of consistent style, meter, and tonality. Further, creating music incorporates performing literacies (singing or playing instruments alone or in ensembles) and listening literacies (analyzing and evaluating the newly created texts).

Contemplating Literacies

Two of the national music standards expect adolescent music students to draw on a range of reasoning skills: *Understanding relationships between music, the other arts, and disciplines outside the arts* and *Understanding music in relation to history and culture*. To meet these two standards, students must not only identify, describe, and classify stylistic features and genres from a variety of music works and aesthetic traditions but also understand and contemplate the interrelations between music and other forms of art by comparing music to dance, visual arts, theater, and the like. Further, adolescents are expected to understand and appreciate music through a range of historical and cultural contexts and also understand how other disciplines are interrelated with music. They can contemplate music's relationship to other arts disciplines, disciplines outside the arts, and history and culture through reading and writing.

DISCIPLINE-SPECIFIC LITERACY STRATEGIES IN MUSIC

The discipline-specific knowledge, skills, and strategies that help students negotiate and interact with text in music classrooms include notation, improvisation, sight-reading, practice, memorization, intonation, expression, composition, and body movement. These disciplinary skills and strategies represent specific approaches by which students enact the literacies used to negotiate or interact with text in their music learning. As shown in Table 9.2, these skills and strategies are consistent with the national music standards that are expected to be taught and supported as vital components of any exemplary adolescent music classroom.

It must be acknowledged that teaching music is indeed complex and that the use of discipline-specific skills and strategies does not happen in isolation. Even as I attempt to organize the skills and strategies in a way that exposes certain purposes, texts, and literacies, musicians utilize these skills and strategies to negotiate texts and enact literacies in complex ways in order to produce musical art. Furthermore, musicians use multiple skills and strategies to interact with multiple music texts and enact multiple literacies to generate one musical act. For example, during

TABLE 9.2. Discipline-Specific Music Knowledge, Skills, and Strategies as Indicated by the National Standards for Arts Education

Discipline-specific knowledge, skills, strategies	Purposes	Texts used or created	Literacies enacted
Notation	To acquire skill in reading and interpreting musical symbols	Instrumental and vocal scores, notation symbols, ensembles	Performing
Improvisation	To acquire skill in making creative decisions about performance in real time	Harmonizing parts, variations, original melodies, instruments	Performing, creating
Sight-reading	To perform written music specifically not seen before	Instrumental and vocal scores, notation symbols, ensembles	Performing
Practice/rehearsal	To prepare for musical performances	Vocal and instrumental literature/scores, ensembles, instruments	Performing, listening
Memorization	To learn music using auditory, kinesthetic, and visual information	Aural examples of music	Performing, listening
Intonation	To perform pitch accurately and to achieve an in-tune performance	Vocal and instrumental literature/scores, ensembles, symbols, instruments	Performing, listening
Expression	To develop expressiveness in musical performance	Vocal and instrumental literature/scores, ensembles, symbols	Performing, listening, creating
Composition	To create an original piece of music	Instrumental and vocal scores	Creating
Body movement	To interact with instruments and communicate to the audience	Vocal and instrumental literature/scores, ensembles	Performing

an orchestra performance musicians might sight-read printed notes and symbols while playing their instruments, interpreting the conductor's gestures, and making decisions about how to incorporate expression, all while listening to other musicians near them. Thus, performing literacies interact with listening, creating, and thinking literacies during a single enactment of musical art.

Notation (Performing Literacy)

Teaching music notation skills to adolescents is not unlike teaching children to speak. Music is a form of communication, but the most effective music communication occurs without using words. According to McPherson and Gabrielsson (2002), reading and interpreting musical notation is a process in which a learner plays music, next reads music, and then puts them together. Jim explains that students will eventually use words, but as with other disciplines that teach active skill sets,

> "the first thing they have to do is experience the thing. They have to do it and then they can describe it. Or it can be described to them … then ask them to try to perform it. They learn to … perform music in the same way they learn to speak. They do it first. There's a sequence to it … we teach patterns and that's how people learn in music … they learn to recognize melodic and rhythmic patterns … first … Having experienced it and then seeing what the notation looks like … they'll attach … the musical notation to it and then … they can … describe it verbally."

Further, Alan complexifies the literacy of reading musical notation. A vocal music student who is required to sight-sing must be able to do this task while interpreting the music notation, in real time, much the same way a reader of a book would perform when reading orally. He explains: "Sight-singing is the ability to read music on the spot (a literate reader) without slow practice (like a slow reader sounding out phonics)."

Jim extends our thinking about negotiating music notation even further by explaining that interacting with notation usually happens while working with others:

> "All of this now has to be … more intuitive and it has to happen—unless it's the rare case where you have a performer without accompaniment—without anybody else, which is almost never—all of this has to happen cooperatively."

Improvisation (Performing and Creating Literacies)

For adolescents, improvisation typically happens during ensemble work as a tool for developing creativity, self-expression, and aesthetic understanding. Engaging adolescents actively in improvisation activities and games epitomizes a constructivist approach to teaching music that allows students to make decisions and problem-solve in real time. For example, students in a jazz ensemble might engage in spontaneous responses or conversations. Artistic sources of inspiration for improvisation can also come from dance, movement, poetry, films, comics, and pictures. Riveire (2006) suggests that these conversations

> "develop an understanding of phrase structure, call-and-response form, various articulations and dynamic levels, and voice leading. Students strive to keep to the established pitch and to repeat parts of what the other has 'said' in their own responses, as people do in real conversations." (p. 41)

Jim describes a strategy for implementing improvisation with adolescents.

> "Musical improvisation at the most basic level is I just learned to play 'Mary Had a Little Lamb.' Now I'm going to play it faster or slower. I'm going to play it louder or softer. I'm going to play it ... with a different sort of articulation ... that's improvisatory. As they're developing ... that impulse, being able to write about that, even in the most general terms gets them to think more about the multitude of possibilities ... combinations of loud and soft, fast and slow, heavy and light and that sort of thing ... if I were to have a kid write about what they were doing either in class or as a homework assignment, I would have them list the various combinations of those dynamic ranges that they could bring to bear on their own interpretation ... which gets them thinking about the finer points of music, arranging and composing, which is something we want them thinking about from the very beginning."

Sight-Reading (Performing Literacy)

Sight-reading or sight-singing, in general, is considered the ability to read music smoothly, steadily, and accurately on first sight like a proficient reader of words would read a sentence. Lehmann and McArthur (2002) present a psychological perspective on sight-reading that involves several literacies, including "perception (decoding note patterns), kinesthetics (executing motor programs), memory (recognizing patterns), and problem-solving skills (improvising and guessing)" (p. 135). Further, there is complexity in the ways musicians think of or define sight-reading. According to Lehmann and McArthur (2002), "It is more helpful to picture a continuum of rehearsal, where playing a piece of music without any preparation would be located on one end of the scale while performing it after rehearsal to the point of overlearning would be located at the other end" (p. 135).

Lehmann and McArthur (2002) make a distinction between sight-reading—to read music one has not seen before—and simply "reading" music, which happens after rehearsal and during performance. For a musician, therefore, reading music ranges in complexity based on amount of rehearsal involved.

Further, Kuehne (2010) found much variation in the amount of time and the instructional methods used in teaching adolescents to read music across the United States. Generally, though, most music teachers agree that proficiency in reading music can translate to easier teaching of performance. In general, in order to read music students learn such concepts as key structure, phrase shape, meter, tempo, form, style, dynamics, and articulation. Teachers use a variety of charts and diagrams and look at the commonalities between pieces of music such as patterns and shapes, and analyze form or compositional techniques. The constructivist aspect of reading music is exemplified when musicians solve musical problems in real time through reading notes, collaborating in ensembles, and using correct fingering based on their understanding of rules and visual, kinesthetic, and aural patterns (Lehmann & Ericsson, 1996). Problem-solving strategies are key to proficient music-reading literacy and, thus, performance.

For Sue, everything having to do with music reading is based upon musical experience.

> "In other words, I don't give them ... quarter notes ... and let's just clap the quarter notes ... now here are eighth notes. It always comes out of musical experience ... you teach a song and then out of that song you extract a musical rhythm ... I start them out and I say to them, clap when I clap ... then I'll start introducing a rhythm syllable."

Jim agrees and explains that the most basic strategy in learning to associate notation with sound, being able to read and interpret notation, is "to use a context that ... helps them to associate with something that's already within their realm of experience."

Rehearsal (Performing and Listening Literacies)

Rehearsal or practice is a strategy employed by adolescents to acquire music proficiency and thereby improve performance. Listening to musical works through such means as professional recordings and teacher demonstrations allows adolescents to analyze performances and apply new learning to their own music.

Rehearsal reflects standards six and seven, which require adolescents to listen to, analyze, and describe music, and evaluate their own performances as well as the performances of others. Rehearsal is the dominant activity for adolescents involved in school music settings. Adolescents make use of different types of practice when rehearsing for music events, such as concerts and festivals. Barry and Hallam (2002) suggest that practice can be more effective if music teachers involve adolescents in metacognitive processes where they think about their own thinking with the goal of becoming more self-regulated learners.

Tutt (2007) concurs and points out that music teachers and their students become frustrated with "too much time talking and writing in a class that we believed was for active music-making" (p. 38). Tutt describes a constructivist approach to teaching students how to listen to, analyze, and describe music and evaluate performances that empowers students to make their own decisions about how to improve their performance. He suggests that music teachers ask thoughtful questions, based on standards that afford students more self-reliance in their own learning. Instead of, for instance, a conductor *telling* the trumpet section "Trumpets, don't rush. Watch!" the conductor can rephrase the statement into a question "What does the accompaniment line have at this point?" (pp. 38–39). In order to answer that question the trumpets would need to listen to the music, analyze who had the accompaniment, come to a conclusion, and adjust their performance accordingly. In that case, students are not only involved in constructing their own learning, but they are enacting both performing literacies and listening literacies and, I would argue, contemplating literacies as well.

Memorization (Performing and Listening Literacies)

Most adolescents memorize music by rote learning, which requires hearing a model and repeating it. Alan describes several mnemonic devices used to memorize music.

"Every-Good-Boy-Deserved-Fudge (or Does-Fine) for the lines of the treble clef and F-A-C-E for spaces in the treble clef. Syllable systems are used for rhythm such as *du-ta-de-ta-ka-di-mi* and for pitch *do-re-mi-fa-so-la-ti-do*. Adolescents use a variety of memorization strategies to enhance their performing and listening literacies."

Memorization allows adolescents to integrate auditory information from listening to musical sounds as they concurrently evaluate the progress of other performers, kinesthetic information such as fingering and other muscular or tactile knowledge, and visual information from images on the written page (Aiello & Williamson, 2002). Other memory strategies include improvisation. Students can develop and practice their improvising skills by memorizing a range of styles of music and then improvising on the basis of the distinctiveness of certain musical styles.

Listening literacies can strengthen memory and help musicians to envision the sounds of a musical work. Sue explains:

> "Music moves so you have to use memory. In other words, if you're listening to something and the composer has said I'm going to bring that whole section back at the end ... it isn't going to have any meaning for you unless you remember how it sounded to begin with ... because it goes and it's gone. We're now moving on to the next thing. So ... as you're listening to something, your perception about what's happening here, which is actually similar in reading related to what you've read previously ... and in music, your perception about this chord, this musical happening is going be influenced by what you heard before. So it's constantly changing, but you can't go back ... and listen to it ... like play the CD again ... it's going and then it's gone."

Intonation (Performing and Listening Literacies)

According to Morrison and Fyk (2002), intonation "can be defined as the ability to distinguish between two successive pitches or two dissimilar examples of a single pitch" (p. 183). The role of intonation in performing music is not unlike the separate roles of pronunciation and enunciation in reading. Much like pronunciation in reading involves choosing the correct vowel or consonant sound within each word that is written, intonation involves choosing the correct pitch within each melodic line that is written; much like enunciation in reading concerns the careful, clear, and distinct production of each vowel, consonant, syllable, and word, intonation in music also concerns the exact precision with which each pitch is produced. Intonation is a matter of both correctness and refinement of pitch. Further, intonation is measurable as a physical property of acoustics. The precise frequency of a pitch can be measured, using an electronic tuner or acoustical computer software, for example.

Alan describes a complex system of hand signs for each pitch in the musical scale or series of musical notes.

"Syllables (*do-re-mi-fa-so-la-ti-do*), letters (A B C D E F G), or numbers (1-2-3-4-5-6-7-8) that distinguish and label each pitch, rhythm syllables (*Ta-ka-di-mi*, *Ta-ti ti-ri-ti-ri*, *Du-ta-de-ta*, or 1-ee-and-a-2-ee-and-a for double rhythms; *Ta-ki-da*, *trip-e-let*, *du-da-di*, or 1-la-li for triple rhythms), Roman numeral assignment to chords built on each pitch of the scale, uppercase for major chords and lowercase for minor (I, ii, iii, IV, V, vi, vii). For scales we assign letters A through G with sharps (♯) and flats (♭) for half-step pitches in between."

Sue further clarifies the use of hand signs as a commonly used strategy to teach pitch.

"A lot of people will use hand signs, especially with choirs, with choral students in high school. Have them hand-sign things … it shows them where the pitch is, but specifically what the pitch is, too. So every pitch … has a hand sign for it."

Expression (Performing, Listening, and Creating Literacies)

Musical expression combines individual voice and personality with principles and techniques like tempo, phrasing, harmonic and melodic tension, patterns of timing and dynamics, articulation, accents, and ensemble timing. Musicians employ musical expression to communicate specific emotions to listeners. Broomhead (2005) defines expressive performing as "the interwoven variations in volume, intensity, timing, tone, color, and more, that make up expressive performing" (p. 64). Broomhead drew on constructivism as he noticed that when he encouraged his students to make their own decisions they became more expressive. He advocates regular and ongoing formal and unprompted opportunities for students to independently problem-solve their way toward more expressive performances.

Composition (Creating Literacy)

Very little attention is paid to teaching students the skills and strategies for creating music at the secondary level (Williams, 2007). A composition can exist in the form of a written piece of music bringing together variations of musical notation or as a single aural event like a live or recorded performance. Composers write music using not only musical notation skills, but also music theory and instrumentation skills with both traditional and nontraditional instruments. Composers can use the latest technology or software programs and other methods of sound production to assist in composition of music. Improvisation is a strategy used by many musicians in the composing process. Sue describes the connection between improvisation and composing and points out the importance of memory in the composing process.

> "I have the literacy tools of the notation to do that ... so in order to compose, you make up something in your head, remembering it, doing it enough times that you remember it so that you keep repeating the same thing, because, otherwise ... it's improvisation. It's different every time because you're making it up as you go along. But you can't share it with anybody until you write it down. It's just yours."

Body Movement (Performing Literacy)

Musicians use body movement as a valuable tool for interpreting their work. They use their bodies to interact with musical instruments and use physical gestures to communicate meaning to the audience, directly or through expressive intention. According to Davidson and Correia (2002), musicians use body movement

> "to communicate the expressive intention (for instance, a sudden surge forward to facilitate the execution of a loud musical passage or a high curving hand gesture to link sections of the music during a pause); to communicate directly with the audience or co-performers about issues of coordination or participation (for example, nodding the head to beckon the audience to join in a chorus of a song or exchanging glances for the co-performer to take over a solo in a jazz piece); to signal extra-musical concerns (for example, gesturing to the audience to remain quiet); to present information about the performer's personality, with his or her individualized characteristics providing important cues (muted, contained gestures or large extravagant gestures, for example); and to show off to the audience. (pp. 244–245)

Sue further illustrates this integral connection between performing and body movement by sharing a tune on the recorder and describing how the body is fundamental to musical performance:

> "If I'm playing this ... little tune ... my fingers are doing something ... my mouth is doing something ... it's very kinesthetic. It should be with music ... listening to music, feeling music, performing music ... should involve the entire body."

PRACTICAL INSTRUCTIONAL STRATEGIES FOR MUSIC

Adolescents engage in literacy learning in music classes through interactive and constructivist processes. Music teachers and directors scaffold adolescents' music literacy learning through implicit modeling, authentic practicing, and the use of cognitive strategies in constructivist ways that afford opportunities for students to become independent decision makers about music. Rote teaching has a place in music teaching, for example, to teach music concepts like melody and rhythm patterns; it requires little thought and provides little or no opportunity for students to make decisions about their own learning. Traditional reading and writing about music are rarely used in adolescent music classrooms, likely because of the heavy emphasis on performance goals in schools (Tutt, 2007; Williams, 2007).

Particularly powerful is the widely accepted instructional strategy of modeling found in scores of educational settings across all disciplines. In interactive music rehearsal or practice sessions the conductor models or demonstrates a concept. Students then demonstrate their music literacy learning by imitating the conductor. This modeling by the conductor is largely implicit prompting or forcing students to use their listening literacies and memorization skills to watch, listen, copy, echo back, and repeat what they hear, shaping the concept until it matches the model, for example, in terms of good and poor pitch accuracy, rhythm control, and so forth. Haston (2007) states that "to increase the performing literacies in ensembles, modeling can be a useful tool to introduce musical concepts and performance skills before students see the printed music." He further suggests "this can be done live or via recordings, in group settings or in individual instruction, or by having older students model for younger students through peer mentoring" (p. 26).

Constructivist approaches to literacy learning are crucial in helping students move toward independent decision making about music. Teachers who design lessons using constructivist approaches provide opportunities for students to construct their own understandings of music. They involve students in cognitive strategies like problem solving, inferring, visualizing, synthesizing, questioning, and making connections about music and find that students are better able to make their own decisions about music literacy learning and can also transfer their learning to other music contexts. According to Wiggins (2007), students need to be able to "synthesize musical ideas" (p. 39). Students need to be involved in real-world music, solving performing, creating, and listening problems (Broomhead, 2005; Tutt, 2007; Wiggins, 2007).

In conjunction with performing, listening, and creating, traditional reading and writing about music can be effective literacies to use with adolescents for interacting with two of the national standards: *Understanding relationships between music, the other arts, and disciplines outside the art* and *Understanding music in relation to history and culture*. These are not performance goals. Contemplating is the primary literacy used to understand the relationships described in these two standards. The contemplating literacies can be supported and extended through traditional reading and writing, especially when appropriately integrated with the other music literacies of performing, listening, and creating.

WHAT COUNTS AS TEXT AND LITERACY IN THE VISUAL ARTS?

If text is "what" gets negotiated in the production of a work of art, then the elements and principles of design constitute texts in the visual arts. In order to create a work of art, artists think about how to convey messages by integrating the components of a work of art, the elements of design—line, shape, direction, size, texture, color, and value—into a certain structure. Artists also need to think about the principles of design—balance, emphasis, movement, pattern, repetition, proportion, rhythm, variety, and unity—since they carry the plan for incorporating the elements, according to the artist's purpose and intent for the work. Materials, techniques, and tools are also employed in ways that help an artist produce a piece of artwork. When asked what counts as text in the visual arts discipline, consider the commentary from coauthors Larry Burditt, Johanna Paas, and Judy Thurston, who are visual arts experts.

Larry counts the specific works from all art fields as art texts: "An art object such as a painting, graphic design, or piece of pottery can be a text to be 'read' or interpreted." Art texts also include traditional print-based texts like textbooks, art-related books, and artist-composed texts such as an artist statement about his purpose and intent. In a graphic design class Larry discusses using traditional print-based text with students.

"I use two types of texts. I do use a more traditional textbook with the students, especially at the lower levels. These books will discuss the principles and history of design. I also use technical books as a resource for the students to learn how to do a specific task on the computer."

Johanna reasons that

"all images are text ... we read them for their meaning ... visuals of it ... elements and principles of design and how they get stacked together ... similar to creating a sentence would be the complete visual, but also thinking of context like metaphor ... reading them in terms of what does it mean?"

Further, art language is negotiated for meaning—text is used to express and understand ideas as in any other discipline. Johanna reflects on the similarities between art language and the language arts.

"Language we use the same as—metaphor, context (in a very hands-on way) ... Students get a course pack ... recipes and methodologies for creating the techniques that we're doing—then, I give them articles ... whether it's narrative stories that they can feed off of to make imagery or talk about the connection between image and text and illustration. So my students get a combination of ... written text ... an instructional manual ... inspirational text ... to get them thinking. And then they have all the images that we look at as source material that they're reading as well. I was really ... caught off guard at how much language we use which is actually the same as literature ... when you think about metaphor, you think about content ... all the same stuff."

Borrowing from the visual arts standards and defining literacy as how we interact with or negotiate text for the purpose of meaning making, visual arts literacy encompasses creating, problem solving, evaluating, reflecting, and critiquing artwork. Adolescents involved in art making engage in each of these literacies as well as the traditional print-based literacies such as reading and writing about art. In order to carry out the reflecting, evaluating, and critiquing literacies related to a work of art, one must "read" or interpret the artist's intent based on certain criteria.

According to Barrett (2011) interpretations of a piece of artwork are not equal. He maintains "we will never get a single right interpretation of it, nor would we want to: interpretations are a matter of ongoing discussions" (p. 40). When interpreting a piece of art a reasonable response might be "insightful, enlightening, a good way to look at it, or, on the contrary, that some interpretations don't make sense, don't fit the work, are without evidence, or are nonsensical" (p. 39). Barrett (2011) describes three criteria used to meaningfully interpret artwork: the artwork should make sense in and of itself (coherence) and the interpretation should fit the work (correspondence) and explain the work, including an account of how, when, and where it was made and information about the artist (completeness).

Interpreting art involves asking questions about the artwork: What does it look like? When interpreting art one must describe what she sees. Johanna explains how she teaches students to interpret and critique other students' works. She develops her own critique templates; then, using these templates as guides, small groups of students circulate throughout the class critiquing their peers' works.

> "They're reading somebody else's image ... basically describe what you see, talk about what that means to you ... what does that make you ... think about and then ... after that, you evaluate ... How could it ... be changed in a way that could be more effective?"

Larry describes art literacy from the perspective of what makes good design.

> "I think most of the experts in design talk a lot about research and the value of research in development of ideas. This takes on a really wide variety of sources. There is also a lot of discussion in the discipline about the nature of design and what makes a design a success or failure. Typically good design has a clear objective and all the visual decisions made in its development are to meet that objective."

Johanna's description of art literacy includes the perspective of art literacy as visual culture:

> "I think ... you can break it down to the elements and principles of design, right? But then I think there's also this other level of visual culture where it's about denotation or connotation ... what does that Coke label mean?"

WHAT DO THE STANDARDS SAY ABOUT TEXT AND LITERACY IN THE VISUAL ARTS?

The National Standards for Arts Education (National Association for Music Education [MENC], 1994) for adolescents in grades 5–8 and

9–12 describes visual arts literacy in terms of applying, demonstrating, evaluating, differentiating, describing, analyzing, justifying, identifying, exploring, comparing, synthesizing, creating, problem solving, critiquing, evaluating, and reflecting about artworks. These standards describe expectations for visual arts literacy activities in which adolescents interact with a wide range of media, techniques, and processes to create and think about artworks of various structures and functions across a number of fields in the arts like drawing and painting, sculpture, design, architecture, film, video, and folk arts. These standards clearly encourage relationships and communication between music and other disciplines, as well as understanding music in relation to history and culture. Further, the arts standards expectations include developing the vocabularies and concepts and visual, oral, and written literacies necessary to communicate through artworks. Table 9.3 represents an attempt to understand more clearly the texts that adolescents need to negotiate and the literacies they would enact to accomplish the tasks put forth in the arts standards. Reflecting, evaluating, and analyzing seem to

TABLE 9.3. Visual Arts Texts and Literacies as Indicated by the National Standards for Arts Education

Standards	Texts (what is negotiated)	Literacies (how text is negotiated)
Understanding and applying media, techniques, and processes	*Elements of design, artworks, media* (materials, techniques, processes), *tools*	*Creating, problem solving*
Using knowledge of structures and functions	*Principles of design, artworks, media* (materials, techniques, processes), *tools*	*Creating, problem solving, critiquing*
Choosing and evaluating a range of subject matter, symbols, and ideas	*Elements of design, principles of design, artworks, media* (materials, techniques, processes), *tools*	*Creating, problem solving, reflecting*
Understanding the visual arts in relation to history and cultures	*Elements of design, principles of design, artworks, media* (materials, techniques, processes), *tools*	*Reflecting, critiquing*
Reflecting upon and assessing the characteristics and merits of students' work and the work of others	*Elements of design, principles of design, artworks, media* (materials, techniques, processes), *tools*	*Reflecting, critiquing*
Making connections between visual arts and other disciplines	*Artworks, media* (materials, techniques, processes), *tools*	*Reflecting*

be the most-used descriptors of higher-order thinking advocated by the visual arts standards. The standards frequently use both evaluating and analyzing as descriptors to indicate an expectation of a particular type of thinking based on certain criteria that results in one's interpretation or explanation of artwork. We chose *critiquing* to represent these similar thinking literacies not only because they are synonymous, but because critiquing is fundamental to the type of thinking that is widely used in the arts. Reflecting, on the other hand, refers to the act of thinking carefully. To that end the visual arts literacies can be represented by creating, problem solving, critiquing, and reflecting.

Creating Literacies

Creating literacies are reflected in three of the six arts education standards, which signify that creating or producing artworks is fundamental to the understanding of visual arts texts in adolescent classrooms. Teaching and learning in visual arts classrooms depends on the creating literacies represented in these standards: *Understanding and applying media, techniques, and processes*; *Using knowledge of structures and functions*; *Choosing and evaluating a range of subject matter, symbols, and ideas*. Creating works of art and thinking about the artwork produced dominates the literacies enacted by visual artists. Visual artists make use of the following skills and strategies in a variety of ways with a range of know-how in order to negotiate or interact with or create visual art: elements of design, principles of design, production of visual art—media, methods, techniques, processes, and tools.

Problem-Solving Literacies

Adolescents involved in the creation of works of art are expected to solve challenging visual arts problems on their own using higher-order reasoning skills. They investigate and define a real-life problem, devise a solution, and carry out a plan. Students must engage in reasoning skills such as analyzing, synthesizing, and evaluating to impact their decision-making about the media, techniques, processes, and tools they will use to solve a range of visual arts issues and problems. In adolescent visual arts classrooms students also engage in solving problems that exist in their daily lives using visual arts principles and functions as indicated in the following creating standards: *Understanding and applying media, techniques, and processes*; *Using knowledge of structures and functions*; and *Choosing and evaluating a range of subject matter, symbols, and ideas*.

Reflecting Literacies

The reflecting literacies suggest thinking in serious or careful ways. Adolescents must think or consider carefully in order to accomplish such standards and expectations as differentiating between historical and cultural contexts, identify artist's intentions, and describe meanings of artworks. Reflecting is required to accomplish four of the six standards: *Choosing and evaluating a range of subject matter, symbols, and ideas*; *Understanding the visual arts in relation to history and cultures*; *reflecting upon and assessing the characteristics and merits of their work and the work of others*; and *making connections between visual arts and other disciplines*.

Critiquing Literacies

Critiquing is a discipline-specific expectation that artists use to interpret art and participate in a wide range of conversations about the art. In order to participate in the process of critiquing one must carry out other thinking skills as well, including analyzing, interpreting, evaluating, assessing, and describing. Critiquing literacies are encouraged by these standards: *Using knowledge of structures and functions*; *understanding the visual arts in relation to history and cultures*; and *reflecting upon and assessing the characteristics and merits of their work and the work of others*.

DISCIPLINE-SPECIFIC STRATEGIES IN THE VISUAL ARTS

The discipline-specific knowledge, skills, and strategies that help students negotiate and interact with text in visual arts classrooms include the elements of design, principles of design, production of art, criticism, aesthetics, and writing. These disciplinary skills and strategies represent specific approaches by which students enact the literacies used to negotiate or interact with text in their visual arts learning. As shown in Table 9.4, these skills and strategies are in harmony with the visual arts national standards expected to be taught and supported as essential components of any exemplary adolescent visual arts classroom.

Elements and Principles of Design (Creating, Problem Solving, and Reflecting Literacies)

The elements of design comprise a set of concepts that provide essential language for interacting with and communicating about art. These vital

TABLE 9.4. Discipline-Specific Visual Arts Knowledge, Skills, and Strategies as Indicated by the National Standards for Arts Education

Discipline-specific knowledge, skills, strategies	Purposes	Texts used or created	Literacies enacted
Elements of design	To acquire the language of the visual arts	Elements of design, artworks, media (materials, techniques), tools	Creating, problem solving, reflecting
Principles of design	To manage the composition of artworks	Elements of design, principles of design, artworks, media (materials, techniques), tools	Creating, problem solving, reflecting
Production— making the art	To learn the methods and techniques to create artworks	Elements of design, principles of design, artworks, media (materials, techniques), tools	Creating, problem solving, reflecting, critiquing
Criticism	To learn how to respond to artworks— critically	Elements of design, principles of design, artworks, media (materials, techniques), tools	Reflecting, critiquing
Aesthetics	To respond to artworks—sensory responses	Artworks	Reflecting
Writing	To articulate what you make and why (artist's statement)	Artist's personal work	Reflecting

components carry the common language that artists use to make decisions about art as well as produce, talk about, reflect, evaluate, critique, problem-solve, and read and write about art. Adolescents must learn the language of these building blocks in order to enact the visual arts literacies. Principles of design help artists figure out how to operationalize these elements into a successful work of art by thinking about the emphasis of the design or how they will craft pattern or unity, or generate movement, rhythm, or balance. Visual arts instructors teach adolescents how to take the elements and principles of design into account when planning an art project, considering the solution to a specific visual arts issue, or meeting the needs of a particular design problem.

Production: Making the Art (Creating, Problem Solving, Reflecting, and Critiquing Literacies)

The act of producing art is not the same for every artist. Adolescents, however, should understand that a generally accepted, fundamental process for creating art exists. According to Barrett (2011) artists share certain behaviors during the making of art. For example, in every project artists engage in "conceiving of a work, deciding its purpose, beginning it, developing it, changing it, staying motivated in the face of problems, finishing the work, showing the work, and deciding its degree of success" (p. 2). Judy reflects on the discipline-specific strategies where production tends to be the strategy that is most emphasized in schools: "critique is one and … art history … art criticism, aesthetics and production … production gets the lion's share of time, but it's the idea that all of them are worth thought and interaction."

Criticism (Reflecting and Critiquing Literacies)

Defining criticism within the realm of the visual arts is complex; disparate points of view exist among art critics. Barrett (2000) holds the notion of criticism as a "lively, ongoing, interesting, valuable, and complicated conversation" (p. 1). He describes criticism as a process that includes the elements of interpretation, description, and judging, the most important of which is interpretation. According to Barrett (2000), interpretation is a complex cognitive process that takes into account two types of information—internal and external evidence. He explains internal evidence as that which is "in the work itself," what would be a description of the work. On the other hand, external evidence is described as "relevant info not within the work," consisting of such information as other works produced by the artist, certain information about the artist, and information about the time period of the specific work (p. 159).

Description and judging also play important roles in the process of art criticism. Since readers may not have first-hand visual knowledge of the subject of a written criticism, it is essential that a picture or photo of the focus piece be included within the criticism. This description provides a visual account of the image being discussed. Judging, another vital element of criticism makes the criteria, reasons for assessment, and assessment protocol clear.

A well-known approach to teaching criticism—the Feldman method—is widely used with all visual arts students. Developed by Edmund Feldman (Feldman & Woods, 1981), this approach is relevant to all types of visual experience and similar to the method discussed previously. Feldman's method is a systematic approach to interpreting visual art involving four distinct stages: description, formal analysis, interpretation, and evaluation.

Step 1 involves students in examining the visual details in a work of art. Students are taught to "make a visual inventory of objects and details in the work" by identifying, naming, differentiating, and describing them (p. 78). Students' thinking is then extended as the teacher asks "questions designed to elicit further noticing, exploring, comparing, and responding" (p. 78).

Step 2 engages students in formal analysis (art criticism) where these concepts and relational terms are developed by analyzing the relationships within and among the forms and objects described in the first stage. Students make comparative observations about forms and objects in which an interest has already been established.

Steps 3 and 4 allow students to move to higher levels of understanding, to interpretation and evaluation. Students use higher-order cognitive skills:

> drawing inferences about what the work means as a whole; hypothesis testing to see whether a tentative interpretation fits the visual facts already adduced; creative problem solving in an attempt to reconcile and synthesize alternate, equally valid interpretations and levels of meaning; and deductive and inductive reasoning to support proposed evaluations of the work. (Feldman & Woods, 1981, p. 79)

Johanna describes her three-pillar system to engage her students in thinking about their art.

> "What is your intent? What is your motivation? On my rubric, there are three main categories. One … is it innovative … the second one is … have you developed it as far as you can? And then the next set of questions … based on the visual product … are you using the elements and principles of design in an innovative way? Is it an interesting product to look at? And then have you actually matched those two things up? Have you matched up how you're making this product with what it is you want to communicate? And then I go into craftsmanship … is it printed well? Is it … appropriate to what you're trying to do."

Aesthetics (Reflecting Literacies)

Aesthetics can generally be described as the sensory responses associated with a piece of visual art. Barrett (2011) describes an aes-

thetic experience as "a unique reaction to an artifact or event that
is disengaged, disinterested, and removed from practical concerns"
(p. 204). I am reminded of the parallel between aesthetics in terms
of "reading" or interpreting visual art and reading and interpreting
literary art or print-based text. Rosenblatt (1978) refers to aesthetic
transactions between readers and texts as those guided by the textual signs and our experiences. If we interact with text and shape
meaning aesthetically, we connect personally through our emotions,
and what we hear, see, and feel. Judy describes how she encourages
students to

> "enter into the work ... I always start with one that's quite literal and
> then get into abstract works ... walking them through the senses.
> What do you hear? What do you taste? What do you feel? What do
> you smell? Do you think they're happy? Do you think they're sad?
> And literally, through the sensory properties ... they write from
> that ... I got some beautiful stuff from kids who had never been
> writers and it changed the way I looked at specific artworks forever.
> I mean, once I saw it ... through their senses and their imagination.
> It blew my mind!"

Writing (Reflecting Literacies)

Visual artists enact the writing literacy to think deeply about their subject
matter. In addition to the discipline-specific form of writing described as
criticism, visual artists learn how to write an artist's statement, "a written commentary by artists about their own work to help them clarify
their own intent and give viewers an entry point to understanding their
artifacts" (Barrett, 2011, p. 24). Adolescents learn how to use specific
guidelines to appropriately observe, think about, and create a personal
statement about their art. Larry commented on the writing literacies
enacted in his classroom.

> "Many of my projects have written components. It might be a process
> book, a client proposal, or just the content for the project, but I feel
> the students' skills at writing can be augmented by incorporating
> literacy as often as possible. They will also do written critiques of
> work as well as oral defenses. They learn to "read" the art as well
> as written text.

Another aspect of writing about art is explained through the context of visual culture. Judy and Johanna describe how writing literacy
can produce texts that signify visual culture. The visual arts standards

acknowledge the influence of the visual world in which students live and the art they produce. Judy begins the conversation about how she gets students to use criticism to write and express ideas.

> "For ... art education ... art criticism ties the closest with language arts. We can really ... get kids to write and to express ... ideas and interpret things and work it through. In fact my art education majors or non-majors wrote a paper on criticism today based on artwork ... [art] can be signs, with visual culture, it can be LED signs or advertisements."

Johanna elaborates on the idea that culture gets represented visually in the world around us in multiple ways.

> "I think visual culture is the ... hot topic of the moment ... and the visual culture ... is pretty much anything and especially in ... this time and place ... everything comes at us visually ... every ad, every Google search, every label on something ... it's all broken down in these multifaceted ways."

Judy continues this thought: "Look at the phones ... the phones have got cameras on them now and computer apps so that you have all the visuals continually."

PRACTICAL INSTRUCTIONAL STRATEGIES FOR THE VISUAL ARTS

Similarities exist across all disciplines, including the arts, in terms of the instructional strategies used to teach adolescents how to interact with texts and literacies. Larry concurs and explains that instructional strategies are comparable across subject areas.

> "I'd say it is the same. I've heard several practicing designers tell me that they feel students going through art institutes are not the best designers because they haven't had all the other information and literacy skills provided by a liberal arts education. Students still need to be able to articulate their thought processes and explain why they made specific choices."

All disciplines including the arts teach certain language systems to construct meaning. Visual artists use language to carry certain messages—to communicate about their work—through traditional print-based literacies like writing, talking, and reading. Hence, one of the practical instructional strategies used to increase adolescents' literacy use is teaching and learning vocabulary. Visual arts standards require that adolescents learn vocabularies and concepts related to a range of works in the visual arts. Their artistic competencies hinge on building fluency in visual, oral, and written communication (National Association for Music Education [MENC], 1994). Teaching and learning of terms and concepts in the visual arts happens through both implicit modeling, such as demonstration, and explicit modeling by naming and explaining the terms in the course of reading, writing, and conversation. Johanna describes an instructional strategy that involves simply practicing art-based techniques learned by watching others:

> "By practicing on other people's artwork like through critique, the purpose is they can then be self-reflective ... when they're actually making artwork ... it's basically a series of problem-solving adventures ... and so by seeing it in other works—what they like, what they don't like, what they think functions well, what they don't— they then can apply it to their own."

Further, visual arts literacy learning is fundamentally based on constructivist approaches and is crucial in helping students develop independent decision making about artworks. The visual arts standards require teachers to design lessons using constructivist approaches to learning. In this way, teachers provide opportunities for adolescents to construct their own understandings of visual arts. When adolescents engage in such cognitive strategies as problem solving, creating, evaluating, reflecting, synthesizing, analyzing, integrating, and assessing works of art, they are better able to make their own decisions about making art, increasing their visual arts literacy learning.

Traditional reading and writing about artworks can be effective literacies for adolescents when used alongside the creating, problem-solving, reflecting, and critiquing literacies, particularly in relation to four of the national standards: *Understanding the visual arts in relation to history and cultures*; *Reflecting upon and assessing the characteristics and merits of their work and the work of others*; *making connections between visual arts and other disciplines*; and *choosing and evaluating a range of subject matter, symbols, and ideas*. Reflecting is a primary literacy used to understand the relationships described in these four standards, which can also be supported and extended through reading and writing.

CONCLUSION

Four instructional beliefs stand out in this chapter with regard to both music and visual arts teaching and learning—students tend to learn better when involved in constructivist approaches; they are expected to utilize higher-order cognitive strategies; teacher modeling is key to student learning; and both traditional and nontraditional forms of text can be used to extend learning. In practical classroom settings these instructional beliefs interconnect in significant ways.

First, much of what we know about best practice in education centers on the constructivist idea that students should have opportunities to build their own understandings about the concepts and issues being learned. Students should be involved in negotiating their literacies in authentic ways, through constructivist processes that allow them to make their own decisions and solve real-life problems (Broomhead, 2005; Tutt, 2007; Wiggins, 2007). Both music and visual arts standards promote a constructivist view of teaching and learning, particularly in the areas of problem solving and decision making.

Through a more constructivist approach teachers will notice increased student engagement, motivation, and achievement. Wiggins (2007) contends that students need opportunities to "solve genuine musical problems (performance problems, creation problems, listening problems that are genuine in that they are problems 'real' musicians solve) with support (scaffolding) of peers and teacher" (p. 39). Many music educators write about the benefits of a more constructivist approach to music teaching and learning and invite teachers in the field to experiment with these approaches (Broomhead, 2005; Reveire, 2006; Tutt, 2007; Wiggins, 2007). Visual arts instruction embraces constructivist approaches to teaching and learning naturally as students consider the elements and principles of design when planning an art project, considering the solution to a specific visual arts issue, or meeting the needs of a particular design problem.

Second, both music and visual arts standards encourage higher-order cognitive thinking in daily instruction. Music students must utilize their problem-solving literacies when making decisions in real time in order to carry out such cognitive processes as improvisation, composing, arranging, and analyzing a varied repertoire of music. According to Reveire (2006), the discovery method of teaching promotes the use of such cognitive processes as application, analysis, and synthesis as well as better listening acuity in music. To teach students to evaluate music, Conway (2008) suggests that teachers make use of good questioning, for example, "What makes a musical work worthy of being studied in a music class?" and "Who says?" (p. 38). Teachers who ask thoughtful questions afford students more autonomy in their own learning (Tutt, 2007).

Secondary music instructors, however, are constrained by the expectations of their schools and tend not to afford their students opportunities to investigate these cognitive processes or the contemplating literacies that their standards promote and demand. In traditional secondary music classrooms where adolescents receive music instruction through participation in large orchestra, band, or choir classes, instruction primarily focuses on rehearsal for upcoming performances like festivals or concerts. It can be challenging for music teachers to disengage from the time-honored mode of rehearse, rehearse, rehearse in order to carve out time for developing improvisational skills and concepts (Reveire, 2006).

According to Winner and Hetland (2008), "arts programs teach a specific set of thinking skills rarely addressed elsewhere in the curriculum" (p. 29). Included in this set of skills are "visual–spatial abilities, reflection, self-criticism, and the willingness to experiment and learn from mistakes" (p. 29). Visual arts students are expected to investigate real-life problems and use higher-order reasoning skills to solve them. In order to participate in the process of critiquing, for example, adolescents must employ thinking skills like analyzing, interpreting, evaluating, assessing, and describing.

Third, modeling is clearly advocated across the arts disciplines. In music, both teachers and peers model certain actions in music making. For example, conductors model or demonstrate concepts in rehearsal or practice sessions with students imitating the conductor as evidence of their learning. Students use their listening literacies and memorization skills to mimic and then repeat what they hear until they have reached mastery of the concept. Conductors also model how to handle and play musical instruments as well as perform the body movements that musicians use to communicate to other musicians, and the audience, during a performance. In the visual arts, teachers model processes and techniques using different types of media and technology, how to use the tools to produce a variety of artistic styles and forms of art, and the thinking involved in the production of art criticism.

Fourth, the arts disciplines can use both print and nonprint texts in meaningful ways. There are opportunities for music and visual arts teachers to use the traditional literacies of reading and writing. Writing is especially useful for engaging students in the higher-order cognitive processes encouraged by some of the specific arts standards. Zoss (2009) explores how we can integrate visual arts into literacy curricula at the secondary level. Underlying this belief that visual arts can and should be included in meaningful ways within disciplines is the idea that visual arts texts can be read and composed to enhance meaning making from print-based text. Thus, visual arts can be used as another means to respond to printed text in ways that extend and expand learning—to translate across text types, to convey ideas in other ways, and to connect thinking across domains (Albers et al., 2010; Zoss, 2009). For example, students can create a painting in response to a poem in a way that captures the poem's essence. Utilizing visual arts texts to respond to print-based text can offer multiple possibilities and media for making meaning. Music texts are used in much the same way in response to an idea or feeling expressed through the written word, for example, composing a musical score that captures the spirit or heart of a story or interpreting meaning from the lyrics of a song by singing it expressively.

Writing this chapter was a quest to make sense of how *text* and *literacy* are viewed and enacted in the music and visual arts disciplines particularly with regard to the teaching and learning of adolescents. Eisner (2005) calls attention to three advantages for learning in the arts. Not only do the arts enrich the lives of those involved, but adolescents who study the arts can develop ways of thinking not commonly taught in other disciplines, like reflecting, making judgments, using visual–spatial literacies, and persisting in solving problems. What's more, the literacies enacted in the arts include ways of communication and meaning making that go beyond logically constructed language, such as responding to print-based text in nonprint ways like drawing, painting, and composing music.

We hope this endeavor to learn more deeply the intricacies involved in teaching and learning in the arts has opened a more inclusive space for meaningful conversations among arts educators about how adolescents learn specifically from arts texts and literacies. Moreover, with this common understanding about how texts and literacies are represented in the arts, arts teachers can enter into the larger conversation with teachers in all disciplines about the literacies adolescents enact and the range of texts they negotiate for the purpose of making meaning.

REFERENCES

Albers, P., Holbrook, T., & Harste, J. C. (2010). Talking trade: Literacy researchers as practicing artists. *Journal of Adolescent & Adult Literacy*, 54(3), 164–171.p. 167

Alvermann, D. E., Phelps, S., & Gillis, V. (2010). *Content area reading and literacy: Succeeding in today's diverse classrooms* (6th ed.). Boston: Allyn & Bacon.

Barrett, T. (2000). *Criticizing art: Understanding the contemporary* (2nd ed.). Boston: McGraw-Hill.

Barrett, T. (2011). *Making art: Form and meaning.* New York: McGraw-Hill.

Broomhead, P. (2005). Shaping expressive performance: A problem-solving approach. *Music Educators Journal, 91(5),* 63–67.

Conley, M. W. (2008). *Content area literacy: Learners in context.* Boston: Pearson.

Conway, C. (2008). The implementation of the national standards in music education: Capturing the spirit of the standards. *Music Educators Journal, 94,* 34–39.

Diket, R. M. (2003). The arts contribution to adolescent learning. *Kappa Delta Pi Record, 39*(4), 173–177.

Draper, R. J. (2008). Redefining content-area literacy teacher education: Finding my voice through collaboration. *Harvard Educational Review, 78*(1), 60–83.

Draper, R. J., & Broomhead, P. (2009, December). *Open, free, and ringing: Teaching and learning choir literacies.* Paper presented at the 59th Annual Meeting of the National Reading Conference, Albuquerque, NM.

Eisner, E. W. (1997). Cognition and representation: A way to pursue the American Dream. *Phi Delta Kappan, 78,* 349–353.

Eisner, E. W. (2005). Opening a shuttered window: An introduction to a special section on the arts and the intellect. *Phi Delta Kappan, 87*(1), 8–10.

Gee, J. P. (1996). *Social linguistics and literacies: Ideology in discourses* (2nd ed.). New York: RoutledgeFalmer.

Feldman, E. B., & Woods, D. (1981). Art criticism and reading. *Journal of Aesthetic Education, 15*(4), 75–95.

Haston, W. (2007). Teacher modeling as effective teaching strategy. *Music Educators Journal, 93*(4), 26–30.

Heron-Hruby, A., & Alvermann, D., (2009). Implications of adolescents popular culture use for school literacy. In K. Wood & W. E. Blanton (Eds.), *Literacy instruction for adolescents: Research-based practice* (pp. 210 –227). New York: Guilford Press.

Hinchman, K. A., Alvermann, D. E., Boyd, F. B., Brozo, W. G., & Vacca, R. T. (2004). Supporting older students' in- and out-of-school literacies. *Journal of Adolescent and Adult Literacy, 47*(4), 304–310.

Kuehne, J. M. (2010). Sight-singing: Ten years of published research. *Update: Applications of Research in Music Education, 29*(1), 7–14.

Lehmann, A. C., & Ericsson, K. A. (1996). Structure and acquisition of expert accompanying and sight-reading performance. *Psychomusicology, 15,* 1–29.

Morrison, S. J., & Fyk, J. (2002). Intonation. In R. Parncutt & G. E. McPherson (Eds.), *The science and psychology of music performance: Creative strategies for teaching and learning* (pp. 183–198). New York: Oxford University Press.

National Association for Music Education (MENC). (1994). *National Standards for Arts Education.* Retrieved November 10, 2010, from *www.menc.org/resources/view/national-standards-for-music-education.*

Riveire, J. (2006). Using improvisation as a teaching strategy. *Music Educators Journal, 92*(3), 40–45.

Shanahan, T., & Shanahan, C. (2008). Teaching disciplinary literacy to adolescents: Rethinking content-area literacy. *Harvard Educational Review, 78*(1), 40–59.

Street, B. (2006). Understanding and defining literacy. *Education for All Global Monitoring Report 2006: Literacy for Life*. Paris: UNESCO.

Rosenblatt, L. M. (1978). *The reader, the text, the poem: The transactional theory of the literary work*. Carbondale: Southern Illinois University Press.

Tutt, K. (2007). Using questions to teach the National Standards in rehearsal. *Music Educators Journal, 93*(5), 38–43.

Vacca, R. T., Vacca, J. L., & Mraz, M. (2011). *Content area reading: Literacy and learning across the curriculum*. Boston: Pearson.

Watson, P. A., Johnson, H., Lesley, M., & Brass, A. (2009, December). Seeking a path to disciplinary literacy: Can we rely on content literacy textbooks to define the knowledge base? Presented at the 59th Annual Meeting of the National Reading Conference, Albuquerque, NM.

Wiggins, J. (2007). Authentic practice and process in music teacher education. *Music Educators Journal, 93*(3), 36–42.

Williams, D. A. (2007). What are music educators doing and how well are we doing it? *Music Educators Journal, 94*(1), 18–23.

Winner, E., & Hetland, L. (2008). Art for our sake: School arts classes matter more than ever—but not for the reasons you think. *Arts Education Policy Review, 109*(5), 29–32.

Index

Page numbers followed by *f* or *t* indicate figures or tables.